of gold & dust

# of gold & dust

SAMANTHA WILLS

A memoir of a creative life

ALLEN&UNWIN
SYDNEY • MELBOURNE • AUCKLAND • LONDON

First published in 2021

Allen & Unwin
83 Alexander Street
Crows Nest NSW 2065
Australia
Phone: (61 2) 8425 0100
Email: info@allenandunwin.com
Web: www.allenandunwin.com

 A catalogue record for this
book is available from the
National Library of Australia

ISBN 978 1 76087 654 8

Internal design by Simon Paterson; handwritten elements by Samantha Wills
Set in 12.25/18.75 pt Adobe Caslon Pro by Bookhouse, Sydney
Printed and bound in Australia by Griffin Press, part of Ovato

10 9 8 7 6 5 4 3

For my nieces,
Naya and Anaïs

contents

introduction

Did you know that the name given to the movement of petals in response to darkness is 'nyctinasty'?—the closing of a flower at night. It's somewhat unfortunate that a definition so beautiful could have such a sharp and dissonant title. Jarring pronunciation aside, the concept of a flower opening in the light and retreating in darker times is as much a human response as it is botanical. It is the very make up of our experiences that sees us made of gold and dust, our elation and our grief. Our daylight and our midnights. Nothing faces the sun all of the time.

Often throughout my career, I have been asked to explain my 'overnight success'. How the Samantha Wills jewellery brand went from Bondi market table to the international stage, seemingly in a flash. I have long resented the question, and eventually my answer became: 'It took me twelve years to be an overnight success.' Most people appreciated this response, while others thought I was simply being facetious. I wasn't. It took me no less than twelve years to find success. But what is success, anyway? The very definition of it has changed in my mind many times over the years—the only steadfast truth that I know about it is that the closer you get to it, the more it looks nothing like you thought it would when you first set out to reach it.

I have known for a long while that the Samantha Wills jewellery brand had a following that extended beyond lovers of accessories. Within that following, there was also a large community of (predominantly female) entrepreneurs, who, like me, were building their own creative enterprise.

It is because of this that I want to share more of the bits in between. Not just the outward-facing yardsticks of success that people have no doubt seen on Instagram or in the press, and also not just the hardships. Because while I feel providing transparency on both is important, what is not often spoken about is the human element. The parallel experience of it all. When the success of a milestone was being celebrated publicly, what was it that was going on personally? What did the silence behind the applause sound like? What happened in the moments between the inhale and the exhale? That's what the stories on these pages are. I'm sure I don't have to tell anyone that it wasn't all highlight reels and high fives. What it takes to build a commercially successful brand has to have an impact on all that surrounds a private life. As above, so below—they do not operate independently from each other.

'The Universe only ever has three answers for us: "yes", "not right now" or "I have something better in store for you".' I have long loved those words, but it took me a great amount of time to really understand the true power of this guidance and an even greater amount of time to truly accept it. And to accept it means to surrender what you think the outcome should look like. For so long I know I was unable to do that, both professionally and, even more so, personally. For the majority of my years, I defined success by whether an outcome happened in the way I hoped it would, in the time I thought it should. What an anxiety-filled and rigid way to exist, don't you agree?

What I came to realise in writing these pages was that the tighter I held on to a set outcome, the more strongly anxiety hugged me back, sometimes embracing me so tightly I struggled to even breathe. Author and teacher Caroline Myss once wrote, 'Just let go. Let go of how you thought your life should be, and embrace the life that is trying to work its way into your consciousness.' That advice really reached me throughout the many (many!) months spent immersed in the writing of this book. It was as though laying each word onto the page was a surrender of sorts, a white flag between me and the experiences in my life that maybe didn't go the way I thought they would. The ink on these pages enabled me to see my experiences—particularly the ones that didn't go to *my* plan—for the guidance, redirection and resilience that each brought. Even through the acceptance of this, it doesn't lessen the disappointment or the pain that a long midnight brings, but the certainty with midnights is darkness, and with darkness also arrives the opportunity for alchemy.

I have long been fascinated by alchemy—as a jewellery designer, it really appealed to me that there was a word for the process by which base metals are converted into gold. I felt the word richly and poetically captured the truth and beauty of my craft—patina metals and bleeding hands that, together, produce sparkling, decadent objects that women adorn themselves with as glam armour. Over the years, though, I also started to appreciate the secondary and emotive part of alchemy, a magical process of transformation, creation or combination.

This transcended the physical or the obvious; it is the alchemy of the human spirit as it travels through the ranges and depths of emotions and experiences, from the dark, dusty hollows, and leads eventually, if we choose to go there, into a golden light that envelopes and recharges the fibres of our very being. It moves us forward. Alchemy comes from the ebb and flow of the human experience. It is not the highlight at the end of a cycle, it is the full spectrum of the experience in and of itself. It is the shadows that take us to the ocean floor, it is the broken hearts that shackle us, the almost-but-not-quite circumstances that we think are hindering our path, blocking us from where we are meant to be going. But they are not blocking it at all. They *are* the path. That *is* the process.

It's a true honour to be able to share my story with you. Having a career in the arts, I have worked across many of their disciplines, and the art of storytelling may very well be my favourite. This is because it is through storytelling that we are able to recognise parts of our own story in another's. If you recognise parts of your own story on these pages, I hope—if nothing else—it brings you a certain kind of calmness, and reminds you that wherever you are on your journey, whether your petals are facing the sun right now or retreating due to what feels like a particularly long night, this too shall pass. I also hope some of these stories might reach you like a hug or a little wink, and in doing so, no matter if you are in light or in darkness, in gold or in the dust—that some of the words on the following pages reassure you that what is meant for you is making its way to you right now. Right this very moment, you are exactly where you are meant to be.

hustler

hust·ler

noun

an aggressively enterprising person; a go-getter

When I was six years old, sick of being an only child, I prayed every single night for God to give me a big brother. Mum and Dad sat me down one day and told me that while my request for a big brother was not possible, I would however be getting a new _little_ brother or sister. I took it as a fair compromise. The following day, I excitedly told all my friends and teachers that I was not going to be an only child anymore, I was going to be a big sister!

Then one day not long after, my dad sat me down in the lounge room with him. 'The baby in Mummy's tummy has gone to heaven, Poss,' he said. That afternoon was the first time I had ever seen Dad cry. I knew from Sunday school that going to heaven meant someone had died, but I didn't know you could die before you were even born.

1

The next morning, when my Year 1 teacher at my very strict Christian school asked me how I was, all I could respond with was, 'The baby's dead.'

'Oh, Sammy. I am so sorry,' she said, crouching down so our eyes were level. 'Please tell your mummy I am thinking of her and will be praying for God to bless her.'

'God's not real!' I yelled. My teacher stood back up as the bell rang for class.

I stopped praying, and my mum never fell pregnant again.

—

By the time I was eleven years old, I was running a business selling handmade jewellery in the playground of my school. Even at that age, I knew this operation would be frowned upon, so I sold my jewellery behind the bike shed—the place all good Christian girls did things they didn't want teachers or the Lord Jesus to see. My mum had enrolled me in a beading class the previous school holidays at the local craft shop in our hometown of Port Macquarie in New South Wales. It's a little surfing town on Australia's east coast, not dissimilar to *Home and Away*'s fictional Summer Bay. I think Mum just wanted some peace and quiet at the price of $8.50 an hour, but those beading classes would have a bigger impact on my life than either of us could have predicted. There, sitting around a table at the back of the shop with a handful of other beading enthusiasts, I learnt the basics of jewellery-making.

Mum and Dad had always run their own small businesses when I was growing up, so it didn't take me long to turn my school holiday craft lessons into a money-making enterprise. Beading classes were to Saturday mornings what church was to Sunday mornings. From as early as I can remember, we would attend church every Sunday morning and every Sunday night. Monday to Friday was spent at my religious school and Christianity was the only religion I knew. I assumed everyone else was Christian, too. The only day I didn't have to put on either a Christian school uniform or my good church clothes was Saturday.

I loved Saturdays.

—

My mum and dad opened a clothing boutique in 1993. I witnessed the entire small business startup process in the months leading up to the opening of the store. Planning and strategising over the dining-room table, brainstorming marketing ideas and poring over résumés, often working well into the early hours of the mornings. When they signed the lease on the store, I helped Dad paint the new space and build the shelving for the back stockroom, and when all the clothes that Mum had ordered started to arrive, I helped with the pricing and merchandising and with filing invoices.

The store was an instant success when it opened. I would go there after school and over the Christmas holidays and wait for my parents to finish work. I figured I may as well make some extra pocket money while I was waiting, so I used to go out the front and squeak my way through 'When the Saints go Marching In' on my flute. I left the flute's red velvet case out to collect donations for my busking and I would stop when I hit my $20 target for the day, which never took too long. One Saturday, I was complaining about how bored I was, as usual, and Dad told me to 'go and make myself bloody useful' and grab a bucket and a sponge and clean the shop's sign. Mum's store was located in an outdoor mall, one of sixteen shops that all had the same glass storefront windows and large signage . . . up on the roof.

I got the ladder from the stockroom and climbed up onto the slanted tin roof, a bucket of soapy water in one hand and a sponge in the other. Dad came out to the front of the store to check on me.

'Wow! Who knew it was so dirty!' he exclaimed, admiring the sign. I had started at one end of the sign and had scrubbed it meticulously right up until the middle, a stark line between clean and dirty—the perfect before and after—like I was showcasing a new soap product on an infomercial.

'I know!' I called down to Dad. 'Look at it! It looks like two different signs!'

'Great job, it's going to look like new!' Dad said. 'I'll come back to inspect it when you are finished.'

'I am finished,' I said.

'No, you're not, you've only finished half the bloody sign!' Dad barked.

I turned around to face him. 'I've finished my free trial, to show you how good it could look,' I paused, 'if you employ my services to wash the remaining side.'

Dad's eyes started to narrow.

4

'For $20. Cash,' I added. I couldn't tell if Dad was furious or impressed.

'Finish the job, you little shit, and then get off the bloody roof before your mother sees you up there and we're both in trouble.' Dad said, heading back inside. That sounded like a deal to me.

As my mind filled with all the ways I could spend twenty bucks, my eye caught the row of dirty signs above all the other shops. Fifteen more putrid signs crying out to be cleaned. Rather than climbing back down the ladder, I proceeded along the roof, washing half of each store's signage in a complimentary demonstration of the value of my service. Then I invited the shop owners out to inspect my handiwork. Fourteen of them gave me $20 to get back up there and finish the job. One of them told me I'd better start running before he called the police.

Dad wasn't impressed with my little extortion stunt but waited in the car for me to finish until well after dark. By the time I was done cleaning all the signs, I was exhausted and my clothes were soaked but I didn't care. I started counting my wad of $20 notes.

'How much did you earn today?' Dad asked.

'Two hundred and eighty dollars!' I exclaimed, holding up the red bills like Scrooge McDuck. I was twelve years old and it was more money than I had ever held.

'Well, actually $300 . . . including what you owe me.'

Dad reached into his back pocket and pulled out his well-worn leather wallet.

'While I think your approach was a little outlaw, I am really proud of the initiative you showed today, Poss,' Dad said.

I was chuffed, and bursting with excitement to add another $20 to my kitty.

'You showed initiative and work ethic,' he said as he snapped a $20 note between his thumb and index finger, 'important traits in any businessperson.' My hand reached out for the note but Dad pulled his hand back. 'But in any good business, there are expenses,' he continued. 'To run today's enterprise, you needed equipment—a ladder, bucket, water and soap—and transport. I guess twenty bucks should cover your costs,' he said, sliding the note back into his wallet and pocketing it as my face fell.

I guess it's true what they say: you can't hustle a hustler.

—

If Mum had time on her buying trips to Sydney for the shop, she would often pick up a bag of beads and jewellery-making supplies to bring back to me. Opening the crinkled brown paper bag was like lifting the lid on a sparkling treasure chest. Inside were the most beautiful trinkets, beads and charms. The craft store in our tiny town didn't stock anything nearly as fancy as what Mum could get in Sydney, and her deliveries felt all the more special because they'd come all that way, just for me. She bought me a little olive-coloured fishing-tackle box to store everything in, and that box quickly became my most prized possession.

Still trying to keep a low profile after my sign-washing stunt the previous week, the next Saturday I took the jewellery I had made that week to Mum's shop with me and created a little stand on the counter. I had handmade swing tags and priced each piece, as well as carefully writing my business name on them: SAMart. I sold five pieces that first Saturday, so I made some more and sent the new pieces in with Mum the following day. Every night over dinner, Mum would tell me what I had sold and on my way home from school the next day I would call past the local craft shop to buy more supplies to keep my business rolling.

I loved designing and creating pieces, seeing what sold quickly and then pulling apart styles that didn't sell to remake them into something new. What I also loved was that Mum's shop was open seven days a week. Staff wages were higher on Sundays, so to save costs Mum and Dad worked on Sundays too. This meant having to go to church much less, which suited me just fine.

—

I started playing representative basketball in high school and every other weekend we would travel to play teams from other regional towns. The rep teams were made up of players from all the schools in the area and I loved everything about being on the team: the long bus rides, the cute public school boys, the non-Christian music blaring from Discmans and battery-loaded stereos and the teen magazines the public school girls would bring along.

On one trip on the rep bus, some of the kids were talking about something I had never heard of before—the process of evolution. I moved up a couple of seats to listen to the conversation for a few minutes before adding to it.

'What do you mean?' I asked genuinely, the naivety of nine years of Christian schooling loaded neatly into one question.

'How Earth was made, you know . . . ?' one of them replied. 'Evolution . . . Science?'

I knew for certain that Earth was made by God. In seven days. I remembered that at Sunday school we had been told that worldly people would try to say that we came from apes and that that was a ridiculous myth. But I'd never heard any more about it. Until now.

'God made the Earth,' I said. It was genuinely all I knew. 'Adam and Eve is where we came from . . .'

Their laughter started only a few seconds after they realised I wasn't joking.

'Ah! Yeah! I forgot! You're like a nun or something!' one of the boys said, sniggering. The laughter continued as the news spread down the bus that I believed that the world was created in seven days by a bearded man sitting up in the clouds.

'What do you mean?' I said. They were confused by my confusion. I was confused because I had no idea what they were talking about. I felt like such an outsider. I went back to my seat and stared out the window, my face burning as I held my breath to try to stop the tears. I hated religion, I thought as the rural Australian bushland whizzed by along the highway.

It turned out that the Christian school I attended taught only a Christian curriculum, which was why I had never heard of evolution. I ended up using this as the cornerstone of my argument to convince Mum and Dad to let me change schools. They finally relented and I started at Port Macquarie High School in the middle of Year 8, where I was much happier, if still a good deal more naive than my classmates.

The grunge movement of the mid-nineties was very influential in our small town. Many kids had nose-rings and bright pink or green hair. Surf-brand clothing and accessories also reigned supreme. Heavily branded surf T-shirts were coveted garments and school folders were covered with surf-magazine pictures and branded stickers. Melanie and I met in my first year at Port Macquarie High and quickly became best friends. Neither Mel nor I were allowed to dye our hair, so what we lacked in hair colour options, we had to make up for in our fashion choices. Mum would baulk at the cost of 'surfie' clothes, so I had to get savvy with my strategy. For birthdays and at Christmas, I was allowed to choose two surf-brand items, and on top of that I was allowed one surf-brand winter jumper a year. Melanie had a similar deal with her Mum, so between us we had a rotation of ten garments. We soon realised that if we very carefully unpicked the internal brand label on our surfie clothes, we could go to Big W, buy some really cheap basic T-shirts, shorts and skirts and carefully sew the surf-brand labels straight onto the outside of them—instantly transforming a pair of $8 Big W shorts into a coveted one-off Billabong item. When other kids would ask where we'd found these never-before-seen Billabong and Quiksilver clothes, we'd say they were a gift from family who lived in Brisbane or on the Gold Coast, and that they weren't available in surf shops in Port Macquarie because, as we would say, 'only the big cities get the full collections'. Pre-internet, it was pretty easy to get away with our self-produced counterfeit clothing operation and it was one of my earliest experiences of really recognising the power of branding.

While I enjoyed school, especially art and creative classes, I lacked focus in some areas. As my report cards attested.

'Samantha is incredibly creative! I only wish she would apply herself to the more technical elements of English study,' wrote my English teacher. 'Her attention to detail and process is not her strength.'

'Samantha, I am unsure how to mark you for this project,' my art teacher wrote as feedback on one assignment. 'While I appreciate the creativity that you have put into your work, you have not stuck to the assignment criteria. You have an incredibly creative mind, but I need you to focus on the technical details.'

Looking back, it was an early indication of how I would approach the opportunities in my career that I was wildly unqualified for. Technical ability didn't concern me so much; I was more focused on how to engage people through emotive storytelling and creative presentation. And creatively present, I did. Once we were given a simple sculpture assignment in art class, and I found a way to run electricity through mine so that the sculpture became a lamp. My senior major work assignment for art—a wearable gothic-inspired costume—was so large that the teachers had to call at my house to mark it as it was unable to be transported or stored at the school due to its size and construction.

They say art is subjective but it turns out you cannot use that argument with high-school assignments. No doubt my art teacher would have described my approach as unorthodox and misguided, but I would have said it was opportunistic and inspired. Over the years, my career would unfold in a similarly unconventional fashion.

In 1997, I was finishing Year 10 and had to choose my subjects for my final two years of school, which would determine the university courses I could apply for. Like a lot of other sixteen year olds, I had no idea what I wanted to do with my life.

Somewhere in my mind, I had determined that some people had careers and some people had jobs. People who went to university were the ones who had careers, the kind you needed a qualification and graduation gown for, and other people just had jobs. The community I grew up in was made up of incredibly hardworking middle-class people with jobs. That is what I knew.

From the minute I was legally able to work, I had a job. I worked at a local ice-creamery, in a galley on the local river cruiser and, during the school holidays, I dressed up as Cinderella at Fantasy Glades. Fantasy Glades was a local theme park marketed as 'four acres of enchanted rainforest'. As a kid, I thought it was the most magical place on Earth. In reality, it was a poor man's Disneyland: four acres of Everglades swampland filled with leeches, mosquitoes the size of pigeons and second-rate backyard-made versions of fairytale-inspired attractions. It was one of Port Macquarie's most popular tourist destinations.

In Year 11, as my peers stacked their senior schooling time-tables with maths and biochemistry to propel them into the best position for university applications—they all seemed to be crystal clear about what they were going to do with their lives—I went in the opposite direction with art, art theory, woodwork, photography and creative writing. I was resigned to the fact that I was probably going to stay in Port Macquarie, get a job straight out of high school and indulge in my creative hobbies on the side.

'Maybe you could get a job as a shift manager at Fantasy Glades?' my geography teacher, who moonlit as a careers advisor, offered in one of our career counselling sessions.

I pictured living out the rest of my days working among the overgrown mosquitoes. I offered a small smile in return. *Fuck,* I thought to myself.

I graduated high school in 1999 still unsure of what I wanted to do with my life. I added to my list of part-time jobs a gig waiting tables at a Hog's Breath Cafe (being a strict vegetarian at the time did not stop me upselling the prime rib if it meant taking home the $20 weekly kitty for the top-selling waitperson), a promotions girl job at an Autobarn on Saturdays and some promo work for the local radio station, Star FM, which involved driving to various locations along the coast to give away free cans of Coke or whatever product I was spruiking on any given day.

Eventually, I managed to land a full-time job at Prouds the Jewellers, who were opening a new store in Port Macquarie. They sent me a 300-page folder and told me I needed to read it before the store opened. It was like an entire encyclopedia of jewellery—no gemstone was left unturned in this *War and Peace*-length tome. Wanting to impress my new employers, I became fluent in all things jewellery over the following three weeks, putting more hours into studying that giant binder than I had into six years of high-school assignments.

'Wow, Samantha. You really have done your homework,' the area manager, Faye, said to me on our first day of instore training. Faye was an elegant woman in her mid-fifties who wore a Chanel silk scarf affixed to her blazer with a pearl brooch. Her eyes widened as I rattled off the names of different chain links and ran through freshwater, cultured and South Sea pearls and the different shapes each came in. I could tell you all about how diamonds were mined and graded and could go into great detail explaining different precious metal elements and stone settings.

'I think you have a big career ahead of you in jewellery,' Faye said, smiling at me like a proud headmistress. I beamed right back at her. The C word. She thought I could have a *career*. There was a resident jeweller who worked on site at Prouds and he kindly took me under his wing. Over the following year, he taught me everything he knew about making and repairing jewellery, while Faye taught me everything she knew about selling it.

I loved working at Prouds, but after a year I instinctively knew that it was not where I was meant to be anymore. I looked at my life and it felt like I was looking at someone else's. I knew there was something else out there for me, something more. I just had to get out there and find out what it was.

Melanie and I used to talk about how we would one day live together in a big city somewhere. We dreamed about what our apartment would look like and the fancy parties we would throw for our friends. I don't think either of us expected this dream of ours to actually come true. Nevertheless, not long after I quit my job at Prouds, we packed as much as we could fit in my Corolla hatchback, including the olive-coloured tackle box Mum had given me all those years ago. The beads and tools inside rattled as I slammed the car boot lid down, willing it to close.

'Good luck, girls!' Mum cried, waving, as we pulled out of their driveway.

'Remember to drive with your lights on, Poss!' Dad yelled. I honked the horn in response. We kept waving until we had turned the corner and then, with Destiny's Child blaring on the stereo, Mel and I looked at each other with a combination of excitement and terror.

'See you soon, Sydney!' Mel yelled out the open window.

'Bye, Port Macquarie!' I shouted.

'Goodbye, Porpoise Spit!' Mel screamed, both of us laughing as we turned onto the freeway. It was time to start a new chapter.

glimmer

glim.mer

noun

a faint or wavering light

Melanie and I moved into a tiny flat in Sydney's eastern suburbs around the same time that I enrolled in a Retail Visual Merchandising TAFE course in the city. Quickly realising that it wasn't for me, I thought I would try my hand at a tourism course instead, and within three months I was officially a TAFE double dropout. With barely enough money in my bank account to cover the following week's rent, I picked up a job at our local shopping centre working at Surf Dive 'n Ski—or SDS—a surf clothing chain. I interviewed with the company's operations director, Todd Liddy, he offered me the job and I started almost straight away. As it turned out, Todd would also help me to land another role three years later, one that shaped my career, and ultimately my life, immensely.

I had been at SDS for three months when I joined a social basketball league with some other girls from the store. I had played thousands of basketball games throughout school and never suffered more than a sprained ankle or a bruised finger. But three minutes into my first game in the social comp with the girls, I was passed the ball and went to pivot, only my shoe stayed stuck to the floor while the rest of my body spun, my knee the connecting point. I hit the ground like a dead weight as my knee exploded. The next two months would see me in a leg brace, unable to work or leave the flat without assistance.

I had a few medical appointments over those two months and Mel very generously offered to take me to them. Mel only had her learner's permit, but because I had my full licence she could legally drive with me in the car. The issue was that Mel could only drive an automatic and my trusty old Corolla was a manual. We were both flat broke and definitely could not afford the cost of taxis back and forth from the hospital, so Mel offered to do something that I am still moved by to this day—she said she'd drive my manual car in Sydney traffic. As I couldn't bend my leg, I had to sprawl across the back seat and instruct her how and when to change gears when all I could see was the car's grey upholstered ceiling. I would scream in pain as Mel bunny-hopped the car, each gear change jolting my shattered knee. Mel screamed in as much anguish at the sight of any upwards incline on the road ahead—her fear of having to do a hill start in Sydney traffic could be likened to most people's fear of death. What should have been a seven-minute drive to the hospital became a forty-minute commute as Mel drove at snail's pace, trying to stay in second gear for as long as possible while following a carefully mapped route that went out as far as the airport in an effort to avoid any hills or inclines. I wished we had filmed it, the two of us in a car travelling at eight kilometres an hour, all the other traffic honking at us, Mel screaming at me and me screaming back at her between our shared hysterical fits of laughter, a welcome respite from our respective pain.

Only five days into my two-month sentence of house arrest, I was feeling very sorry for myself. Already sick to death of daytime TV, I remembered the little olive-coloured fishing tackle box I had brought from Port Macquarie. It had been sitting on the top shelf of my wardrobe untouched.

As I had to use both hands to put my entire body weight onto my crutches in order to walk anywhere, after I pulled the box down, I had to carry it with the handle in between my teeth as I made my way back down the hallway. Its contents rattled and shook with every movement, as if the beads and crystals inside were jumping around, excited to have been remembered. It must have been a sight indeed, me in an old T-shirt and undies—as trying to get anything else on over the leg brace was too difficult—hobbling down the hall on crutches with a fishing tackle box in my mouth. That afternoon, in an attempt to quell the boredom, I sat at our kitchen table and started making jewellery again.

'What are you doing?' Mel said when she arrived home from work to find me at the kitchen table. 'How did you get there?! Holy shit! Did you make all these today?' she asked, spotting the pile of pairs of earrings next to me.

'Hey! Why are you home? Is it after 5.30 already?' I had completely lost track of time.

'Yeah, it's nearly 6.30. These are amazing!' Mel said, holding up a different pair of earrings to each ear and inspecting herself in the window's reflection. 'Can I wear these tomorrow night?'

'Yes, of course. I just made them for fun,' I said. 'I am going out of my mind and still have six weeks to go before I get this thing off my leg.' Mel had stopped listening to me and was now pawing through the pile of jewellery like a coupon queen at a bargain bin.

'Remember when you used to make jewellery in high school?' Mel asked as she held up a large crystal pair. 'These are so cool! Maybe you could start selling your jewellery again?'

'There is no way anyone would pay money for something I made on our kitchen table,' I said, securing the final component to the pair I had been working on. 'Speaking of which, let me clean this mess up so we have somewhere to eat dinner tonight.'

'Oh, don't worry about clearing off the table, you'll probably make more tomorrow!' Mel said.

'Are you sure?' I asked Mel, conscious that the beads and crystals were covering the whole table. She didn't even hear me as she was still excitedly sorting through the pile. 'I'll clean it all up tomorrow,' I promised.

We didn't know it at the time, but we would never eat another meal at that table again. From that afternoon on, it was only ever used as a jewellery-making design desk.

—

By the end of my eight-week recovery, I had unintentionally made a stockpile of jewellery that could have filled a small store. The kitchen table was stacked high with metal oven trays full of sparkling statement earrings, but with the leg brace finally off, I was back at work at the surf store five days a week. Getting home from my first day back, I found Mel in the dining room with Sophie, a friend of hers from work. Oven trays were spread across the table and Mel and Sophie picked up and inspected pieces as if they were shopping in a prestigious department store.

'This is Samantha,' Mel said, introducing me to her colleague.

'Mel's been telling me about your jewellery. It's amazing!' Sophie said. 'How much are these?'

'Oh, thank you!' I said. I blushed at her compliment but was slightly embarrassed that she thought I was trying to sell them. 'Oh, they're not—' I started.

'They're not *priced yet*,' Mel said, cutting me off. 'How much did you say these were going to be? Sixty dollars?' Looking at me, she held them up.

Sixty dollars! Was she kidding? I thought, expecting Sophie to laugh.

'Okay, great, can I get them and also these two pairs?' Sophie said, holding up two other pairs of larger earrings.

'Of course, those ones are $90 each, that's right isn't it, Samantha?' Mel said, shooting me a look. Before I could answer her, Sophie took $240 out of her wallet.

'These are really great! Thanks for letting me come over and shop,' she said, handing me the money. 'I have a few friends who

I know would *love* these, would you mind if I bring a few girls over later this week?' she asked. I was stunned.

'Yes, of course!' was all I could manage in reply. Mel caught my eye, in the way only best friends can, and gave me a silent, knowing smile.

—

I used the money from Sophie's purchase to buy more supplies and make more jewellery. My manager at SDS let me leave early on Friday and with the few dollars I had left in my bank account, I picked up a bunch of supermarket flowers, some cheese cubes, Jatz crackers and the cheapest bottle of wine I could find. I felt like I was hosting an Avon party, just like Mum used to in the late eighties. Alana, a colleague from SDS who was also a graphic designer, had kindly made some swing tags and business cards for me, glossy olive cards with my name in large white letters. I'd never had a business card before and when I took one out of the box and held it in my hand, it gave me an unexpected pang of pride.

Wow, I thought once every piece of jewellery on the table had a swing tag attached. They looked like something you might buy in a store. I heard Mel's voice as keys turned in the front door and the sound of conversation filled our flat.

'Hi, love!' Mel chirped as she threw her handbag down near the door. 'Samantha, this is everyone!' she said, gesturing to the stream of women coming through our front door. 'Everyone, this is my best friend and jewellery designer extraordinaire,

Samanthaaaa!' she added, introducing me like a game show contestant.

'Hi! Hello!' ten women chorused.

'Er . . . hi!' I said, as our guests made a beeline for the kitchen table.

'Oh my god! Look at these!' one said.

'They are stunning! If you don't take them, I want them!' another said.

'These ones are perfect for that dress you are going to wear on Saturday!' someone else squealed.

Mel winked at me and went straight into sales mode. 'Oh, you should get those ones for sure,' she said. 'And these, I mean they are both perfect for you!' Mel really was the best that night.

The buzzer to our flat sounded and I shimmied through the crowd of bodies to push the intercom.

'Hey! It's me!' Alana's voice came through the speaker, 'I hope you don't mind, I brought some friends!' I hit the button to let her in. A few moments later, Alana appeared at our front door with five women and hugged me hello. 'Sorry! Hope it's okay I brought this many people,' she whispered quickly in my ear. 'I told them I was coming to a jewellery party and they insisted!'

A jewellery party? I didn't have time to question it further. I smiled at Alana's quintet and stepped back to let them in. The women flocked towards the table like ravenous birds.

Browsing soon turned to purchasing. Melanie had found the tissue paper and was wrapping up the earrings like a department store cashier on Christmas Eve.

'Where'd all these new people come from?' Mel asked, in disbelief.

'They're Alana's friends,' I replied as a line started to form at our makeshift register. I took over wrapping and Mel took payments—our combined retail skills playing out seamlessly in the dining room of our tiny flat. What was happening felt like the Boxing Day sales. With nearly twenty women and only sixty pairs of earrings, no sooner would someone put a pair down on the table than someone else would scoop them up.

'Samantha, this is amazing! How can I book a party?' one of Alana's friends asked. 'My girlfriends would go crazy for these earrings!'

Mel and I exchanged a look.

'Yeah, of course . . . a party . . .' I stammered. 'Um, when were you thinking?'

'What about next Friday night?' she offered.

'Next Friday? Okay, great! Next Friday. Say 7 pm?' I said, knowing I would not get out of work until 6 pm.

'Great! This is your email on the swing tag, right? I'll email you tonight so you have my details. Can't wait!'

'Can I book one too?' another shopper piped up.

'Yeah, I want to book one too!' said another.

'We want to book one too!' said a woman at our 'register'. 'We have three other sisters and four sisters-in-law, not to mention our cousins, so we would have at least twenty-five women at our party . . . and that's just family!'

That night we sold forty-eight pairs of earrings, took $2740 and booked six jewellery parties. Everyone had been too busy shopping to worry about my cheap wine and Jatz cracker catering, so after everyone had left, Mel and I flopped onto the couch and opened the bottle.

'To jewellery parties!' Mel said, as we clinked glasses. 'I know you don't believe it, but I really think what you're doing is going to turn into something big.'

—

Mel's premonition started to take shape, and quickly.

I was twenty-one years old and would work at SDS Monday through Friday, host jewellery parties three or four nights a week and on the nights that I wasn't driving around Sydney with Tupperware containers full of jewellery, I was working into the early hours of the morning making more stock. The jewellery rattled away in the boot of my Corolla as I whizzed out along Parramatta Road to host a party in Sydney's western suburbs, or over the Harbour Bridge to host parties in the northern beaches area. I not only loved creating the jewellery but also a brand. I had stickers and flyers made, along with branded tissue paper and gift bags, which made at-home jewellery parties a proper retail experience. All the money from the parties went back into making more stock. I kept a basic inventory of what I had sold and made follow-up calls to confirm the parties each week. I was effectively operating a business and although my actions reflected that, my thought process did not. I loved what I was doing but I thought there was no way I could turn it into an actual long-term career. It was impostor syndrome at its finest. I was convinced I needed to keep a steady job, a job where you could rely on a weekly pay cheque—specifically paid by someone else—and which offered stability and security. Even though I was making more money from the jewellery parties than in my retail job at SDS, in my mind they were just a bit of fun. After all, what did I know about running a business?

When I didn't have a jewellery party booked on Sunday afternoons, Mel and I would often head down to Bondi Beach. The Bondi Markets were known as a launching pad for many young designers and artists. You could spend hours wandering around and rummaging the stalls to the sound of live musicians playing for the market crowds. Over 200 stalls were filled with vintage and new clothes and wares from independent designers; nothing was mass-produced and a lot of the stock sold was handmade. After we had trawled the markets on a Sunday, Mel and I would walk a few blocks over to Gould Street, where the best clothing shops in Bondi were.

One of these stores was Tuchuzy, a pioneering boutique when it came to supporting local designers. While other twenty-two year olds were idolising Robbie Williams or Justin Timberlake, I was all about brands, their founders and the stories behind their businesses—and Tuchuzy was the retailer that stocked them. To be stocked in Tuchuzy was the ultimate goal for any young Australian designer. If I saw a new brand in Tuchuzy, I instantly wanted to know *how* they got to where they were and, back in 2003, this information was predominantly accessed through one channel: print magazines. The big titles such as *Vogue, Harper's Bazaar, Cosmopolitan, Cleo* and in the following years *Madison* and *SHOP Til You Drop* would all publish monthly editions which usually featured a beautifully styled profile of a local designer. I knew when each publication was due to have a new issue hit the newsstands and I would be at a newsagency first thing on those mornings to grab my copy. I read the magazines cover to cover and then took to them with a pair of scissors, cutting out the profiles of female designers and pinning them to a corkboard I had hung on the wall above the kitchen table.

The corkboard became an inspiration board, one I would look up at when I was making jewellery for hours on end. It had interviews with Jodhi Meares on how she started Tigerlily, as well as Heidi Middleton and Sarah-Jane Clarke from sass & bide, Ruby Smallbone, Sarina Suriano, Lisa Ho and Collette Dinnigan. Even though the possibility of my little jewellery party venture ever becoming a proper brand seemed a world away, I would find myself studying these female entrepreneurs. They were who I wanted to be, if only in my wildest dreams.

Trucker hats were very on trend at the time. Mel and her boyfriend had started customising them, adding paint, patches and stencilled patterns to the blank hats. They started out just making the hats for themselves, then their friends started to buy them and, just like what had happened with my jewellery, their small business started to grow organically. Our little flat quickly turned into a creative hub, with Mel and her boyfriend painting and producing hats in the living room, and me making jewellery in the dining room. Soon enough, Mel and I were ready to become stallholders at the Bondi Markets ourselves.

It was before the days of online registration so in order to get a prime position for our stall, we'd get to the markets at 3.30 am every Sunday morning, rain, hail or shine. We took folding chairs to sit in while we waited in the line for over four hours until the gates opened and we could finally get in and set up. We treated our stall like a retail store, not like a 6 by 4 foot space with folding tables and wooden racks. Each Sunday, it was $50 to rent the space and that outlay was usually recouped in my first sale as soon as the markets opened at 10 am. I invested in a fancy calico and timber umbrella from Bunnings, jewellery displays and a vintage silver handheld mirror with a hummingbird and winding vines embossed onto it. The days were long and the 3 am wake-up time was brutal, but I loved every minute of it. What I didn't love was my Monday to Friday job at SDS. It wasn't that I hated it, but for the thirty-eight hours I was there each week, I was always thinking about my new design ideas or how to make the jewellery parties better.

The success of the jewellery parties and at the markets felt like green lights. Things were going well and the business was growing organically. Rather than follow that momentum, however, I chose to stay in my safety zone, refusing to take the leap to pursue a jewellery-making career full time. I clearly hadn't learnt the lesson that if you stay in your comfort zone too long, the universe eventually forces you out of it, one way or another. It had been almost a year since I'd broken my knee, which at the time felt like a massive setback preventing me from what I thought I was meant to be doing. In reality, my injury was actually clearing my path and giving me space for what was to come.

Blowing out my knee was the universe's effective, albeit aggressive, way of guiding me back to making jewellery. The universe didn't just deal in physical pain, however. She would have many more tricks up her sleeve to ensure I was heading in the right direction.

fu·el

noun

a thing that sustains or inflames passion, argument,
or other emotion or activity

It's funny, isn't it? The things that fuel us. And not fuel as in what
sustains us, but 'fuel on a fire'—the things that happen in life
that ignite us into action.

For almost a year, my Sundays were spent at the Bondi
Markets selling earrings from our stall. Every night, I was either
handmaking jewellery to replenish the stock or I was selling it
at jewellery parties, all while still working at SDS fulltime on
weekdays. I didn't have much of a personal life, but by now I
was used to my crazy routine.

In the public speaking I do now, one of the questions I get
asked most often by people wanting to start their own business
is, 'When do you know it is the right time to quit your "real"

job?' My answer is that there is never going to be a right time. There will always be a voice in your head that tells you to keep up the juggling act for *just a little while longer.*

What if my business doesn't work out? that voice says. But the universe will only put up with this idleness for so long before she sends something or someone to propel you forward. Maybe a better question for the voice to ask would be: *But what if it does?*

Justin Chung was a local distributor for a few Australian fashion brands and he often had a stall at the markets where he would clear excess stock and samples from past seasons. Mel and I would sometimes chat to him as we all waited in the stallholder line each Sunday. Australian Fashion Week was fast approaching—an event I would watch from a distance, as the who's who of the Sydney social scene appeared in the weekend papers looking glamorous at all the designer shows and parties. It was a world away from my small-town upbringing and a scene that intimidated me greatly. One Sunday afternoon, as the lunchtime market crowd was starting to thin, Justin approached my stall.

'Samantha! I've been meaning to ask you. I have taken a showroom in the Source at Fashion Week. I am putting six of my brands in there and I have a small panel still vacant. I was wondering if you would want to take it? Maybe display your collection to get it into some retail stores? The panel is about the size of a door,' he went on. 'It's not huge, but it's the perfect size for jewellery.'

'You think I could display at Fashion Week?' I asked, mouth agape. 'You know I just handmake it all on my kitchen table, right?'

'I know,' he said, 'but your stall is always so busy, I really think you could present to retailers. Anyway, you don't have to decide now. Have a think about it and shoot me an email,' he said, handing me his card. 'The available panel would be $500 and would easily fit your collection, and the trade show goes for four days.'

I was flattered that Justin would think I even had a 'collection' to present, let alone something worthy of being shown at Fashion Week. That night I sent him an email thanking him for thinking of me, but that I didn't feel I was nearly ready to take him up on his offer. I suggested he look for someone else to take the spare panel at his booth.

Around this time, I had been on a few dates with a guy, Jack, who ran the door at a club in the city that Mel and I had been to a few times. He was twenty-nine and I was twenty-two. It all seemed very glamorous and grown-up and I was thrilled when he invited me to an exclusive show that was taking place the following Wednesday evening and said he would be in touch to arrange the details. But Wednesday came and went and I never heard from him. He didn't respond to the text I sent him either, a last-ditch effort to try to get some kind of explanation.

'Maybe I'm not, I don't know, cool enough for him,' I said to Mel at home after he ghosted me. 'I mean, why would he want to date someone like me?' I focused my eyes on a spot on the floor while trying desperately not to cry.

'You listen to me right now,' Mel said with a conviction that commanded me to look up at her. 'Stop talking this rubbish. You are beautiful and funny and talented and amazing and he should be so lucky to date you!' She grabbed both my shoulders and gently shook them as she spoke. 'I am *sure* there is a simple explanation for this that has nothing to do with you. He might have just been really busy with work this week. Or he might have something going on with his family, an emergency or something,' Mel said hopefully, as she went through every single possible reason a boy didn't call when he said he was going to. The next few days passed by slowly. My heart felt heavy and there wasn't much I could focus on besides wondering why he had just disappeared.

On Sunday morning, Mel and I were back at Bondi Markets and Mel went to get us coffees while I held our spot in the stallholder line.

'Here you go,' Mel said, returning with two lattes and the Sunday papers.

'You're the best! Thank you!' I said, taking a coffee and one of the newspapers from her.

No sooner had Mel settled herself back into her folding chair, coffee in one hand and social pages in the other, than she gasped dramatically.

'What?' I said, curious. 'What is it? Are you okay?'

'Oh, yes, yes! All fine,' Mel said, closing the paper. 'It's going to be a beautiful day, don't you think? This sunrise, I mean . . . spectacular!' she added, putting the paper on the ground and taking a sip of her coffee.

'Is everything okay?' I asked, immediately suspicious.

'Yes, of course! Great! Why?' Mel said. She was a terrible liar.

'What's in the paper?' I asked.

'Oh, there's nothing in there, boring, nothing worth reading at all,' she said, unable to look me in the eye.

'Melanie. Give me the paper.'

'Okay . . . okay,' she said, picking it up slowly. 'But before I give it to you, I'm going to tell you something,' she added, as if about to inform me of a death in the family, 'and it's not good.'

'Okay . . .' I said. Her tone was making me nervous.

'Okay. Well . . . I know why Jack didn't take you to the show,' Mel said, her voice calm and quiet. 'It's, um, it's . . . it's because he took someone else.' She carefully opened the paper and tilted it towards me. The glitterati had descended on the opening night of Wednesday's show and there Jack stood, smiling for the cameras with his arm wrapped tightly around the waist of gorgeous *Home and Away* actress Tammin Sursok.

My stomach churned in a blend of nausea and hollowness, as though I had suddenly lost several vital organs. I wished I could have gone on thinking that maybe Jack had just mislaid his phone or something and that's why he never reached out, but now I had a lovely photo of the happy couple to clear up any misconception I may have had. It was brutal.

'I'm so sorry,' Mel said, moving her chair closer to mine as I fought back tears.

'Those papers always have bad news anyway,' Mel said, 'but the *good* news is, we *never* have to see him again.' She got up and threw the paper into the closest bin, then put her arm around me and I rested my head on her shoulder. We didn't move until they opened the market gates at 8 am and we filed in to set up for the day.

The universe really does have a sense of humour, and while I didn't see a funny side at that moment, when the cosmic choreography on the universe's dance card that afternoon was revealed it would be nothing short of poetic.

The afternoon rush at the markets was slowing down, and I had just finished with a customer when Mel appeared beside me.

'You know how I said you'd never have to see him again?' she said, quickly and through clenched teeth.

'See who? What?' I said, confused.

'Him, Jack!' she said urgently. 'Well, he's here, he's with her! They're coming this way!'

Before the final word had even left Mel's mouth, there on the other side of my market-stall table stood Jack and Tammin.

'Sam ... hi!' I heard him say. He stood smiling at me like we were old school friends that hadn't seen each other since graduation.

'Hey,' was all I could muster as I tried to smile back.

'So, this is the little hobby you were telling me about?' he said, eyeing my table of jewellery.

'Um,' I said, another wave of nausea rising in my stomach. 'Yeah, these are my designs.'

'Very cool,' he said, as he put his arm around Tammin. 'Well, good to see you, and you know, good luck with it all.'

Tammin nestled her head into his shoulder as they walked away.

His words cut into me sharply, sucking all the air from my lungs.

'Would you mind covering my table for a few minutes?' I said to Melanie.

'Of course, my love,' she said softly.

I ran to the school toilets, which doubled as the amenities for the Sunday markets, stood in front of the stainless-steel sinks and sobbed until my face was blotchy and wet with tears. I cried because his words made me feel so disposable, but in that moment something more powerful overrode the hurt that I felt. I was mad. Mad that he didn't call me to let me know he had made other plans for Wednesday night and really mad that he had just dismissively referred to my business as a 'little hobby' in such a flippant way.

I'll show you what I'm going to do with my 'little hobby', I thought. My anger was adding fuel to a fire that I didn't even realise was ignited.

I wiped my face, took a deep breath and started to make my way back to our stall. Just as I returned to my table, Justin walked past, and this time I heard the universe's message loud and clear.

'Justin!' I called out, the words out of my mouth before I could even think about them. 'I'm in!' I said. 'If the offer still stands and that space in your Fashion Week showroom is still available, I'll take it!'

It was. And I did.

It's funny, isn't it? . . . The things that fuel us.

Fashion Week was only six weeks away and as I vowed to never refer to my jewellery as a hobby again, I had a lot to get done—if I truly meant business, the first step was to actually register it as a business. I called Dad and he walked me through everything I needed to do to become a legitimate working entity.

I logged into my bank account and saw I had $509 in available funds. My wages from SDS were due the following day and I didn't want to lose the spot at Fashion Week, so with a deep breath and a silent prayer, I transferred the $500 to Justin.

Colette, a fashion assistant at *Cleo* magazine, had contacted me to book a jewellery party. She wanted to have it at lunchtime at her work, in the Australian Consolidated Press offices in central Sydney. So a few days after booking my space at Fashion Week, I walked through the heavy double-glass doors that opened into the giant marble foyer of the ACP building, then home to the most coveted magazine titles in the country. All the pages and designer profiles I had tacked to my inspiration board had been produced in these offices.

Surrounded by ultra-glamorous chic women, I was suddenly very self-conscious of the floaty bohemian print dress I had chosen to wear that morning.

'The boardroom is through this way,' Colette said, taking me up to *Cleo* headquarters. 'Let's get you set up, and then I'll send out an email and let the girls know when they can come in.'

'Thank you so much for hosting this today, Colette,' I said as she swiped her security card to open the boardroom door. 'I really appreciate it.'

'Not a problem at all. Everyone is very excited,' she said, flicking on the lights above the huge twenty-four-seat boardroom table. 'I'll leave you to it. Shout if you need anything.'

A few minutes later, a parade of women dressed much better than I'd ever been in my life started to pour through the board-room door. The jewellery party I thought I was doing for Colette and a few of her *Cleo* colleagues turned out to be the biggest media showing I would ever do. Colette hadn't just sent the invite out to her *Cleo* workmates, she had sent it to the entire building. All of Australia's major fashion editors came to the boardroom that day. For the next hour, the room was buzzing with everyone from interns to editors of Australia's biggest fashion publications, all oohing and ahhing over the jewellery I had displayed on the table. By the end of the showing, the boardroom table that had been filled with jewellery one hour before was now all but empty.

'That went great!' Colette said afterwards, beaming at me. 'I am so glad the *Women's Weekly* girls came up! Everyone *loves* your designs!' Colette gave me a hug and headed back to her desk as I stood there alone in the boardroom, completely overwhelmed by what had just happened. I counted the money I had collected. It was exactly how much I needed to cover the costs for Fashion Week.

The universe had already outdone herself that day, but she wasn't finished yet. By the time I got home that afternoon, I had two emails waiting in my inbox.

TO: Samantha Wills

FROM: Colette Harvey

SUBJECT: Today + call in

Babe—thanks again for today!

So . . . confidentially, we are shooting Nicky Hilton next week.

My Fashion Director LOVED your work today and has asked

if you can send in some statement pieces for the shoot.

Let me know if possible!

C x

TO: Samantha Wills
FROM: Fashion Assistant AWW
SUBJECT: Product request
Hi Samantha,

I met you today at ACP. My Fashion Director has asked if you could please send in a selection of peach/gold-toned earrings. Only thing is, we would need them here tomorrow morning as we are shooting tomorrow afternoon. Please let me know if you can have a selection to our receiving dock by 9 am?

Regards,

Nicole

I couldn't believe what I was reading. I stayed up all night making the pieces for each request. After wrapping them as though they were being delivered to the Queen herself, I finally put my head on the pillow at 4.15 am. By 6 am, I was up again, bundling myself and all my packages into my car to beat the morning traffic and drop the deliveries off in time.

'This one is for *C-l-e-o* m-a-g-a-z-i-n-e,' I said, pronouncing my words as though the guy behind the desk at the receiving dock was hard of hearing. 'And this one is for the *A-u-s-t-r-a-l-i-a-n W-o-m-e-n's W-e-e-k-l-y*.' I handed the second package over like it was my firstborn baby going to day care for the first time.

'No worries, love,' the guy behind the desk said, taking the parcels from me with a smile. He then tossed each package into a plastic storage tub with the respective magazine title spelt out on the side with peeling packing tape.

I drove to work with a different kind of energy that day—not even the Sydney peak-hour traffic could dampen my mood.

I couldn't believe my designs had been called in by a magazine! For the first time, I started to feel like maybe Mel was right about this jewellery thing. Maybe I *was* on the verge of something big.

—

One afternoon three days out from Fashion Week, I checked my Nokia mobile phone:

19 MISSED CALLS

15 VOICE MESSAGES

The fifteen voicemails were all from different women wanting to buy the pair of earrings Delta Goodrem was wearing in the latest issue of *The Australian Women's Weekly*. With no idea what they were talking about, I scribbled down the numbers and names of the callers, jumped into my car and sped to the nearest news-agency. Alongside the grated metal frames displaying the front pages of the national newspapers, there was Delta Goodrem on the cover of *The Australian Women's Weekly*. At the age of eighteen, Delta, then an actress on *Neighbours*, had recently revealed that she was undergoing treatment for Hodgkin's lymphoma. The nation was cheering for her to make a full recovery. I grabbed a copy of the magazine and flicked through to the main feature. There it was, a glossy full-page image of Delta wearing my earrings—the gold fans with peach-coloured crystals cascading from them that I had stayed up through the night a few weeks ago to make and then deliver to the ACP dock. In the corner of the page were the credits for her outfit. *DELTA WEARS: COLLETTE DINNIGAN AND SAMANTHA WILLS EARRINGS.*

I spent the rest of that day making as many pairs of those earrings as I could and calling back the customers who had left messages. I made thirty-eight pairs that day. Thirty-seven of them were allocated to customers, and one pair was for my collection at Fashion Week. By the end of the day, there was a waitlist for forty more pairs.

I barely slept a wink the night before Fashion Week, but at 8 am, I walked into the Overseas Passenger Terminal at Circular Quay with an official Australian Fashion Week Exhibitor security pass around my neck, a jewellery collection that I had handmade on my kitchen table and a carbon-copy triplicate order book. It was 2004, I was twenty-two years old and I had absolutely no idea that the next four days were about to change my life.

Fashion Week itself was equal parts exhilarating, intense and exhausting. After the four days were over, I sat at my kitchen table on the Sunday evening and I flicked through each page of my carbon-copy order book, my handwritten orders scrawled across each page.

'This can't be right,' I said to Mel.

'What can't be right?' she said, getting up from the couch to peer over my shoulder.

'This,' I said, showing her the calculator. 'That's the total from all the orders I took this week. This is the third time I've added it up.'

'Holy shit,' Mel said, staring at the display. I punched the numbers in one more time just to be sure.

Still the same: $17,489.

'Fuck,' I said, to no one in particular. Mel and I sat speechless as I flicked back though my order book. Above each order I had written the store's name and their requested delivery date. All the pages said the same thing.

DELIVERY: Two Weeks.

In my inexperience and with my focus just on selling the jewellery, I had promised *every* buyer a two-week delivery from the date they placed the order. I had not taken into account the logistics and lead times required for me to handmake $17,489 worth of orders.

If the overall dollar total was intimidating, seeing the styles broken down by unit quantities was even more so, with orders for the bestselling style alone tallying up to sixty pairs. *That's 120 individual earrings just in the one style*, I thought, staring at the numbers in front of me.

I started to panic, wondering how in the hell I was going to manage to do all of this *and* keep my full-time job at SDS.

'I just remembered! I've got something to show you!' Mel said as she disappeared and returned quickly with that Sunday's newspaper.

'Oh god,' I said, wincing at her. 'Please don't tell me Jack and Tammin are in there *again*?'

'No! Forget about them!' Mel said dismissively. 'Have a look at *this*.' She placed the paper in front of me, opened at the weekly astrology readings.

SAGITTARIUS   Nov 23–Dec 21

If you don't believe in your plan, how can you expect
anyone else to? How can you sit idly by while it is being
doubted and denigrated? It is time to reassess your
relationship with the fence. If you continue to perch so
precariously on it, you will surely develop a real pain in
the . . . well, let's just say that you now need to give your
heart and soul to the pursuit of an essential objective.
Add effort to faith and you just can't lose.

There, right in front of me, was the answer to my problem.
There was no way I could complete the jewellery orders *and*
continue to work my SDS job. The universe had been trying
to get my attention for a while, and now she had spelt it out in
black-and-white print for me. *You now need to give your heart and
soul to the pursuit of an essential objective.*

I handed in my resignation at SDS the following morning.

leap of faith

leap of faith

noun

an act of believing in something whose existence cannot
be proved, or attempting something when the outcome
cannot be known

In all the time I spent worrying about what would happen if I quit
my 'real' job, not once did I think, *What if this jewellery thing goes
really well?* No, it was always worst-case scenario. This basket of
fears that we carry around with us—continually adding different
reasons as to why we shouldn't try something new—can become
a very heavy load. We often don't actually realise how heavy
that burden is until we let go of it. Once I made the decision to
focus all my energy on my jewellery business, I didn't look back.
Stripped of my safety net of a guaranteed weekly salary, I had
no choice but to dive into the deep end and swim.

I wanted to symbolically mark the decision, so I went to Officeworks and purchased a large desk to store all of my beads, crystals and metal components in. All of a sudden, the kitchen table was no longer my place of work; the dining room became my office and my new desk became my workbench. I looked around, pleased with my new workspace. This was no longer a hobby: it was a business. I had an Officeworks desk to prove it.

Over the next two weeks, I barely moved from that desk. I worked till at least four o'clock every morning, slept for a few hours, then got back to it. Every afternoon at 4.30, I would race down to the post office and send off whatever orders I had completed that day, just in time for the 5 pm post. The repetitive movement of the plier handles quickly created blisters on every finger and in the palm of my right hand. Not having had any time to heal, they would be reunited each morning with the weapon that caused them such pain. I wrapped my fingers in fabric bandaids, which I had to replace every hour. Either the handle of the pliers would wriggle the bandaids off, exposing the open wound, or blood would start to soak through them. But by the end of the fortnight, all the orders had been shipped. On the evening of that final post run, I removed all the bandaids from my hands and slowly submerged them in a bowl of Dettol. They stung as the seeping blisters drank in the whisky-coloured antiseptic. It was both a physical initiation and a warning of what was to come.

That year, 2004, was also when the Australian model Jennifer Hawkins was crowned Miss Universe. Shortly after she'd won, I saw a promo for her first exclusive appearance back in Australia, to take place on the hugely popular panel TV show *The Footy Show*. Jennifer was the toast of the nation, and I wanted nothing more than to get some jewellery to her. She was to appear on the show that evening and I had a friend who worked on the set. Prefacing that I knew it was a long shot, I asked him to give some of my jewellery to Jennifer on my behalf.

For the next six hours, I carefully made eight pairs of earrings. Wrapping them like a department store gift, I whizzed across the Sydney Harbour Bridge to the Nine Network studios, parked the car in a no-standing zone and ran to the studio's courier dock. I made it with about three minutes to spare before they closed for the day. My friend made good on his promise and got the parcel to Jennifer. I knew this not just because he told me, but because for the next week, Jennifer appeared in the paper each day as the media reported on her various appearances—and in every photograph, she was wearing a pair of earrings I had made for her. I couldn't believe it. I added the newspaper clippings of Jennifer into an 'As Worn By' folder I had started with the Delta Goodrem shoot.

The biggest surprise was when, a few weeks later, Jennifer appeared, just like Delta had, in a feature in *The Australian Women's Weekly*. She must have taken the earrings I had given her to the photoshoot, because there she was, the most talked about celebrity in Australia in the country's most read magazine, wearing Samantha Wills earrings. My phone didn't stop ringing. This time, orders not only came in directly from customers, but also from the retailers who had placed orders at Fashion Week wanting to order more pairs. A few weeks later, a handwritten note arrived all the way from New York City. It was a card from Jennifer Hawkins—a fellow small-town girl whose success I admired greatly—thanking me for the earrings.

Like most Australian twenty-somethings, Mel and I had booked a backpacking trip. We planned to travel for a few months exploring the world. The deadline was looming for the final payment for our trip and I so badly wanted to go with her, but Samantha Wills jewellery was really taking off and I knew if I took a few months off to travel, I would lose all the momentum I had already built with the brand. I decided to stay and give everything I had to the business, but it wasn't easy to wave Mel off at the airport and head back to my desk, choosing a set of pliers over my passport.

It was around this same time that, while having drinks with friends at the local pub, I met Andrew. We hit it off straightaway and meeting him certainly distracted me from the fact I had decided to stay at home and work when all my friends were uploading photos of their European adventures to their Myspace pages. Within a month, Andrew and I were officially dating. Meanwhile, the brand was going from strength to strength. By the end of 2004, my designs were stocked in thirty retailers across Australia. Such momentum in my first year of operating the business as a sole trader came as a shock to me. Andrew was incredibly supportive as my days got busier, and when I didn't think I could keep up with the demand, he would often spend late nights sitting at my workbench helping me cut wires, thread swing tags and pack orders. His support meant the world to me and his generosity made me fall in love with him even more.

As I didn't have any capital behind me at startup, building a wholesale business meant I had to accept orders with thirty-day payment terms, so credit cards became my cashflow.

To get by, I was relying heavily on the money I made from jewellery parties, but I also knew that retailers would not continue to stock a brand in their stores that was also sold via a party plan model. As a way of getting around this, I decided to keep the Samantha Wills brand just for retailers and I rebranded the jewellery for the parties under the name Bamboo Oyster.

Running two brands as a 23-year-old inexperienced sole trader was tricky, and with the Samantha Wills retailer stockist list growing, I struggled to meet the demands of production while still making sure all other areas of the business were functioning. I did not understand the power of sometimes simply saying no. I worried that declining an opportunity would mean I would lose it forever.

The brand continued to grow in profile, but there was a mounting pile of work to go with it. I was receiving a constant flow of emails from retailers wanting to reorder, return a faulty item, order a special colour combination for a VIP customer or chase their orders, and my phone rang nonstop. It would have been a normal day-to-day business for a team of people, but I didn't have a team—it was just me. I was the designer, manufacturer, salesperson, warehouse manager, accounts department, marketer, personal assistant, courier, cleaner and stock manager. The most time-consuming part was making the stock. I was too small an operation to look at outsourcing the manufacturing entirely, but I definitely needed an extra set of hands to help with the production.

I decided to bring Melanie's stepmum in to assist me. Her name was Grace but everyone called her Bunda, which is the Indonesian word for mother. Bunda was a very talented seamstress who was excited to help out. She focused on the production of Bamboo Oyster while I looked after Samantha Wills and her help took a huge weight off my shoulders.

I still needed more help on the business side, though. What I really needed was a jack-of-all-trades to help me get through the backlog of tasks that needed to be done. One of the biggest hurdles I'd had while wearing all the hats as a one-woman show was the tricky balance of working as both the salesperson *and* as accounts receivable. Building strong relationships with retailers, then having to call those same retailers and tell them their accounts were overdue was not ideal for the relationship.

To help manage accounts receivable, I did something that was conceivably, and almost definitely, illegal. It would be considered fraud at worst, catfishing at best. But one evening, neck deep in trying to get through a pile of unpaid invoices, I had an idea. I invented a fake employee. Renee was her name and I thought she was the perfect candidate. Renee was promptly given the title of accounts receivable manager and she was to play the bad cop to my good cop, thereby protecting the relationships I was building with retailers. Renee got an email address that evening and got to work straightaway, emailing our retailers from her new email address to introduce herself and tell them she'd be running the accounts department and cc'ing me. I thought that adding the word 'department' made us—us being Renee and me—sound more legitimate, like we were working from a bustling fashion head office rather than from a small room near my kitchen. The introduction of Renee to the business—albeit illegal—proved a great success and we quickly became a formidable team. Retailers would often comment that the new girl, Renee, worked very strange hours, as they would often receive account reminders from her well after midnight. I would just tell them that Renee was *very* dedicated. It was all going well until people started calling to speak to Renee, wanting to pay their account over the phone by credit card.

'Good afternoon, Samantha Wills Designs,' I answered the phone one afternoon.

'Hello, I'd like to speak to the Accounts Department,' the voice at the other end of the line said. 'Can you put me through to Renee please?'

Fuck.

'Um . . . yes,' I stammered. 'Hold the line, please.' The phone did not have a hold or mute button, so I just put the phone face down on my desk, counted silently to ten, put the phone back to my ear and said, 'Hello, Renee speaking', in what I hoped was a slightly different voice.

I was beyond relieved when by the end of that phone call Renee had seamlessly processed our first credit card transaction and the retailer had thanked her very much for her time. She really was doing a great job. I just hoped no one showed up wanting to meet with her.

There was one particular retailer that I really wanted the brand stocked in. I figured I needed to do something special to get their attention, so I decided to bedazzle the bejesus out of my lookbook, the catalogue you give to buyers that showcases photographs of the whole collection. So I made a quick trip down to Spotlight and had a rummage through their clearance bin, and found a roll of dark red heavy tapestry-type material. That afternoon, I cut the fabric into 500 pieces and dropped the pieces off to a local screen-printer who emblazoned the Samantha Wills logo onto the fabric in metallic gold. Two days, sixteen cans of spray adhesive and one piercing headache from aerosol glue fumes later, I had 500 regal red lookbooks ready to send out to media and buyers. Well, I thought they were ready until I caught a whiff of them. I hadn't anticipated the overwhelming smell of the industrial-strength glue. Not wanting retailers to experience the same when they opened the envelope, I got out the folding clothes line and draped the lookbooks over it and every other available hanging surface in our flat. I strung up rope from handrail to door handle, hung the little crimson books over them and let them flap in the breeze. By morning, thanks to a combination of night air and Febreze air-freshener, they were ready to be mailed out. That night air must have done them the world of good because a few days later, the buyer from my dream retailer called. They wanted me to meet with them the following week.

'Hi! I'm Amelia, the buyer's assistant,' a young woman who was about my age said as she walked into the boardroom in their offices. 'I think we spoke on the phone?' Her attention went straight to the jewellery I had laid out. 'The pieces are beautiful!' she exclaimed, before I could introduce myself.

'Thank you!' I replied.

'So, when is Samantha getting here?' Amelia asked, looking up from the product and staring straight at me.

'Pardon?' I said, thinking I'd misheard her. 'Samantha? Is she running late?' she asked. 'The buyers will only deal with the designer, not the intern . . . you understand, right?'

'Um, I . . . I am Samantha,' I said, almost shrugging my shoulders in apology.

'*You're* Samantha? Samantha Wills?' She sounded as shocked as she looked.

'I am SO sorry, I had no idea,' she said. Her cheeks had turned the shade of my lookbooks. 'Let me go get the buyers.'

She practically ran out of the room and returned a few minutes later with the buyers. It took them the same amount of time to tell me they wouldn't be stocking the range in their stores.

'It's not right for us,' they said, through tight, forced smiles.

I knew they had a problem with my age, which in fairness to them, I kind of understood. Their store stocked international designer brands. A retailer of that stature didn't want to do business with a kid and, whether their level of self-importance was elevated or not, it was clear to me that these buyers saw the meeting as a waste of their time.

I was twenty-three years old and I never wanted anyone to doubt that I was capable simply because of my age. That afternoon, I decided the brand needed some embellishments— something that would address any concerns buyers might have about doing business with a twenty-three year old who ran the operation from her dining room. If I were going to be taken seriously, 23-year-old me figured that adding foreign countries beneath the logo was a great first step at appearing international and alluring. Sydney was a given, London seemed to be on every international designer's list, so that was in, and lastly, I chose Munich because I thought the umlaut above the 'u' in München looked very fashion-chic. Next, I gave myself a fancy title that suggested the opposite of intern. I was no longer Samantha Wills, Jewellery Designer—now I was Samantha Wills, Managing Director. I added the words 'Global Head Office' next to the address of the flat and gave us a numbered 'Suite' to make it sound like our headquarters were in a fancy high-rise building. It was as if that list of cities was an order sent direct to the universe—call it the law of attraction or a sheer coincidence but what happened next was truly incredible.

Three days after ordering my new and improved business cards with the new global office details, the phone rang.

'Good morning, Samantha Wills Designs,' I said.

'Hi, can I speak to Samantha please?' a friendly voice said.

'Speaking!' I replied.

'Samantha, hi! My name is Belinda,' she said. 'I have a sales agency in Germany that represents Australian brands. I'm from Sydney originally and am back here in Sydney for the week and I saw your work in a store in Surry Hills and loved it!'

'I'm calling,' she continued, 'to see if you would be interested in having sales representation in Germany?'

I couldn't believe it. I sat there stunned as Belinda took me through the logistics of her agency before asking if I had any questions for her.

'Just one,' I said, biting my lower lip. 'What city is your showroom located in?'

'We're in Munich,' she replied.

I was walking on a cloud when I went down to the post office to send out the day's orders. I was about to call Andrew to tell him about what had just manifested when another email caught my eye.

It was from Coco Ribbon, an exclusive boutique in Notting Hill, London, that stocked exclusively Australian designers and counted Elle Macpherson and Sienna Miller as regular customers. They wanted to know if I'd be interested in being stocked by them. I had an article about Coco Ribbon pinned to the inspiration board above my workbench. The store and its founder featured in magazines regularly because of their celebrity following. I emailed Alison, the owner, back immediately with lookbooks and order forms, telling her I would be absolutely honoured.

It was a surreal day. New business cards, a German distributor, a London stockist and the feeling that the universe was always eavesdropping.

The business continued to grow, as did the amount of space I required. More orders flowed in, which meant more components, more packing boxes and more paperwork. I'd outgrown the dining room, so I started looking for a small studio space to rent, and quickly found one in Alexandria in Sydney's inner west. Andrew and I celebrated our one-year anniversary at the same time that Mel returned from her overseas travels, and I couldn't have been happier. Mel told me all her amazing stories from her European adventures and I filled her in on everything that had happened over the past few months. It was so great to have her back and, now that the business was moving into its own studio space, it felt like Mel and I had our little flat back—and could, for the first time in a year, once again actually use the dining room. Mel helped me pack up all my jewellery supplies, Andrew loaded it all into a van and together we set up the new Samantha Wills global headquarters in a gorgeous split-level studio in Alexandria.

As sales continued to boom, I appointed a sales agency, Homfrays, to manage sales across all Australian states and territories, allowing me to focus on the design, marketing and production sides of the business. Libby, the founder of Homfrays, suggested that I needed to get more press, the kind of profiles that focused on me, the designer, rather than the jewellery. 'Profile PR' would attach a level of luxury to the brand, she said. Soon afterwards, I got an email from the features editor of *SHOP Til You Drop*, a retail-focused fashion magazine. She wanted to profile me and the business structure I had built around the jewellery parties. It was exactly the type of press Libby had suggested, but while it would have been great exposure, Samantha Wills Jewellery and Bamboo Oyster were now two separate entities by necessity, and my appearing in the magazine piece would be confusing to the consumer and detrimental to the Samantha Wills brand. Mel, bless her, agreed to appear in the Bamboo

Oyster profile on my behalf and posed with a bunch of models to replicate a jewellery party in a very stylish, very glamorous magazine shoot. The editor told us the piece would be published in three months.

That weekend, Andrew lugged the last of the paperwork and my filing cabinet upstairs into my new design studio, where he also set up my desk, printer and phone lines.

'It's definitely minimal, babe!' Andrew joked. Occupying a dining room was one thing, inhabiting an entire studio was another.

'I know, I will have to get a couch and something to display the jewellery on,' I said, looking around the empty space.

'Well, I have a surprise for you,' Andrew said as the studio's buzzer sounded. 'You can't have a global head office without furniture!'

Andrew smiled at me as two delivery men started to carry in an assortment of furniture and shelving. Not wanting me to sit in an empty office space all day, Andrew had bought me a beautiful couch, coffee table and display unit to put in the main section of the studio.

'This is too much,' I said, my eyes filling with tears. 'I don't even know what to say. Thank you so much.' I didn't know what I'd done to get so lucky with Andrew.

'You deserve it,' he said, kissing my forehead, 'I'm so proud of you.'

—

Just as I couldn't have predicted my transition from kitchen table operation to international stockists and official headquarters, there was also no way of forecasting what happened one Sunday evening in early November, only a few months after Andrew surprised me with the new furniture. We had spent the day together down at Bondi Beach and were heading back to his house to order a Sunday night pizza and rent a movie.

'What do you think about one margarita and one BBQ Chicken?' I called from the kitchen. He didn't reply. 'Babe? You there? I'm starving! What pizzas do you want?'

'I'm here,' he said quietly, appearing in the doorway of the kitchen.

I turned to face him, still holding the pizza menu. His face was drained of colour.

'I'm sorry. I can't do this,' he whispered, barely able to look at me. 'I think we should take a break.'

'What?' I whispered. The pizza menu dropped to the floor.

'I'm so, so, so, sorry,' Andrew said. His shoulders slumped and his eyes were fixed on the ground. 'I'm so sorry.'

I couldn't breathe. It felt like someone was suffocating me from inside my body. I didn't see it coming and, more than that, I didn't understand it at all. I don't remember driving home that night and I don't really remember the days that followed either. The break turned into a break-up, and I allowed that break-up to break more than just my heart.

tsunami

tsunami

noun

an arrival or occurrence of something in overwhelming
quantities or amounts

The wave of grief didn't wash over me, it pinned me down and
wouldn't let me resurface. I couldn't bring myself to go to the
office and be surrounded by the furniture Andrew had given
me only a few months earlier. I just stayed in bed. I would drift
in and out of sleep during the day, having not slept a wink the
night before. Mel would gently knock on my door and put tea
and toast on my bedside table where it would still be, untouched,
when she returned home a few hours later. My bedroom in
our little flat faced west and the afternoon sun would fill it,
trapping heat between the four walls. My body felt as though
it had fused with the mattress, and the buzz of the oscillating
fan provided a numbing soundtrack. At twenty-three, it was my

first experience of adult heartbreak and I didn't know how to navigate the darkness I felt closing in around me.

My phone buzzed with a text message. 'Hi Sam, it's Libby. Just wanted to make sure you got the first of the orders?' I stared blankly at my phone. I hadn't been to the office in well over a week. When you're a solopreneur, your business doesn't care if you're injured, have a broken heart or are in the midst of a personal crisis. You can't call in sick to the boss—you are the boss.

'Hi Libby!' I typed, faux cheerfully, relieved I could text rather than call her. 'I'm so sorry!! I have been a bit under the weather this past week or so and haven't been at the office. Hoping to be back in tomorrow!!' I hit send, rolled over and went back to sleep.

The next morning, I stood in front of the bathroom mirror. It was the first time I had seen my own reflection in a week and it was the first time ever that I really didn't recognise the person looking back at me. Her face was gaunt and her collarbone and shoulders protruded much more severely than usual. I took a deep breath, willed the girl in the mirror to pretend that she was someone else for the next few hours and promised her we could go back to bed soon.

When I turned the key in the door to my office, I was greeted by the sight of all of the furniture that Andrew had bought for me, taunting me. There was a pile of papers in the tray of the fax machine. The orders had been streaming in while I was away—a whole forty-nine of them. *Fuck*.

'Hi Libby, back in the office, feeling much better,' I lied. 'Just want to check I haven't missed anything, I have 49 orders here. Is that everything?'

'Yep, that's all,' Libby typed back.

Thank Christ! I thought, breathing a small sigh of relief. 'Fantastic!' I tapped out. 'I will get started on them today and will let you know when shipped. Thank you!'

My phone beeped again. Another message from Libby. 'Brilliant! Will send thru the orders from the rest of states over the next two weeks. The new buyers loved the collection, really excited to be representing the brand!'

I flicked through the forty-nine pages in my hand, only now noticing that all the store addresses were from just one state, New South Wales. Libby still had Queensland, Victoria, Tasmania and Western and South Australia to show the collection to.

Over the next few weeks, the orders continued to stream in—and I continued to fall apart. Putting a sales agency on was a great move to grow the revenue and distribution, but growth only works if you have the logistics and structural back end in place to support it—an area my operation was sorely lacking in. The break-up, the demands of the business and the front I was trying to maintain to juggle everything all got too much. I would be on autopilot during the day but the minute I got home, I would crumble. It felt like there was a shadow always hovering and that no matter how fast I moved, I couldn't escape it. I often burst into tears as soon as I walked through the front door, then again in the shower and sometimes again at 3 am as I stared at my bedroom ceiling, unable to sleep.

Mel was worried and called my mum, who was horrified when she arrived to stay with us for a few days.

'I really need you to try to eat something, darling,' Mum said gently, touching my bony shoulder blade. 'You've lost a lot of weight.'

I had lost fifteen kilograms in a month. But as my body continued to repel food, it wasn't just my weight that was impacted. I was emotionally and mentally unable to process the stress and anxiety that was playing out internally, so it started to force its way out of my body physically. My hair was falling out in clumps and infected scabs started to cover my legs and arms. It was awful. Mum stayed for the next week and, even in my detached state, I could hear her and Mel talking quietly about how worried they were.

'Maybe I should take her to the hospital?' Mum suggested to Melanie one afternoon.

'I don't need to go to the hospital, Mum,' I interrupted. 'I'm fine.'

I knew that if I was going to relieve Mum of her worry, I needed to find a way to get back on my feet. I mustered every ounce of energy I had and promised Mum it was fine for her to go home and that I was going to be okay. Meanwhile, my emotions continued to hit me like a tsunami—waves of tears would flood down my face and I struggled to breathe. Some waves would last for a minute, some closer to an hour; some felt deeper than others, but there was always a calmness that followed each release. I would let the tears fall and lean on my desk when I needed to. Afterwards, still bleary-eyed, I would continue to thread beads onto wires as I worked on my next collection of jewellery. This had become my new routine. I was in complete survival mode.

The *SHOP Til You Drop* issue with the Bamboo Oyster feature came out and it looked fantastic. I texted Mel to let her know as I got to the office, some twenty minutes after I'd picked up the magazine at a newsagency. I opened both my Samantha Wills email and also the separate inbox I had for Bamboo Oyster, which contained 278 unread emails.

What? Am I in the spam folder? I thought. *This has to be a mistake.* I hit refresh. 303 UNREAD EMAILS.

I started scrolling through them—they were all messages from women around the country who had seen the *SHOP Til You Drop* feature and wanted to book their own Bamboo Oyster jewellery party. The magazine couldn't have been on newsstands for more than two hours.

I hit refresh again. 323.

I snapped my laptop shut as though it was full of snakes and backed away from my desk. But open or not, by the end of the week, that laptop had received over 7500 emails from women all over Australia. The basic website I had up for Bamboo Oyster, with just our contact details on it, crashed. I had no idea how to handle something of this scale, even with Renee's help! The feeling of being overwhelmed was so severe that there was only one thing to do. What I did next felt like an out-of-body action, even as I think about it now.

I don't know how many more emails were ever received at that address because that afternoon, I logged out of the Bamboo Oyster email account for the last time and had the Bamboo Oyster website taken permanently down on the spot. 'Page not found' was the message that would pop up thereafter if someone typed in the website address. The jewellery parties were no more.

By the start of 2006, with Bamboo Oyster now little more than an urban legend, there was a gaping hole in cashflow. The revenue that the jewellery parties used to bring in was no longer coming in, but the retail orders were. At this point in the startup journey, I should have simplified and honed my focus on the Samantha Wills brand, but the mode that I was in—and had been in from the very start—was frenetic and reactive. As the Samantha Wills retailers list grew, so did the number of stores placing orders whose aesthetic or core pricepoint fell just below where the brand was positioned—we had to decline them. I saw these declined orders as an opportunity to pick up some of the revenue we had lost when I'd closed Bamboo Oyster. My plan was to take the styles that I knew sold well at the jewellery parties and build them into a commercial collection, with the aim to have all these pieces priced under $100 in stores. Doing this not only allowed Homfrays to say yes to the retailers seeking a more accessible pricepoint, it also allowed us an offering to stores that had wanted to stock Samantha Wills but couldn't because another retailer nearby already stocked the brand. I named the new range Papaya and had Bunda take over Papaya production as I focused on making jewellery for Samantha Wills. In 2006, at twenty-four years of age, I had no idea what the term 'market share' even meant. But by having the Samantha Wills brand retail for $99 to $250, and with the Papaya collection priced at under $100, I had unintentionally created a portfolio that had a significant market share of the mid-tier costume jewellery market within Australia.

The fax machine would ring and ring and ring. The orders were flowing in consistently. I would make jewellery for eighteen hours a day. The old wounds on my hands were no longer required to be covered in bloody bandaids because the wounds had hardened to calluses. My hands had become tougher, and slowly so had I. At 4 pm every afternoon, I would alternate between going to Bunda's apartment to drop off components to her or collect finished Papaya stock and heading to the post office to mail out Samantha Wills orders.

But despite all the hard work, I was falling deeper into debt. I had no proven track record, so couldn't secure a bank loan. Instead, my five credit cards were used for cashflow. Where my approach *should* have been proactive, instead my head was down, working frenetically to just try to get everything done in the quickest time possible. My approach to everything was reactive. Rather than looking ahead and putting a plan in place for the long term, strategically forecasting what I might need to buy in bulk to obtain better margins, I instead purchased components at full retail price so I could instantly fulfil the orders that came in. The result was that the debt on my credit cards was hovering at around $50,000. The standard payment terms were that retailers had thirty days to pay me, the wholesaler. But even with that in place, most took three months or longer to pay—even with Renee chasing them. Despite this, I told Libby I wanted to do a show at Fashion Week, even though I was aware it would come with a significant cost to produce—around $20,000. But I was confident it would be worth it, as the publicity it generated would grow the brand's presence and visibility. But the thing that I took so long to learn was that the growth of a brand's profile is worthless if you don't have the means to fulfil the orders that result from it and actually deliver the product.

The last thing I needed to be doing was a Fashion Week show. What I really needed was a better business structure to support the increasing demand, but I thought that if I simply continued to turn over *more* money, it would magically alleviate the financial strain on the business, and eventually reduce the strain on me. I think a part of me wanted to do the show purely for the validation. Validation that I had made the right choice in pursuing the business, validation that my high school art teacher was wrong, validation that this wasn't just a 'little hobby'. I thought that I required all of this validation from others, but the reality was, the validation I was seeking was my own.

I had three months to create fifteen couture pieces for Fashion Week; three months of alternating between manufacturing stock for orders and making high-fashion jewellery costumes that were inspired by what can best be described as a Victoria's Secret show taking place at the Moulin Rouge. The show was called Birds of Paradise, and it would showcase jewellery that would then be available in a new collection that was as colourful and decadent as the pieces in the show, but in a smaller-scale, more wearable format.

The day the invites were posted out, I made sure to include one addressed to Andrew. It had been a few months since we had broken up, but I held hope that he would come to the show.

Standing backstage on the night of the show as the make-up artists put the finishing touches on the models, I tried to stop and take it all in. It was my first standalone show, I was twenty-four years old and I should have been feeling over the moon with excitement. But I didn't feel anything. I was utterly numb. I wasn't happy or excited; I was just exhausted. I hadn't eaten a proper meal for the past four months and the dress I was wearing that once hugged me now gaped around my body like it didn't want to touch me. I had used extra-hold hairspray to carefully stick down pieces of my hair to cover the bald patches on my scalp where it had continued to fall out—all signs that my body was screaming, trying to tell me something incredibly important. Trying to tell me to slow down and take better care of myself, but I just ignored it. Instead of focusing on my health, I focused on the hope that Andrew would be in the audience and that the media would say complimentary things about my work. I was convinced that if those two things happened, everything would be alright. It's a dangerous game, handing that type of power over to things you cannot control.

The houselights went dark as the music started and the spotlight came up, illuminating my name emblazoned across the back wall of the runway. The models strutted out, each wearing an outfit as opulent as the next, and beneath the professional lights and on a Fashion Week runway, the pieces all came to life in a whole new way. Even I found it hard to believe they were crafted on the workbench in my little studio. The crowd applauded as the models walked out together in the finale and I came out from backstage to take my bow.

Cameras flashed as media and buyers filed backstage after-wards, congratulating me with double air kisses and toasting their champagne glasses in my direction. Libby told me that a few publications had already expressed interest in a feature. With a look that was part sympathetic and part chin-up, she also informed me that Andrew had been a no-show.

'You better go,' she said, nodding towards the growing group of media trying to get my attention.

'Samantha! Over here! Big smile for me!' a photographer yelled out.

'Samantha! Over here, please!' another voice said.

'Samantha! A little to your right!' said another. I shuffled in his direction. *Flash. Flash. Flash.*

'Samantha Wills, congratulations on an incredible show!' a reporter said, thrusting a dictaphone in my face. 'You must be on top of the world!'

When I got home that night, I went straight to the bathroom and sat in the bath under a shower until the temperature turned cold. The water splashed over me, but I didn't feel a thing.

The media had become very interested in the young Samantha Wills 'overnight success' story. No sooner had one article been published, we'd be contacted about another. The more magazine profiles I appeared in, the more red-carpet events I received invitations to, and the more red carpets I was photographed on, the more orders were placed by retailers. I would often go to the event, get my photo taken, say hello to a few people and then head straight back to the office to continue making jewellery to ensure an order could be sent out the following day. Anyone looking on would have thought I was on a dream run: going overnight from Bondi Markets to being stocked by retailers and walking red carpets across the country.

But I was up to my eyeballs in debt and had no idea how to get out of it. It was closing in around me like a fog that thickened each time yet another one of my credit cards was rejected. I would pay only the minimum amount off each card every month, and would just hope like mad that the bank wouldn't shut it down.

'Sorry, that card isn't working either,' a sales assistant behind the register snapped at me one day.

'Here!' I said quickly, shoving my fifth and final credit card at her like a blackjack dealer, 'try this one.' She rolled her eyes as an acknowledgement to the queue of people behind me as she swiped it. I needed these supplies to finish the orders that were due to be posted that afternoon.

'Declined,' she declared. *No more bets.*

The shop assistant was clearly bored with the card game we had played for the past ten minutes.

'Oh, there must be something wrong with the magnetic strip!' I said, laughing in a bid to get her to laugh along with me. She didn't. 'I am just going to run down to the ATM and get some cash out, I will be right back!' I felt the heat creep up around my neck and kept my head down in embarrassment as I left the store.

This was it: checkmate. I was still owed $27,000 from retailers but with the decline of my final credit card came a paralysing realisation. Even if my overdue retailers all paid me at once, it wouldn't put a dint in the $80,000 I now owed the banks.

I couldn't afford the rent at my office anymore. One week after letting my landlord know, I packed up my workbench and all the furniture Andrew had bought for me and within three hours Mel and I had completely cleared out the studio. Two and a half years after I first launched at Fashion Week with a panel in Justin's booth at the Source, I was back to where it all started, working from our dining room, only now with an added $80,000 of debt. Lunches and dinners became toasted baked-bean jaffles. I added cheese if it was a good week. I put my head down and kept making jewellery and Renee kept emailing people who owed us money.

In my desperation, I asked everyone I could think of if they knew any business-minded individuals who might like to get involved in a fashion startup. A friend told me she would put me in touch with Toby, the CEO of a pharmaceutical company, and the following week, I sat on a very expensive leather couch in the reception of Toby's very fancy office in the Sydney CBD.

Toby was warm and welcoming and dressed in a suit that looked as though it could run a business on its own.

'Thank you for meeting with me,' I said.

'My pleasure! I've heard a little bit about your story, but why don't you tell me in your own words,' Toby said.

So I told Toby the story of the Samantha Wills brand so far, careful to leave the debt part until as late in the meeting as possible.

'I owe $79,998,' I blurted, opting for a sub-$80,000 figure to make it seem less offensive. As soon as the amount left my lips, I was ready to thank him for his time and escort myself out of his office, but he didn't even seem to flinch.

'I'll tell you what,' Toby said, sitting back in his chair. 'I think you're an incredibly talented designer, Samantha. And, clearly, there is demand for what you are doing. I believe you are going to be a success, and I would love to add a fashion brand to my business portfolio and, in doing so, I could help you clear your business debt.'

He could WHAT? I was gobsmacked.

'I'll send you an email this afternoon to put the offer in writing and let's arrange to meet up this time next week. Does Friday work for you?' Toby asked.

'Yes, that's great, thank you so much,' I said, trying to sound professional while perilously close to bursting into tears of relief.

Holding Toby's draft contract in my hand that afternoon, the only thing I could think about was the fact that next Friday, I was going to *finally* be debt-free. I read over the details of his proposal. With the amount of debt I was in, it felt like I was barely able to keep treading water. Toby's offer felt like the lifeline I had been waiting for. I grabbed it with both hands and signed the document. When I went to bed that night, it was the first time in two years that I didn't feel as though a lead weight were pushing down on my chest.

divine intervention

di·vine in·ter·ven·tion

noun

a purported miracle caused by a deity's active
involvement in the human world

The next day, I could hear my phone ringing but couldn't find it
for the life of me. Just when I thought my voicemail was going
to intercept it, I saw Toby's contract vibrating on my desk, my
phone underneath it.

'Hello, Samantha Wills Designs,' I said.

'Willsy! It's Todd Liddy! Long time, no see!' Todd said.
I hadn't heard from him in the three years since I left Surf
Dive 'n Ski. I was shocked he remembered my name, let alone
had my phone number.

'Todd! Hi! . . . How are you?' I said.

'You must be wondering why I'm calling you,' he said, as
though reading my mind.

'Um, yes! Yes, I am!' I said, laughing.

'Well, I'll cut to the chase. I am no longer at SDS. I'm now working for Icon, you know the jewellery brand that's stocked through every single surf store in the country. We're opening our own retail stores and we are launching a women's retail range. I've seen the incredible brand you have built and was wondering if you would be interested in doing some contract design work for us?' Todd said. 'I know you are all rich and famous now, and surf jewellery is probably not really your thing—'

'Yes!' I replied before he could even finish his sentence. 'Yes, I'd be really interested! I'm familiar with the brand,' I said. Icon had been stocked in every surf store in Port Macquarie when I was a teenager.

'You would?' Todd replied, sounded slightly surprised and a little relieved. 'Well, great! Okay. The company has just been bought by new owners and we are headquartered up in Ballina, near Byron Bay. I know it's short notice, but do you think you could possibly pull together some creative mood boards over the weekend? Nothing fancy, just something we can show the owners? Then we could fly you up here on Monday so you can meet the team and the new CEO?'

'Monday? As in the day after tomorrow?' I said, hoping he meant the following one.

'Yeah, look, I know it's not a lot of notice, the timeline on it is really tight . . . I could see if we can push it out a few days?' Todd's voice trailed off.

I didn't want to miss this opportunity by quibbling over a

few days. I had worked through the night to get things done before—I knew I could get this done in time.

'This Monday is fine!' I said. 'If you could email me a short brief, I'll get to work on the presentation this afternoon.'

'You're the best!' Todd said. 'Oh, and just as a courtesy to manage expectations, I guess I should be transparent with you on the financials.' Todd sounded very serious. Financials hadn't even entered my mind. I was excited to work creatively for another brand and, besides, my own financials were about to be taken care of thanks to Toby. 'I know it's probably much less than what you are raking in now, but the salary for the contract role is $75,000 a year.'

$75,000 a year?

'Willsy, you still there?' Todd asked

'Yep. Yes! Yes,' I replied. 'I'm still here.'

'Okay, well, that's what the ballpark is on the salary. I'll email you the brief, plus your flight details now. Thanks again, Willsy, look forward to seeing you Monday.'

—

'Willsy!' Todd called across the Icon office. 'So great to see you! How was your flight?'

'Hi! It was great!' I replied. 'I'm excited about today, thanks for thinking of me for this opportunity.'

'Of course! Who'd have thought we'd possibly be working together again?' Todd said, smiling. 'Now, let's get you set up in the boardroom.'

I'd timed it so that I got to the boardroom twenty minutes before the meeting was due to start and could set up my mood boards and design concepts calmly and carefully. The company's new CEO, Geoff Bainbridge, was a big deal—his reputation preceded him. Todd had also given me a brief run-down on him. But I had to put his big reputation aside for the minute. I was just hoping he liked turquoise. Turquoise had been the bestselling stone colour in all the Samantha Wills and Papaya collections, so I had included it heavily in the Icon design concepts.

'Geoff is running a little late,' Todd said, as he walked into the boardroom with some other members of the Icon team and then made introductions. 'Let's just get started without him, he won't be far off.'

First, I talked about the journey of my brand to give them an idea of how my aesthetic tied into the surf aesthetic they were looking for in their new retail collection. I told the Icon team about my surf industry background and how I envisaged creating pieces for the Icon brand that brought surf and fashion a little closer together. I started to click through my presentation, projecting the mood boards onto the boardroom wall. Geoff didn't even glance at me as he walked in and took a seat at the head of the table. Todd gave me an encouraging nod, so I kept going.

'Turquoise is a really strong palette at the moment,' I explained, pointing to the myriad of blue and aqua stones I had included in the presentation for reference.

'Turquoise doesn't sell,' Geoff said, his feet up on the board-room table, scrolling emails on his BlackBerry.

Was that a question? I thought, panicked.

'Um, well,' I said nervously. 'In our retailers, it has been the bestselling colour and—'

'In my experience, it doesn't sell,' Geoff cut me off and tossed his BlackBerry on the table. He sat through the rest of my presentation in silence, moving only to check his phone, which he did often. He walked out of the boardroom as soon as I asked if anyone had any questions.

What an asshole, I thought. Maybe this role wasn't for me after all. I couldn't get on the plane back to Sydney fast enough. As the plane took off late that afternoon, I was grateful that at least I would never have to see Geoff Bainbridge ever again.

—

'Hello, Samantha Wills Designs.'

'Samantha, hi, it's Geoff Bainbridge from Icon.'

Fuck.

'Hi. Geoff . . .' I replied, 'how are you?'

'Great, buddy!' Geoff replied jovially. 'Listen, I just wanted to give you a quick call to say thank you for yesterday, I thought your presentation was fantastic!'

'You did?'

'I sure did! I would love to find a way for us to work together.' I checked the caller ID to make sure I was speaking with the same person I had met the day before. I was. 'So, as I'm sure Todd told you, we're on a pretty tight time frame with this retail project. What would the possibility be of you developing the concepts you presented into some sample options and flying back up here Thursday so that we can agree on how best to move forward?'

'I guess I could do—' I started to reply.

'Great!' Geoff cut me off. 'I'll have someone organise your flights, look forward to seeing you Thursday.'

The presentation went without a hitch and Geoff seemed slightly more impressed than he'd been a mere three days before— and by that, I mean he stayed for the entire presentation and only checked his BlackBerry three times. The rest of the team, thankfully, loved the collection. After the meeting, Geoff, Todd and I sat down and agreed on the terms of a contract whereby I would design six collections a year for Icon. I would work closely with their design team and spend one day a fortnight up in the Icon offices.

'Samantha, follow me,' Geoff said once the contract was signed. 'Let's grab lunch.'

'Okay . . .' I said cautiously, still scarred from his brusqueness at my first presentation. I was hoping that Geoff would also invite Todd or some other members from the team, but no one else followed us out of the office.

Geoff seemed like the type of guy that ate lunch at Michelin-starred restaurants in big cities, not the type of guy who lived in a small coastal town and ordered hot chips out of a bain-marie at a two-star Yelp-reviewed cafe, but that's exactly what he did at the sandwich shop we found ourselves in ten minutes later.

'You can have some of mine, trust me, they're really good,' he said. He didn't seem like the type of guy to share his chips, either, and I wasn't prepared to drop my defences with him just yet. We sat down at a table covered with a red and white plastic tablecloth that felt as sticky as it looked.

'It's not exactly five-star, huh?' Geoff said, wiping the tabletop with some napkins.

'I don't mind it,' I said, smiling. 'It actually reminds me of the town I grew up in.'

'Oh, yeah?' Geoff said, as the lady brought out our sandwiches and his hot chips. 'And where was that?' he asked, offering me a chip.

'Port Macquarie,' I said, taking a chip. I figured it would be rude not to at that stage.

'Ah, that makes sense,' Geoff said.

'What makes sense?'

'Your surf background thing,' Geoff said, 'and, you know, your whole small-town girl trying to make her way in the world thing.'

'You're right, these are good,' I said, acknowledging the chip and his recommendation, but also avoiding responding to his comment.

'Tell me more about the Samantha Wills business,' Geoff asked.

He sat back in his chair, not unlike the way he did in the first presentation in the Icon boardroom. I was half-expecting him to kick his feet up on the table, and if it weren't for his hot chips sitting there, he probably would have. I couldn't read him at all. I didn't know if he hated me and my turquoise designs, or if he liked me and I was being interviewed. As I had rehearsed a shiny version of the Samantha Wills brand story for Toby just a week before, I kicked into gear and retold it to Geoff, steering the conversation back to him before I was forced to get into financials.

A little bit of research had told me that Icon was currently valued at $11 million. It made sense that someone with Geoff's business acumen would acquire a company like that, but I thought he was just a numbers guy, the guy they bring in to increase revenue or oversee a big restructure—I definitely didn't think he would have an appreciation for brand. I had just assumed that someone in his position and with his head for numbers wouldn't be interested in the branding or the creative side of the business. My initial impression was that Geoff and I would have nothing in common at all. I was starting to think that maybe I had him pegged all wrong.

'So, why does a *fashion girl* like you want to design women's surf jewellery?' Geoff asked, finishing off his chicken sandwich and ready to kick off a second round of interrogation. The way he said 'fashion girl' triggered something in me, and my reply came out a little sharper than I had intended.

'Oh, I'm *not* a fashion girl,' I snapped. 'I grew up in Port Macquarie, I know the surf industry because I grew up in it and now I know a *little* bit about the fashion industry because I've spent the last two years building a brand, but the truth is . . . it's not actually the fashion industry I love, it's creating and storytelling. I want to create a brand that people want to be a part of, the same way I wanted to be a part of brands that I loved. That's why I started the Samantha Wills brand.'

Geoff paused for a while, a tactic I would see him deploy again and again in the years to follow. He paused to elicit a more fulsome, truthful response from people, similar to the way a top interrogator would coax a confession out of a murderer. Geoff was always three steps ahead in the conversation waiting for everyone else to catch up.

It felt like the perfect time to tell Geoff about tomorrow's meeting with Toby. *He's going to be so impressed that I have secured this business deal*, I thought.

'So, anyway, I feel like I've taken the business as far as I can get it. It's stocked in sixty retailers and while I'm struggling to keep up with production and at times it all seems too much, I truly do love it.' I paused, waiting for Geoff to say something. But he didn't. He just kept slowly eating chips, so I just kept talking. 'I mean, the cashflow is tight and while I know the brand could be so much more, I don't yet know enough about the business side of things to structure it the way it needs structuring. But the good news is that I've actually found someone, an investor, who is going to come on board. His investment will clear all the debt!' I said proudly.

There were a few chips left on Geoff's plate, and he slid the plate towards me. I shook my head.

'And what does this *investor* want in exchange for his *investment*?' Geoff asked, picking up the last chip and putting it in his mouth.

'Well, to clear *all my debt*,' I emphasised, just to be sure he understood the scale of the offer, 'he only wants 51 per cent of the company.'

Geoff suddenly stopped chewing and then, after what seemed like hours, swallowed the chip and put both his elbows on the table.

Deadpan, he looked me straight in the eyes and said, 'If you sign that contract, it will be the fucking dumbest thing you ever do in your life.'

'What?! Why?' I protested. 'My business is in $80,000 worth of debt! If I don't take this offer, I will have to close it,' I confessed. *Shit, he was good.*

'So close it,' Geoff said.

'What? No!' I replied, shocked at how calmly he suggested I walk away from something I had poured literal blood, sweat and tears into building. 'I've put everything I have into it. *Everything.* But as I said, I'm landlocked. The bank won't give me any more credit, and without any more money I can't keep the brand going.'

'Okay. So you're $80,000 in debt?' Geoff asked.

'Yes,' I replied.

'It's really not that much for business debt,' he said calmly. 'Do you want my advice?'

'You have more?' I asked, half-sarcastically, half-embarrassed by my naivety.

'I do,' Geoff said, 'I think you should close the Samantha Wills business and come and work for us, not as a freelancer, but full time as the creative director at Icon. We can find a way to pay off your debt in your salary package. You know the surf industry and you would have full control of the brand and design. It would be everything you are doing with the Samantha Wills brand, but without the debt. We could look to start your salary at $85,000.'

$85,000! My mind screamed in celebration.

'I can't.' The words were out of my mouth before I'd even thought them through.

'You can't what?' Geoff asked.

'I can't close the Samantha Wills brand,' I said quietly. 'That is a very generous offer, thank you, and I am truly flattered, but I can't close the brand. I have put so much into it.' The words were pouring out of my mouth, but my heart was doing the talking. 'I just know it can be something big, I don't know exactly what yet, but I just *know* it can be so much more. I'm not done with it. I can't walk away from it just yet.'

'Okay, well, that decision is yours,' Geoff said. 'And if we can work with you on a contract basis for the retail collection, then that's great. But what I *do* think is that you are a really talented designer and could make an incredible creative director.'

It was one of the nicest things anyone had ever said to me. The inner voice that constantly told me I was a fraud and an impostor was momentarily silenced.

'Thank you,' I said, 'that means a lot, especially coming from you.'

'At the very least, do yourself a favour, do *not* sign that contract tomorrow,' Geoff said. 'At least trust me on that one.'

I walked out of the cafe, my hands sticky from the plastic tablecloth and my mind confused as I tried to weigh up Toby's and Geoff's offers. In bed that night, I stared at the ceiling as if willing the answer to fall out and hit me on the head. Debt-free and a clean slate for my business with Toby, or a full-time creative director role with Geoff at Icon?

$85,000 to design jewellery? Yes! my head screamed. *That is exactly what you have always wanted! And Geoff is offering you more money than you will ever see in your lifetime.*

No, my heart whispered in return. *You haven't come this far to only come this far.*

—

'Hello, it's Samantha Wills calling, would Geoff be available please?' I was speaking with the receptionist at Icon, phone in one hand, Toby's contract in the other.

'What did you decide?' Geoff's voice came down the line.

'What about you?'

'What about me, what?' he said, confused.

'What about *you* come on board the Samantha Wills brand as my business partner?' I said. 'I don't want any money from you, not a cent. I just want your advice, that's it. I'll give you equity in exchange for advice.'

'Fuck no,' he said, without even so much as a pause. 'No way. I'm far too busy.'

'Will you at least think about it?' I replied.

'I have thought about it. No.'

'Okay. Well, I'm back up at your offices in a fortnight to present the next part of the collection; I am going to ask you again then,' I said.

'If you create great Icon collections, you can ask me as many times as you want,' Geoff said. 'And for fuck's sake, dial it down with the turquoise, would you? I'm telling you, it doesn't fucking sell.'

I sat down that afternoon, took a deep breath and emailed Toby, politely explaining that after consideration I was not in a position to bring on an investor at this stage, and thanking him for his offer. As I hit send on the email, I ripped up the contract I had signed a week earlier and placed it in the wastepaper bin under my desk. For the first time in a long while, even though the debt was still there, I felt like my head was above water. The events that had unfolded over the past seven days had been perfectly timed, like characters in a play arriving for their scenes on cue. The call from Todd at exactly that moment changed the trajectory of everything, and the lunch with Geoff at a shitty little cafe in Ballina (albeit with good chips) would be a milestone in the Samantha Wills brand journey and the start of one of the most treasured (and, at times, tormenting) friendships of my life.

Working with the Icon team to create and produce collections for their retailers and stores was like a fast-tracked apprenticeship in how a commercial jewellery business was meant to be run. The thousands of hours spent meticulously handmaking jewellery over the past three years faded as I saw how a commercial design supply chain works. I would create a sample, either by constructing or sketching it. A design assistant would then 'spec it up', taking my design and deconstructing it onto a page with precise measurements, weights, plating specifications and pricepoint. The spec sheets would then be sent off to an offshore production house and, about four weeks later, an entire sample set would arrive. I would either approve it or make changes, then we would order the stock, which arrived in the warehouse ready to send out to retailers ninety days later.

I was up in Ballina working at Icon headquarters every second Friday, which meant I would see Geoff every two weeks. We had managed to forge a special friendship, one with a similar dynamic to Mr Miyagi and the Karate Kid. On my fortnightly visits to Ballina, I would seize every opportunity to extract advice from Geoff's infinite pool of business knowledge, following him around with a notepad and list of questions I had compiled over the past fortnight. He usually rolled his eyes, but there was an abundance of generosity underneath that brusque exterior. What he gave me in those early days was an unofficial mentorship that money couldn't buy.

'I've been thinking,' Geoff said to me one Friday afternoon. 'Why don't you start to run the Samantha Wills production through one of our production houses? That would free up a huge amount of your time, not having to handmake everything.'

'That would be amazing, you'd be okay with me doing that?' I said, almost bursting into tears at the thought of not having to spend thirty hours a week hunched over a table making jewellery.

'I have no problem with it,' Geoff said.

'Does this mean you've thought any more about coming on board as my business partner in Samantha Wills?' I asked hopefully.

'No,' he said, without any further explanation.

It was the fifth time I had asked him.

baptism

bap·tism

noun

a person's initiation into a particular activity or role,
typically one perceived as difficult

Transitioning from handmaking product in your dining room
to manufacturing it offshore is much more emotional than you
might think. It's like raising a small child, then sending it off
to international boarding school. The distance between the two
of you means you have to relinquish some control and, for most
creative founders, that is not an easy thing to do. The minimum
order quantities when working with offshore production houses
are high, so I also had to get smarter in the design process.
I needed to start consolidating the components I was using and
select fewer of them; the components needed to work across more
styles. The goal in this transition was to get as much of the work
done offshore as possible but also to allow for versatility in what

could be made from each compilation of components. Soon I was producing quantities that I would never have been able to make by hand. It was a move that saw supply and demand increase and, in turn—slowly—so did revenue.

Moving the production offshore was my first step into the big league of commercial business. It felt a long way away from where I had started, with the olive-coloured fishing tackle box full of beads and crystals that my mum had given me when I was eleven years old.

In addition to moving most of the production offshore, I finally employed a freelance bookkeeper and I also engaged a PR consultant, Matt, to help build the brand's profile. Matt was in his early twenties and had just started his own PR company. I admired his drive and determination and now with my Icon contract retainer coming in each month, I could afford to bring good people in to help with the business. When it came time to shoot the new collection, rather than booking a model to shoot the campaign, Matt managed to convince me to be the one in front of the camera. He was adamant that consumers needed to get to know the person behind the brand.

'What do you think?' Matt said, as we went over the photographer's edit a few days later.

'I don't know,' I said, looking at myself in the photographs, nervous that naming a brand after yourself felt obnoxious enough, let alone starring in your own campaign.

'The Samantha Wills brand is a persona. It's you. It's your voice,' Matt replied, as we made the final selections for the campaign shots. '*You* need to front this thing. *You* are the commercial advantage.'

The media response to that campaign was overwhelming. Matt was right, putting a face to a name was very helpful in securing more profile press, and more and more interview requests started to filter in.

It was still quite the juggling act, designing for Icon as well as running and taking a more public role with the Samantha Wills brand. Now, though, I felt like I could actually see everything in front of me, whereas before I felt as though I was doing it all in the dark.

—

Geoff had a theory that you never really know someone until you travel with them. As a kind of secondary interview process for any key role in his businesses, he would take a work trip with the 'candidate'. He would later tell me that this gives a huge insight into a person: their resilience being away from home, their ability to be organised and how they adapt to their job while outside of their normal routine. My baptism of fire came in 2006 when Geoff told me he was going to Hong Kong for a trade show, and that I was going with him. Held in a huge convention hall near Hong Kong airport, hundreds of international jewellery suppliers and trade vendors would come in from mainland China, India and the Philippines and set up booths. Vendor stands filled two pavilions and you'd traipse around them, searching for new suppliers and meeting with existing ones. It sounded like a dream come true to me—when Geoff told me we were going, I felt like I'd won an overseas trip on a game show. I had no idea it was intended to be a test of character, but I was sure as hell about to find out.

I had been standing in the check-in line at Sydney airport for almost an hour. My guesstimate was that I was still about sixty people from the front of the queue. Beyond the crowd in front of me, I caught sight of Geoff walking up to the counter on the other side of the economy desk, BlackBerry to his ear as he handed the check-in clerk his passport and she seamlessly handed it back to him with his ticket inside. It was as smooth as a gold medal Olympic baton change.

'Geoff!' I yelled, flapping my arms in the air. 'Geoff! Over here!' Geoff didn't hear me, nor did he see me waving my arms in a manner not dissimilar to the way you signal when you are drowning. 'Excuse me!' I said, flagging down a Qantas staff member who was walking through the sea of bodies checking we all had the correct documentation. 'Hi! My boss, he is over there. He just checked in,' I looked over to where I was pointing, but Geoff was no longer there. 'Um, well, he was just there before.'

'In the first class check-in, you mean?' she said, looking over to the white marbled counter as though it were a mirage in the desert.

'Ah. *First class* check-in,' I said, looking down at the work-out tights and old baggy cardigan I had chosen for the nine-hour flight ahead.

'Have a safe flight,' the attendant said. 'Shouldn't be too long to the front of the line, another thirty minutes or so.'

My phone buzzed. It was Geoff. 'Where are you?' his text read.

I quickly plugged in a response: 'Still checking in.'

A moment later, my phone pinged again. 'Okay,' Geoff replied. 'I'll see you at the boarding gate.'

I was well aware of a rumour I had caught wind of at Icon: apparently, because Geoff travelled so often, his tolerance for spending any amount of inefficient time at airports was minimal to zero.

'How'd you go?' Geoff said an hour later as we stood in line waiting to board the plane.

'Good! Check-in was a breeze!' I lied.

Geoff had a pair of Bose headphones around his neck, a copy of the *Financial Review* in one hand and his passport in the other.

Where were all his snacks for the long-haul flight? His magazines? Where were his multiple bottles of water and wet wipes? His neck pillow? I thought, as I stood there like a packhorse with a bag in each hand and my travel pillow around my neck.

'What the fuck is in there?' Geoff said, nodding at the bags. 'You know this is only a nine-hour flight, don't you? We're going to Hong Kong, not central Africa.'

Earlier that week, the Icon production manager had told me that I had to guard the development samples and spec sheets with my life on this trip. Checking them in was a death wish, because if my bags were lost, so was the entire collection and a whole season's work. It was only the third international flight I had ever been on, and the other two had only been to Bali and Fiji, classic Australian holiday destinations. Wanting to ensure I was well equipped for what I thought was a long flight, I had crammed my laptop, the binder full of design sheets, and sample components for the new Icon and Samantha Wills collections into one bag, and in the other I had packed enough snacks, water and magazines to feed, hydrate and entertain not just myself but probably the entire economy cabin.

'It's just development samples,' I half-lied, trying to make the bag appear feather light as I shuffled down the aerobridge.

'Welcome back, Mr Bainbridge!' the Qantas flight attendant said warmly to Geoff when we reached the plane. 'Good to see you again!'

'Alright. See you on the other side,' Geoff said to me as he turned left, towards first class. He didn't look back. My baggage and I turned right. I found my seat, at the back of the plane in the centre of the row. I had managed to jam one of the bags into the overhead compartment, doing so with a silent prayer that if anyone opened the overhead bin mid-flight, my bag would not knock them unconscious. It turns out that travelling through airports with metal jewellery components is not the smartest way to travel, but nevertheless, I was on board and couldn't have been more excited that I was taking an international flight for an actual work trip. I still couldn't believe it.

'Hello!' I said cheerfully to the lady next to me. 'What's taking you to Hong Kong?'

'Just stopping over there en route home,' she said curtly, clearly annoyed that I hadn't interpreted her book as the universal sign for *do not disturb*.

'I'm travelling for work!' I said, answering a question she hadn't asked. She smiled tightly, turned back to her book and popped her complimentary headphones on for good measure.

I'm travelling for work, I thought to myself again. I couldn't stop smiling.

—

'What the actual fuck did you pack?' Geoff said, as my suitcase finally arrived on the baggage carousel. 'You know we're only here for three nights, don't you?'

'Yep, yes,' I said, wrangling my suitcase off the moving carousel while trying not to trip over my two carry-ons. 'Yep, three nights. I know.'

'Alright then, let's go,' Geoff said. His bag had arrived ten minutes ago, its 'FIRST-CLASS PRIORITY' tag doing its job perfectly.

'I've just got one more bag,' I said, craning my neck to see if it was in the jumble of bags tumbling down the conveyor belt.

'You've got to be fucking kidding me,' Geoff said. 'I'll see you at the hotel.' His compact black suitcase behaved like a well-trained dog, spinning around as he did and following him without incident.

'What?' I said. The panic in my voice was audible. 'Wait! Where are we staying?'

'The Langham. You'll work it out!' And just like that, Geoff disappeared, exiting through the sliding glass doors at Hong Kong International Airport. My journey to the hotel, which should have taken forty minutes, ended up taking three hours. I learnt two very important things about Hong Kong in that three hours: first, that taxis there do not take credit cards nor Australian dollars and, second, that there is more than one Langham Hotel in Hong Kong, a fact that Geoff knew very well (and something I should have researched before touching down). It was after 1 am by the time I got to the second—and correct—hotel.

'Ms Wills,' the woman behind the reception desk said when I finally arrived. 'Welcome to The Langham, Mong Kok, we've been expecting you.' She smiled warmly as she tapped my name into the computer. The anxiety of the last few hours I'd spent blindly navigating a foreign city melted away as I took in the most beautiful hotel foyer I had ever seen.

'Here is your key, we will have your bags taken up to your room straightaway.'

'Thank you so much,' I said, taking the key from her. My hair was at peak frizz level from the Hong Kong humidity and the perspiration was causing my clothes to cling tightly to me. I must have looked like a hot mess, especially in contrast to the luxury of the surroundings I was in.

'Oh, and Ms Wills,' I turned back towards her. 'Mr Bainbridge left a message here for you,' she said, her perfect English spoken with a native Cantonese accent. She reached for a piece of paper. 'It says, meet him downstairs at 7 am for breakfast. And don't be fucking late.' She looked up from the note and smiled again. 'Good night. Enjoy your stay!'

—

'Good morning,' I said, as Geoff spotted me in the restaurant. I had been at the table since 6.30 am, too nervous to be late. After unpacking and repacking all of the samples and spec sheets to make sure everything was perfect for our first day at the trade show, I had set my alarm for 6 am so I would be on time for breakfast. I'd had a total of one hour and forty-five minutes' sleep.

'Morning,' Geoff said, *The Wall Street Journal* under his arm. 'You find your way last night from the airport okay?'

'Well, I'm here!' I said, smiling calmly as I took a sip of my second coffee of the day. 'No problem at all.'

'Yes, I guess you are,' Geoff said, sitting down. 'I didn't think you had it in you,' he added. That made both of us liars.

That trip to Hong Kong was the first of many I would take. Those three days were like a masterclass in jewellery production and logistics. The vendor trade show booths had everything from clay beads to displays of leather-weaving techniques; a smorgasbord of infinite possibilities for executing creative ideas. I sourced new suppliers for both Icon and Samantha Wills, discovering new techniques and craftmanship that would suit each brand respectively. At the end of our successful trip, Geoff and I hopped in a taxi to head back to the airport.

'Good book?' Geoff asked, nodding to the book that was poking out of my bag.

'I've just started it, but, yes, I'm enjoying it,' I replied. It was a book of profiles of female entrepreneurs.

'Why are you reading it?' he asked.

'Because I find their stories interesting,' I said.

'Is that what you want to be?'

'What?' I replied. 'An entrepreneur?'

'Yeah.'

'Oh, I don't think I could ever do that!' I said. 'I'm creative, not a businesswoman. I don't think I could ever do what these women have done, but I find their stories really inspiring.'

'Interesting,' Geoff said. I didn't know what he meant by that, and I didn't ask. We travelled in silence for a few minutes. Geoff read a newspaper and I stared out the window as Hong Kong Bay flew by.

'For what it's worth, my observation of you,' Geoff said, keeping his eyes trained on his newspaper as I turned to look at him, 'is that there is a whole world inside of you that you really underestimate.'

Not only could he see something in me that I couldn't, I also didn't know how to respond. We travelled the rest of the way to the airport in silence.

—

At the end of 2006, I went home to Port Macquarie to spend Christmas with my family. It had been a year since Andrew and I broke up and, while it had taken the better part of twelve months, my heart had slowly mended—a combination of time, newfound resilience and growth for both myself and my hair, which had finally grown back after falling out in clumps. I noticed the dramatic difference between where I was at now and where my head had been at the same time the year before and felt immeasurably grateful for all that had happened over the past twelve months. I thought about how close I had come to signing over a controlling share of the company and about how the universe had stepped in to intercept what may well have been the biggest mistake of my life. Although I had now asked Geoff more than ten times to get involved in the Samantha Wills business and he had said no each time, his unofficial mentoring made it feel as though I had a great supporter on the journey with me. I think I appreciated that more than anything—no longer feeling like I was doing it all on my own.

It's funny, the way the world works sometimes. Just when you manage to get yourself out of the fetal position, the past usually comes calling.

'The phone's for you!' Dad yelled out to me from the kitchen.

'Hello?' I said, picking up the phone in the living room.

'Hey,' said the voice. 'I thought you'd be at your folks' . . . I . . . I just wanted to call to wish you a Merry Christmas.'

It was Andrew.

After that first call and many more, Andrew and I decided to give things another go and got back together at the start of 2007—this time as different people. The past and our year apart often seemed too rocky to dig up, so we didn't talk much about it, preferring the much more pleasant route of focusing on building our new world together. Melanie and her boyfriend had decided to move to London, and when she moved out, Andrew and I moved in together.

On the business front, sales had increased and things were at the point where I could move 100 per cent of the Samantha Wills production offshore, a decision which gave me the time to revisit how I was running the business with fresh eyes.

My sales agent, Libby, and her husband had made the decision to close Homfrays and relocate overseas. The timing coincided with me wanting to expand the distribution. I was now able to appoint a localised agency in each state, rather than just having one national agent, which had been the set-up with Homfrays. The sales agency I appointed for New South Wales led me to meet Misha, a young woman who worked in their Sydney-based office. Misha was the full package: she knew the sales and delivery process from having worked at the agency and she became my first Samantha Wills employee.

On top of that, twelve months after I'd had to move out of my design studio because I could no longer afford the rent, I signed a new office lease, again in Alexandria. Misha and I set up a few desks in our new space and no sooner had we plugged the phone in, customers started ringing. Retailers' orders were still coming through via fax but it was also around this time that people were abandoning their Myspace profiles and signing up to a new platform called Facebook. Every time a piece of Samantha Wills jewellery was featured in a magazine or a profile interview was published, my Facebook page would get an onslaught of friend requests. Long before brand pages were introduced, my own personal Facebook page turned into the unofficial Samantha Wills brand account and my status updates began to focus on the brand and our new collections. The 'friends' interacting with my posts were people I had never met in real life, but I felt as though we knew each other. I didn't realise it at the time, but these initial interactions would form the entire basis of what the Samantha Wills brand was about: speaking *with* our consumer, not *to* her.

—

'We really need to get an online store,' Misha said one day as we were packing orders to send the new collection out to retailers. 'Every second phone call is someone placing a direct order.'

Ecommerce was only just starting to emerge in Australia but Andrew knew just the guy to help us set up our site and so introduced us to Dave. Dave was fresh out of university and reminded me of a Doogie Howser of the tech world. He offered to build us what we needed for a fraction of the price of what some people wanted to charge, and he promised to get our site up fast.

Three weeks later, he was back in our office to show Misha and I how to drive our new online store. It seemed simple enough, and Misha and I stayed up late uploading the new collection. By the next morning, we had eight online orders.

My Facebook page soon hit its 5000 friend limit and the online presence and website was also driving traffic into our retailers, resulting in shop sales increasing significantly. By now, this experience of rapid growth wasn't new to me and I was all too aware that things could just as quickly get out of hand. The business felt like a caged tiger clawing to be let out. I had grown it to this point and knew it needed a bigger cage. I didn't know how to build a bigger one—but I knew exactly who did.

outside the box

out·side the box

idiom

to explore ideas that are creative and unusual and that
are not limited or controlled by rules or tradition

Misha and I would work together Monday to Thursday on
Samantha Wills and my Fridays were spent up in Ballina with
Icon. I had done a few more trade show trips with Geoff, always
with him turning left at the front of the plane and me turning
right. On one of our trips, Geoff explained to me that he wanted
to turn Icon into a full-scale accessories brand, expanding it
beyond just jewellery.

'It's not going as well as I'd hoped,' Geoff admitted to me one
Friday afternoon as the design team and I were coming out of
the boardroom. 'The product looks great, but the brand is . . .'
he paused, 'non-existent. Retailers love the new range, but they
want to buy into a brand and right now we're just product.'

'I hear what you're saying,' I replied. He looked tired. 'Let me have a think about it over the weekend and see if I can come up with some ideas.'

But it wasn't ideas I needed to come up with. I already knew what Icon required to expand as a brand. What I needed was a strategy to implement it. The idea I had would solve my business concerns *and* Geoff's. I had till next Friday to get it all down on paper.

'Have you got twenty minutes?' I asked Geoff a week later as we passed in the hallway of the Icon offices.

'I have fifteen,' Geoff replied, his eyes not leaving his BlackBerry. 'What do you want?'

'What you said last week, about Icon being a product, not a brand,' I replied, practically jogging to keep up with his walk. 'I've been thinking about it and I just wanted to show you some ideas I had.'

'I'm all ears,' Geoff said, as I followed him into the boardroom. 'You've now got fourteen minutes.' I quickly opened my laptop, hooked it up to the projector and fired up my slide deck.

'We have to pull it down . . . break it. Rebuild it,' I said, as the first slide of my presentation projected onto the wall behind me. The presentation outlined what Icon had been for the past thirty years, a product that serviced a need in the surf industry. Anyone who had set foot in any surf store in Australia would be able to tell you there was jewellery in there, but no one would have been able to tell you what it was called. Because that was all it was: a product. There was no brand structure or strategy behind it and no story being told around it. The logo was not recognisable, and its swing tags were functional but forgettable. The product was generic; everything to everyone. Being a brand is about communicating *who* you are and *what* you stand for; when a brand tries to please everyone, they end up appealing to no one, because there is nothing that defines it. The presentation outlined my idea to break Icon into two parts. The first part would be the surf jewellery division, with a rebrand of its name and packaging. I proposed that Icon surf jewellery would become Classics77, an homage to its product offering and the year the company was established. The second part was to evolve Icon from a surf jewellery product into an urban accessories brand. I clicked through the slides that showed my vision for the second part of the brand, using mood boards and sketches, product examples and a new corporate logo.

'Presenting the next iteration: Icon Brand,' I said, as the new logo I had designed appeared on the screen. Geoff didn't say anything. 'So . . . in summary,' I continued, to fill the silence, 'we are essentially taking a product offering, and splitting it into two *brands*. Classics77 honours where we have come from, and Icon Brand is the direction we are heading in. They would naturally sit in different retail channels. Icon Brand is the premium offering, and could easily sit in department stores and boutique fashion retailers, whereas Classics77 would be surf chains, mall kiosk and airport retail. Having two brands will allow us to double our distribution, revenue and market share.'

Geoff hadn't taken his eyes off the presentation since he sat down. The fluorescent lights buzzed as I turned them back on.

Geoff was still staring at the wall where the final slide of the presentation remained, the new Icon Brand logo filling the wall.

'It's fucking brilliant,' Geoff finally said. 'It's really fucking brilliant.'

I didn't say anything. I knew what his hesitation would be and waited for him to bring it up.

'There's only one thing . . .' he said, as if on cue.

Perfect. 'What's that?' I asked.

'This is a big job . . . I mean, a really fucking big job. It's not just a rebrand, it's a rebrand *and* a whole new launch,' he said. 'We've tried to recruit a creative director for Icon the past six or more months, remember? We need to be strategic with this. Without someone leading this project properly, there's no way it's going to work.'

'I thought you would say that and I agree with you, but I think I know just the person for the job,' I said, smiling.

'You found someone? Who?' Geoff asked.

'Me.' I replied.

Geoff looked at me, his eyes narrowing.

'Well . . . as I see it,' I continued, '*you* need a creative director to create this new brand and *I* need a business director to help with the Samantha Wills offering.' Geoff remained silent—the longest he'd ever done so since I'd met him. 'So, I will take on this project as creative director in exchange for you taking 30 per cent equity and an unpaid advisory role in the Samantha Wills business.'

It was the fourteenth and final time I asked Geoff to be involved in my company.

The following week, I signed 30 per cent equity of the Samantha Wills business over to Geoff. I also signed on to direct the Icon rebrand in the role of creative director, a position I would hold until 2011. My partnership with Geoff as co-directors of the Samantha Wills business was to officially begin on 1 January 2008 and it would mark the start of an eleven-year working partnership.

'Samantha manipulated me with this amazing presentation!' Geoff would joke years later when telling people how we came to be business partners.

'It wasn't manipulative,' I would reply. 'It was strategic.'

—

Geoff requested the financials from the firm I'd engaged to manage the Samantha Wills accounting.

'Exactly *how many* credit cards do you have?' Geoff asked me, scanning the reports.

'Five,' I replied.

'Choose one and give me the other four,' he said. I handed over the cards one by one, placing them on the table like I was a blackjack dealer in a casino.

'Okay. Here's what we're going to do,' Geoff said after he'd reached for a pair of scissors, cut each of the cards in half and tossed the plastic shards into the wastepaper bin. 'The sales agents are doing a great job; the forward sales indents are really strong. But the GP across the business is currently too low: we need to get it to 75 per cent. I am going to email you an Excel spreadsheet this afternoon with formulas plugged in to calculate the costs of goods—it will read as COGS in the file. Start with what you want to sell the piece for at retail and work back from that. Every product needs to enter this building after freighting with a 75 per cent GP, 71 per cent at the very lowest. Do you know how to do a VLOOKUP in Excel? If you don't, you need to learn. You will drive the outcome of the GP from design, so you need to sit with the suppliers and work out how you can get the quality materials you need with this commercial outcome.'

While I was familiar with these terms from Icon, it had never been my job to be responsible for them—at Icon, it was the production and operations managers who looked after this stuff. It was clear that it was no longer going to be enough to kind-of know what they meant, I had to understand them inside out. *Sales indents, GP, COGS, VLOOKUP* . . . I took notes as quickly as I could.

'All make sense?' Geoff asked, as he closed his computer.

'Yep, got it,' I replied.

Geoff sent the spreadsheet over that afternoon and I spent the entire evening googling all the terms he had used in our meeting and trying to apply them to what he'd sent me. That spreadsheet became my bible—its set formulas allowed me to design with much more commercial intelligence.

The next thing Geoff wanted to do was recruit a general manager and we ended up hiring a woman named Sarah Moore. Sarah had worked for other Australian brands, building wholesale businesses, and she was the perfect fit for us. Geoff tasked her with two main objectives for her first year with the company. The first was to implement procedures and processes to ready the business for the second task, which was to increase sales nationally by 180 per cent within the first twelve months and internationally by 250 per cent within twenty-four. Sarah recruited two more junior team members to manage customer service, and suddenly we were a team of five: me, Misha, Sarah and the two juniors. Six, if you included Renee.

By the end of April 2008, Samantha Wills was a cash-positive business for the very first time ever. Geoff sent me the profit and loss sheet and had highlighted the zero balance owing on the credit card debt I had amassed in the startup years. As tears of sheer relief threatened to start streaming, I picked up my phone to call him.

'I just got the P&L,' I said, my voice shaking as I tried to hold back from crying. 'I can't thank you enough. I don't know how you did that so quickly,' I added, wondering how he'd been able to turn around the remaining $65,000 credit card debt without us investing any money into the business.

'You don't have to thank me,' Geoff said. 'The P&L just needed a bit of . . . restructuring. This could be a really profitable business and it's all because of the brand you have built.'

'I think you are being overly kind in that statement!' I said, laughing a little as a tear escaped down my cheek. 'Well, I guess I knew how to build a brand, but didn't know how to run a business, huh?'

'I don't know many people who would have *known* how to run a business at twenty-two,' Geoff said, 'and the good news is, you can teach someone to run a business, but from my experience, it's near impossible to teach someone how to build a brand.'

—

I split my time between working on the Icon rebranding project one week and then focusing on Samantha Wills design and creative the next. I started doing more work travel, going to not only Hong Kong but also mainland China, where Icon's factories were.

When I was in China for work, I was guided—and interpreted—by a Chinese local, Ella, who was based in Qingdao and had previously worked as an account manager in one of the production houses we used. We'd made her an offer to come and work for Icon and employed her as our quality control manager, responsible for liaising directly with our production teams. Most production houses in China are owned and run by men, but I was adamant that for Samantha Wills, we partner with a production house that had female management. On one trip, I had charged Ella with helping me with this goal and, all credit to her, we managed to find one factory with a female owner and another nearby with a female manager. While I hadn't thought we would be spoilt for choice finding females in senior positions, I did not think they would be as scarce as they were. I returned home with a great appreciation for what each of these women had overcome to reach the levels they had in their careers, and we ended up signing these two production houses as the main manufacturers for Samantha Wills.

The more time I spent on the ground in Qingdao, the more I not only learnt about but also began to appreciate the production process—how many hands had touched each piece, the master craftspeople who hand-carved the moulds, the art of polishing and shaping each stone that was set—from the sampling process through to bulk production.

—

'What's this?' I asked, looking at a hand-carved wooden box that was sitting on my desk.

'It arrived for you yesterday from India,' Misha said. 'I think it's from a supplier you met at the Hong Kong trade show.'

The actual delivery was of pendants and bead samples that the supplier hoped we would want to buy, but it wasn't the beads I was interested in, it was the box they arrived in. It looked like something out of *Jumanji*. Oak in colour, the box's mango wood sides were smoothly polished and tiny flowers and vines had been intricately carved into the lid. The brass hinges were silent as I slowly opened the box and inside, the pendants and beads rested on the black felt lining like little treasures. There was something magical about these boxes and I fell in love with them immediately.

'What the fuck do you mean you want every piece of Samantha Wills jewellery to come in a hand-carved wooden box?' Geoff said the following week when I told him my idea. 'Do you have any fucking idea the logistics involved in freighting wooden fucking boxes from India? And not only that, packaging should be flat packed! You know what you can't flat pack? A fucking wooden box! So you know what you are essentially suggesting we ship in from India? Wood and air!'

'I just think that no one is doing really incredible packaging,' I replied, holding the box up the same way Mufasa held Simba in *The Lion King*. 'I mean, look at it! Can you imagine buying a piece of jewellery and then it arrives in *this*? It would be like getting a surprise gift with your purchase every single time.' Geoff had stopped listening to me and had returned to the email he was typing. 'I truly think if we used this as our packaging, it would really put the brand on the map.'

'I suggest you go and look at where India is on a fucking map,' Geoff said, not even looking up.

I was confident that the boxes were going to work, I just needed to prove it to Geoff, so I went ahead and ordered a couple of hundred boxes to test them out. A few weeks later, three large pallets of hand-carved wooden boxes arrived at our office. True to my style, I had once again jumped in without checking the depth. Three large pallets of wooden boxes were not insignificant in size and I hadn't given any thought to where we were going to store them. With jewellery already filling every available tub of our IKEA-bought storage warehouse solution, there really wasn't any space for the boxes, which actually took up more room than the jewellery did. Determined that they wouldn't be in our office for too long anyway, somehow we squeezed them in. I then gave a few boxes to our sales agents to show retailers. I decided not to tell the agents that we were in the testing phase; I simply explained that this would be the new Samantha Wills packaging moving forward. One of the first retailers to see the new collection was the prestigious Australian department store, David Jones. They loved the packaging so much they placed an order on the spot. The new collection had the packaging price absorbed into it, but it only increased each item by a few dollars. I anticipated that retailers would comment on this, but when they saw the new packaging they had the same reaction as me—nothing else mattered.

'Our customers are going to LOVE this!' retailers would coo. 'How soon can we get this instore? Any chance we can pull it forward?'

The fax machine was getting jammed up with new orders. The season that we introduced the wooden boxes, our sales tripled.

'Samantha, I need to chat to you,' Sarah said one day after I returned to the office after a lunch meeting.

'Sure, what's up?' I said.

'Um, well, I need to talk to you about . . . Renee,' Sarah said, with the awkward tone of someone about to tell another about their offensive body odour.

'Renee?' I confirmed cautiously.

'Yes,' Sarah said slowly. 'Renee. See, people were calling for her, and it was mentioned that if anyone calls for her, customer service is just supposed to say that Renee is not in today, but you can get her on email . . .'

I felt like a kid being sat down to be told that her imaginary friend could no longer sit at the dinner table. I told Sarah the whole story about Renee. She laughed in parts and looked concerned in others. After being with me almost from the very beginning, that was officially Renee's last day with the company. As far as any of our retailers knew, she went on maternity leave, effective immediately, and any enquiries for her were redirected to someone available to take a phone call. I didn't hear from Renee again, but I believe she is doing okay for herself and is now trying her hand at writing.

Between new employees and wooden boxes, we were growing so fast that we needed to find a new office and warehouse space. I had seen a beautiful old electrical substation advertised for lease, so I got on the phone to get the details. The real estate agent explained that it had recently been gutted and was a completely blank canvas. It was stunning: white-washed walls and floors over two huge levels full of natural light, and the back of the building had French-style doors that opened into a courtyard. It was exactly what we needed. Two weeks later, the substation became our new office premises.

In business, whether you are feeling like you are clinging to a lifeline or are juggling everything like a pro, your business still demands the majority of your focus and attention. All my time and energy went into mine and Andrew was immersed in his own startup. Even though we understood each other's work demands and were each other's biggest supporters, it didn't leave either of us much bandwidth to focus on our relationship. We'd pass each other in the hallway at home saying things like, 'Your dinner is in the oven!' and 'It won't be like this forever, our businesses need our focus right now'. Whoever coined the saying 'You can have it all' needs to add a small print disclaimer: 'You can have it all, just not all at the same time.'

Over the coming years, I would learn the ins and outs of running a business, but I would always add the most value on the creative side. I also learnt to surround myself with people who were good at the things I was not. By the time we closed the Samantha Wills office for the 2008 Christmas break, we had twenty-six employees and had turned over $1.1 million that year.

—

I had been a long-time fan of the singer P!nk and in 2009 she was due to come to Australia for the stadium tour of her *Funhouse* album. She was scheduled to film an appearance on the music program *Video Hits* and I was friendly with one of the hosts, Faustina Agolley, from attending some of the same social events. I gave Faustina some jewellery to pass on to P!nk and the following Saturday morning I settled in front of the TV at home to watch the show.

At the end of her interview with P!nk, instead of throwing directly to the commercial break, Faustina reached down to pick up a bag. 'Before you go, I actually have a gift for you,' she told P!nk. 'It's from the Australian jewellery designer, Samantha Wills.'

'What? No way!' P!nk said.

'What? No way!' I screamed, dropping my half-eaten Vegemite toast face down on the carpet. I had given the package to Faustina thinking she would give it to P!nk *after* the interview, not on camera on national television!

'That's so kind! Wow, what is this . . .' she said, as she pulled out the large hand-carved wooden box. The Samantha Wills logo was unintentionally but perfectly positioned to face the camera. 'Wow! Look at this box!' P!nk said, admiring our packaging like it was the most beautiful thing she had ever seen.

'There's jewellery inside,' Faustina said.

'What?' P!nk exclaimed, 'I thought the box was the gift!'

My phone started buzzing with messages—'THIS IS THE BEST ENDORSEMENT EVER!', and 'I CAN'T BELIEVE P!NK JUST OPENED THAT ON NATIONAL TV!' I couldn't believe it was happening either.

P!nk went on to wear the rings I'd gifted her to all of her public appearances on that tour and the best thing about a singer wearing rings is that they are always holding the microphone, making the ring front and centre in every photo. Her personal assistant contacted our office shortly after and said that P!nk loved the pieces so much, she wanted to purchase one of everything from the collection. I said we would happily send the jewellery to her as a gift but she insisted on paying for it. As a young designer, this was the highest compliment you could receive. Her support and generosity is something I have never forgotten. I named our following collection 'Brille en el Air', French for 'Glitter in the Air', which was my favourite song from P!nk's *Funhouse* album.

ex·pan·s·ion

noun

the action of becoming larger or more extensive; a thing
formed by the enlargement, broadening or development
of something

Our celebrity portfolio was starting to fill up. We were getting
calls from stylists in both Australia and the United States,
requesting pieces for celebrities they were working with for
magazine shoots or red-carpet events. When I saw the invoice
for the costs of sending samples over via FedEx, it was clear that
the money we were spending on freight would be better spent
on a monthly retainer for a celebrity services showroom in the
United States. I had a trip to Los Angeles coming up and had
compiled a list of twelve highly recommended celebrity services
firms based there. I was adamant that I was going to sign an
American PR firm before the week was through.

A few weeks later, I'd just had a quick coffee meeting in West Hollywood with Karen, an Australian PR colleague who just so happened to be in LA at the same time, and I was madly trying to flag down a taxi. I had secured a meeting with my top agency of choice; this was no time to be running late. My phone buzzed: it was the agency informing me they had double-booked themselves and had to cancel.

Fuck! I cursed internally, waving the taxi that had slowed down to keep going. I replied, asking them when we could reschedule, frustrated that this would throw a spanner in the works of my already tight itinerary. Just as I sent that message off, my phone buzzed again with a message from Karen: 'Are you still close? The woman I am meeting with wants to meet you. We're at the tea house on the next block down.'

In true LA style, the tea house had a back courtyard full of people who didn't seem to have office jobs, drinking tea poured from ornate teapots into tiny cups. I spotted Karen, who was sitting opposite a woman who looked exactly like Gwyneth Paltrow. Karen introduced us: Gwyneth's lookalike was Annelise Peterson. Annelise—who was toned, tanned and stunning—was casually reclined on a cane couch, her white jeans and T-shirt crisp and spotless against the white cushions.

'Hiiiiiiiii, Samantha! Karen was just telling me about you!' Annelise said. 'I MUST do your PR here. It's not even negotiable! I love your work. I just saw Karen's ring and I was like, "Who made that!" She said you did! And I said, "Where is she?!" And she said she just had coffee with you and I said, "You just had coffee with her? Call her! Get her back here!! I need to represent her!" Tell me everything! Why are you standing up? Sit down!'

I sat down like a slightly terrified puppy.

'Here's my details,' Annelise said, handing me a crisp white business card. *Was everything this woman owned white?* I wondered. I took the business card from her. It felt like linen and was embossed with 'ANNELISE PETERSON Inc' and her mobile number. 'Aren't they great cards?' Annelise said, noticing me staring at it. 'I just introduced the printer to Reese Witherspoon so she could get her cards done there too! Oh, I'm so glad this worked out. This is great! I love Aussies! Do you want tea?' Annelise waved down a waiter before I could even reply. 'She'll have tea!' Annelise told the waiter. I looked at Karen who gave me a little smile and shrugged.

Back at my hotel, a quick google gave me in-depth insight into the powerhouse that was Annelise Peterson.

Annelise had held marketing and strategy positions at Calvin Klein, Alberta Ferretti, American *Vogue* and Valentino. She was known as a brand and PR expert and mingled at fashion events and parties in LA and New York with the industry's best-known names, all of them in her Rolodex. It didn't take much searching to see that she also had a Bachelor of Economics from Columbia University. I clicked into an article about how she had organised the forty-fifth anniversary of Valentino in Rome and jumped as my phone buzzed. It was Annelise.

Shit! Can she see me? I slammed my laptop shut just in case. 'Hello,' I answered, as coolly as I could.

'Samantha! Hi! It's Annelise,' she said.

'Oh, hi!' I said, trying my best to sound surprised.

'If you don't have plans tonight, I would love you to join me for dinner,' Annelise said.

My thirty-minute reconnaissance mission had just revealed that this woman was one of the most powerful women in fashion branding in the country. She has dinners with the likes of Sarah Jessica Parker and Uma Thurman. *Why on earth would she want to have dinner with me?*

'Me? Um, yes! I mean, no, no I don't have plans tonight!' I said. 'Yes, I would love to join you for dinner.'

'Great! Sunset Tower Hotel, 8 pm!' Annelise said. I only knew the Sunset Tower Hotel because I had seen just about every famous celebrity ever photographed leaving it in the weekly gossip mags. The property had been the long-time venue of the infamous *Vanity Fair* Oscars afterparty and while the hotel's dining room provided the utmost privacy for its famous clientele, the paparazzi out the front did not offer the same courtesy. It was where the rich and famous hung out and I had to be there in three hours. All of a sudden, I felt very out of my depth.

Two hours and fifty minutes later, I walked into the dimly lit dining room and instantly saw Annelise. Her skin was glowing and her long blonde hair was worn in a stylish blunt cut. Her elegant black dress was gorgeous and I suddenly felt very underdressed and unglamorous and unsure why someone like Annelise would want to have dinner with someone like me.

'Hi! I'm so glad this worked out that you were free tonight!' Annelise said as I approached the table, greeting me with a huge hug and an even bigger smile. 'Sit! Sit!'

Annelise and I chatted for three hours. I admired her hugely for all she had achieved and knew I could learn a lot from her. Given the global brands and designers she was used to working with, I don't know what she saw in me or in the Samantha Wills brand but she insisted that she wanted to represent the brand in LA. Sitting opposite her that night, I knew that my earlier cancelled meeting was another of the universe's magical interventions. I was meant to work with Annelise.

'So, you've been in New York since college,' I said as the waiter brought over our bill. 'Why are you in LA now?'

'Well . . .' It was the longest pause she had taken since the moment I'd met her. 'Twelve years in New York . . . it kind of wears on you, you know?'

No, I didn't know, I thought to myself, but I nodded anyway.

'So I moved out here to sunny California,' she continued. 'I am just doing some PR consulting for smaller brands at the moment,' she paused again. 'It's a different pace. I mean, it's not New York, but . . . it's what I needed for a bit . . .' The end of her sentence trailed off and she looked away.

I started to reply, just to fill the silence. 'I haven't been to New York yet but—'

'I lost my brother and my fiancé in 9/11,' Annelise said. Her eyes looked at me and through me at the same time. I didn't know what to say and I felt my hands reach up to my chest and clutch at my heart. How does someone process losing two loved ones in the same tragic event? I wanted to speak, but I couldn't find any words.

'Then I lost my Dad a few years after,' Annelise continued, her voice soft.

'Annelise,' I said, almost in a whisper. 'I am so, so sorry.'

'Thank you. It's okay. I'm doing okay now,' she said, 'but at the time, I didn't deal with any of it. I just didn't want to . . . I couldn't. So I just kept pushing forward. I wanted to pretend it didn't happen. Just keep running, you know?'

No, I didn't know, I thought. There was so much I didn't know.

—

As soon as I got back to Australia, I arranged for two sample collections to be sent to Annelise. Two weeks after they arrived, I received an email.

TO: Samantha Wills

FROM: Annelise Peterson

SUBJECT: Eva Mendes wears SAMANTHA WILLS 'Bohemian Bardot' Ring

Hey SW,

Just received the images from last night's red carpet. Eva wore the Bohemian Bardot Ring and Bella bangle set.

It was styled by Rachel Zoe, she is a celebrity stylist out here, have you heard of her?

Photos look great! See attached.

Chat soon, Annelise xox

Eva Mendes?! Bohemian Bardot?! Rachel Zoe?! What???

Rachel Zoe had a reality show that had just launched, and followed her behind the scenes of her career as a celebrity stylist.

I was a huge fan of the show. Getting product into the hands of Rachel and her team was a big deal.

I remembered designing the Bohemian Bardot ring, but hadn't thought too much about it since. It was a large teardrop-shaped ring with oxide gold casing. The one Eva wore featured a peach stone. Our celebrity portfolio was quite extensive by this point; each placement brought with it a spike in sales on the featured item but I could never have predicted the journey this was about to take us all on. The images of Eva wearing the Bohemian Bardot appeared on my screen, the ring prominent as she walked the red carpet at the Giffoni Film Festival in Italy. *OK! Magazine* Australia had said they would run the images of Eva in their next issue. The morning it came out, our website crashed and we had sold out of the Bohemian Bardot ring by lunchtime.

That placement had an impact on the brand—and, in turn, on the course of my life—like no other placement or initiative did. It was like that ring had a life and purpose all of its own. Over the next ten years, we would see close to one million Bohemian Bardot rings produced in over 300 different colours, and that ring would later spark an entire movement in our dedicated online community. For an entire decade, the Bohemian Bardot ring never left the top of our bestsellers list—as too did turquoise as one of our bestselling colourways, a fact I would never let Geoff live down. The ring, along with the wooden boxes, became the most iconic product in our brand's history.

Back in LA, Annelise had organised a media presentation for our new collection and she wanted me there for the meet and greets. The day was a steady stream of fashion media, stylists and their assistants coming through and taking notes, pulling samples or collecting lookbooks.

'Samantha, this is Aaron, he is Patricia Field's assistant,' Annelise said, introducing me to a young guy who was looking at the collection. Patricia Field was an iconic stylist, most renowned for the work she did on the television show *Sex and the City*.

'Lovely to meet you, Samantha!' Aaron said, reaching his hand out to shake mine. 'Pat will just love all of this! We're working on a little something at the moment, do you mind if I pull some earrings to show her?'

We often loaned product to wardrobe departments, happy to do so for the chance that it might appear on screen, but we did it with the knowledge that, due to the amount of product in film set wardrobe departments, it likely would never be returned. Patricia Field could have borrowed my car, house and a vital organ as far I was concerned. We loaned out a lot of product that day, but I wouldn't think of Aaron or Patricia Field again until the same time the following year.

—

The hand-carved wooden boxes continued to gain momentum. There were online chat forums dedicated to them, we received photos from women who had requested a replica of the Samantha Wills hand-carved wooden box as their birthday cake, and our most dedicated customers started to amass personal collections of them and come up with creative ways to incorporate them into their homes. A mother of two made Samantha Wills hand-carved wooden box bedheads for her daughters. Another created a large wood-panelled wall hanging and one customer even sent us a photo of her family using the boxes as a giant Jenga game. The boxes and the Bohemian Bardot ring had become the brand's two signatures and we understood that nurturing them was paramount to maintaining an identifiable brand.

But as our celebrity portfolio continued to grow, so did the problem of counterfeiting. Many Chinese manufacturers were keen to copy celebrity fashions, turning a cheap replica of the product around quickly and then distributing it globally on sites like Alibaba and eBay. In Qingdao, Ella would often report that she'd seen replicas of our metal castings and casings in the local marketplace, often alongside a printed photo of a celebrity wearing it. This meant that someone had purchased our product, replicated moulds for it and was trying to sell it to factories to do bulk production for large international chain stores. No matter where you manufacture, most brands have their production and packaging produced in the same country for ease of logistics. But with our production houses in China and our wooden box packaging produced in India, what was burdensome with logistics became a blessing for counterfeit protection. In both China and India, we had artisans who were master craftspersons of their trade, so competing factories in China could not replicate the wooden boxes and Indian jewellery factories could not replicate the jewellery. The jewellery on its own was a product, the jewellery *with* the signature wooden box made it a branded offer, and one without the other became a quick means of identifying counterfeits of each.

'Urrrrrgh,' I grumbled one afternoon as my eyes scanned the counterfeit figures in our monthly management report. 'The number of replicas is increasing month on month.'

'That's a good thing,' Geoff said, reading the same report.

'What? Why would you say that?!'

'You should be worried when people are *no longer* counterfeiting our product,' Geoff explained, looking up from his report to me. 'The minute you no longer have a counterfeiting issue, you have a brand health issue. As long as people are ripping off your work, you know that the brand is in demand.'

I would look at that report very differently from that moment on.

Towards the end of 2009, the growth of Samantha Wills Pty Ltd was significant. We had thirty-five staff and a turnover of $3.5 million.

'I think we need to combine the back-of-house functions,' Geoff said to me after our final management meeting for the year. 'Combine the SW and Icon warehouse space up in Ballina.'

It made sense—not only did it feel like the right time to bring all functions under the same roof, it would also free up the Sydney office and give it space to refocus its direction. We went on to recruit managers and teams for standalone marketing and PR, accounting and sales functions. The outsourcing and agencies had taken us this far, but it was time to operate as a fully inhouse-managed brand.

Icon was in full swing and we had opened an office in the UK to service Europe, which saw the profile of the brand and revenue increase significantly. The Samantha Wills brand was following with the same momentum, but instead of Europe, our biggest demand was coming from the United States. Geoff suggested I start to spend more extended amounts of time there. His actual words were: 'Someone needs to get on a fucking plane and work out what this brand looks like in the USA! Because right now we are sending product over there with absolutely no fucking clue how it is being represented in the marketplace!'

He was right. Drew Barrymore had been snapped wearing six different pieces of Samantha Wills in one week, Rihanna was photographed coming out of the Chateau Marmont wearing one of our rings and Katy Perry had just worn one of our cuffs to an awards show. When celebrities wear brands, America responds, and when America responds, Australian media pays close attention. Local press coverage of the brand was increasing by the week, including one feature with the daunting headline: 'SAMANTHA WILLS IS TIPPED TO BE OUR BIGGEST EXPORT SINCE VEGEMITE'. It felt like big shoes to fill, but the media attention also added more weight to Geoff's concern about who was driving the brand in the United States. I knew I had to start spending much more time there.

I was due to be in Los Angeles in January 2010 to present our collection at the GRAMMY Style Studio, an invitation-only event where brands would come and display their collections and celebrity stylists would source pieces for their clients to wear to the GRAMMYs and all the accompanying parties. Andrew was as busy working on his business as I was on mine. When Mel told me that she could get a few days off work to come and meet me in LA, I was as excited to see her as I was relieved to have her help. The event was set up in Smashbox Studios and our allocated booth was right next to the Australian fashion designer Toni Matičevski.

Toni, Mel and I had a great week together, working the Style Studio by day then hitting LA's bar scene at night. Many celebrity stylists came through the suite and selected pieces. Ke$ha was just new on the music scene and came through with her mum because she didn't yet have a stylist and they picked a few of our pieces. Our suite at the studio also included two complimentary tickets to the GRAMMYs, which were due to be held at the STAPLES Center in downtown LA. Mel and I couldn't believe our luck when the Studio founder, Kate Nobelius, who was pregnant at the time and exhausted after four days on her feet, told us at the last minute that we could take her GRAMMYs tickets—tickets which were in the front row, stage left.

With our last-minute ticket upgrade, Mel and I felt like we were recreating a scene from *Pretty Woman* as we headed to Rodeo Drive. I purchased a long-sleeved black sequinned minidress that I knew I would never ever wear again, but also rational-ised I would probably never ever be going to the GRAMMYs again, so made peace with the price tag. Mel and I had our hair and make-up done at our hotel while drinking champagne and exchanging looks of excitement and disbelief. It was a long way from the early morning line we had sat in at the Bondi Markets and an even longer way from our childhoods in Port Macquarie.

At the STAPLES Center, Kate's tickets saw us sitting a few metres from Beyoncé and Jay-Z. We watched as Lady Gaga found her seat with help from an assistant, because her silver costume and orb hat did not allow for a clear line of vision—for her or for anyone sitting behind her. We saw that where Britney Spears was meant to be sitting was actually being occupied by a seat filler (an actual GRAMMYs job) because Britney attended the event for all of fifteen minutes before leaving. That night, we also saw a very young Taylor Swift win four GRAMMYs, including Album of the Year, the youngest artist to ever do so at twenty years of age. Beyoncé performed, Elton John and Lady Gaga played together on twin pianos and Bon Jovi sang 'Livin' on a Prayer'. It was a night full of once-in-a-lifetime experiences and felt like being at the most exclusive music showcase in the world. Then the most incredible thing of all happened. P!nk took to the stage in a sequinned nude bodysuit, and was hoisted up to the ceiling of the STAPLES Center on a trapeze to sing 'Glitter in the Air', the very song I had named our collection after. As part of her performance, she was lowered into water under the stage and, as she emerged and flew above the crowd while singing, beads of water caught the light and droplets cascaded from her across the auditorium. The entire evening was incredibly surreal.

After the awards, Mel and I headed back to our hotel, swapped our glamorous dresses for bathrobes and ordered room service, then settled in front of the *E! News* red-carpet wrap-up on TV.

'Now, let's take a look at what the stars wore to the infamous Clive James party!' *E! News* host Giuliana Rancic said.

Mel and I sat there in our fancy hotel robes, clutching each other's arms in anticipation that they might feature Ke$ha. I was eager to see if she had ended up wearing any of our jewellery. We didn't have to wait long.

'And WHAT is that necklace, girl?!' Giuliana started, as Ke$ha appeared on the red carpet wearing a Samantha Wills couture neck piece I had handmade. 'I mean, she looks trashy!!! That necklace is all kinds of ugly!! Seriously, no, seriously, it's awful. What was she thinking?! It's a hard no from me!'

I froze, as the adrenaline high from the evening quickly disappeared, Giuliana moved on to the next celebrity, and Mel slowly reached over to the telephone.

'Hello, yes, we're in room 217,' she said into the receiver. 'We're going to need another bottle of wine.' She paused as they took the request. 'Yes, the same again, thank you. Oh, and as quickly as possible would be great!'

There are an infinite number of things I admire about Mel, but her ability to produce a bottle of wine in under six minutes that night is my favourite.

starry-eyed

adjective

naively enthusiastic or idealistic; failing to recognise
the practical realities of a situation

I was on my way to New York for some meetings with Annelise,
who had moved back to the East Coast and was running her
consulting and PR business from the Big Apple. She was the only
person I knew in the city and she had kindly taken me under
her very fashionable wing. One night, she insisted I join her for
one of New York Fashion Week's biggest opening parties. 'There
will be lots of fashion business people there tonight—people you
need to meet,' Annelise said, moving effortlessly in her stilettos
along the icy footpath in the Meatpacking District. I waddled
beside her like a baby penguin learning to walk, desperately
trying not to slip on the pavement. 'Penthouse, please!' Annelise
said as we got into the lift of The Standard hotel.

Annelise's friends were the who's who of the New York social scene and it intimidated me greatly. We reached the top floor and the elevator doors opened to a golden hallway. I felt way out of my league.

'You'll be fine!' Annelise said, sensing my trepidation. No matter what I had achieved in my career, I never felt like a 'real' designer. If I was Annelise's plus one, Impostor Syndrome was mine. Fashion parties left me feeling anxious and wishing that I was safely at home on a comfortable couch.

I quickly lost Annelise in the sea of glamorous (real) designers and celebrities. I didn't know what to do with myself. With my champagne untouched, and Impostor Syndrome by my side, I craned my neck to try to spot Annelise as I slowly made my way through the crowd. And there, through a sea of sequins and champagne flutes, was Rachel Zoe.

The woman who had styled the Bohemian Bardot ring on Eva Mendes and whose show I was a huge fan of was just a few metres from me, having a drink with her assistant on a lounge. Before I knew it, my legs were moving as if they were propelled by something beyond my control and I started to walk towards them.

'Um. Hi. Rachel. Hi. Um, you don't know me, um, my name is Samantha,' I stammered.

'Hi Samantha, nice to meet you!' Rachel replied warmly, reaching up to shake my hand.

'Oh! You too! Um, I'm so sorry to crash your conversation, I just wanted to say thank you. I'm a jewellery designer and you styled one of my pieces on Eva Mendes last year, and well . . . it really propelled our business in such an incredible way,' I said, barely drawing breath. 'Anyway, um, it pretty much changed my life, so, um, I just wanted to introduce myself. Okay. That's all. I'll go now.'

'Oh, okay!' Rachel said, her friendly smile a very generous exchange for my awkwardness. 'It's lovely to meet you! What is your brand called?' she asked.

'It's called Samantha Wills,' I replied.

'Samantha Wills. Okay! I'll keep an eye out for it in my studio! Nice to meet you, Samantha, and good luck with it all!' Rachel said, as she turned back to her conversation. Her assistant looked at me and rolled her eyes as she turned back to talk to Rachel. I couldn't have been more awkward, and she couldn't have been more lovely. I couldn't wait to get out of there.

A short dash across the snowy pavement and a quick taxi ride later, I was back in the apartment and in the shower, recovering from the experience. Wrapped in a towel, water still dripping off my face and my hair soaking wet, I felt like a girl who had just survived a near drowning by way of the New York social scene.

I spent the rest of that trip visiting New York boutiques and department stores, making notes of the jewellery brands they stocked, the pricepoints and the way the jewellery was merchandised. I researched every brand I could find that I thought might be a competitor to us in the US market. I spoke with bored sales assistants who were happy to spend twenty minutes chatting, asking them how each brand performed. At the end of each day as the snow fell outside, I would sit in my rented midtown apartment wearing every article of clothing I had packed to try to stay warm and work on what became a comprehensive overview of the American jewellery and accessories market.

One night as I typed the last of the day's notes up on my laptop, a Skype call came in. It was Sarah.

'Are you sitting down?' Sarah asked as she appeared on my screen.

'Yes, why?'

'You will *never* guess what we just received in the mail!' she said, holding up an envelope to the screen. I squinted my eyes as Sarah slowly pulled a card out of the envelope and opened it. On the front was a colourful illustration of four women and an abstract illustration of the New York skyline. 'One hand in the air for the big city, thanks for making us look so pretty!' Sarah read, the excitement in her voice increasing with every word. 'Love, Patricia Field and the *Sex and the City* Wardrobe Team!'

I had seen in the media that they had filmed a sequel to the first *Sex and the City* film but I had completely forgotten about Patricia Field's assistant visiting us in LA the year before.

'What else does it say?!' I asked Sarah.

'Nothing!' she said excitedly, turning the card over. 'That's it!'

'Do you think they actually used one of our pieces in the film?'

'I don't know,' Sarah said, still smiling, turning the card over again, as if it was a still-developing Polaroid containing yet more good news. A few members of the team waved as they walked behind Sarah, everyone clearly excited at the prospect of us having product in *Sex and the City*. Seeing everyone's smiling faces made me feel homesick. The Australian office was bustling, a team of people working together. I missed working with the team we had built and being in New York by myself felt similar to the early isolation of startup. I thanked Sarah for calling and said goodbye to a very excited team. I closed my laptop and headed to bed, keen for a good night's sleep ahead of more store visits and research the next day.

Towards the end of my stay in New York, Rachel Zoe was set to launch her first apparel line in collaboration with QVC, a juggernaut American home-shopping channel. Annelise made a call and got me a ticket to the filming, which was being done live from the main Fashion Week tent at Bryant Park. I sat and watched the entire process with awe as Rachel presented her collection to camera—but she wasn't just presenting the clothes, she was telling the story behind each garment. Seeing how product and storytelling came together on a retail platform inspired me greatly and I imagined seeing the Samantha Wills brand do the same one day.

I was flying back to Sydney a few days later and very happy to be heading home. I met Annelise for breakfast the morning of my flight.

'Did I tell you I spoke to Aaron a few weeks ago?' she said, stirring her peppermint tea. 'A pair of the earrings they asked for are going to be in the new *Sex and the City* film!'

'No. Nope. You definitely did not tell me that,' I said, wondering how she could forget to tell me such big news.

'I didn't? Weird. Anyway, Pat just LOVED your collection.' Before I could ask Annelise how such a fact could simply slip her mind, she pushed on. 'Also, I told my friend that you would email her your new lookbook and that she could choose a few pieces. She's awesome, you'll love her. She's on a show here, *Gossip Girl*—do you get that show in Australia? Anyway, I'll intro you now,' Annelise said, as she typed away on her BlackBerry. I felt my phone buzz with Annelise's introduction before she had even finished her sentence.

Shortly after breakfast, I was on my way to JFK to take a red-eye flight to China. Catching up on emails in the car, I hit reply-all on Annelise's introduction email, attaching the new Samantha Wills lookbook and telling Annelise's friend I would love to send her a few pieces if there was anything in the collection that caught her eye. Her friend was Blake Lively.

—

At the Australian premiere for *Sex and the City 2* in 2010, the atmosphere was electric and the red carpet was lined with every fashion publication in the country. The fashion media knew we had product in the film and I think the reporters who covered it were thankful that I shared a name with one of the show's main characters because all the press we received the next day came with a variation on the same headline: 'OUR SAMANTHA, A STAR IN SEX AND THE CITY'.

Even as we sat down to watch the film, I still had no idea which piece of our jewellery Patricia Field and her team had chosen. The movie diverged from the characters' New York habitat and was set in the Middle East. The costumes were elaborate and glamorously bohemian and while the film got less than desirable reviews, it was a perfect platform for our statement earrings. With oxidised gold metal, black crystal and onyx stones, they appeared on Cynthia Nixon's character, Miranda Hobbes, who wore them in the scene that the most widely used still shot from the film came from, where the four main characters were standing on a hotel balcony. The celebrity factor and placement in a major motion picture aside, having the Samantha Wills brand affiliated with the *Sex and the City* franchise came with a tonne of cultural cachet and gave us credibility with buyers, media and consumers internationally. A hardcover coffee-table book was released showcasing every outfit featured in the film and the Samantha Wills brand was listed next to CHANEL, Jimmy Choo and Prada.

The *Sex and the City* placement made it clear that if we wanted to build a global brand, we needed to commit to a global market, meaning I would have to spend most of my time in the United States. Try as I did to invest in every area of my life, it was hard to keep up as the brand took off. Andrew's business was also doing well and demanded just as much of his time. Our updates on each other's lives and businesses started to come by way of rare dinners with our friends. Someone would ask Andrew about how his work was going and he would talk about a new client he had signed or project he was working on or would give an update on a family member.

'That's great, babe!' I would say, joining our friends in their congratulations as we all heard his news for the first time. Andrew and I loved each other but we were both putting all our time and energy into our businesses. And now we'd come to a crossroads. I knew the Samantha Wills business needed me to spend more time in the States and that Andrew's required him to be in Sydney, so it was with a very heavy heart that for the second and final time, we ended our relationship.

A few weeks later, with little more than my laptop and a suitcase, I boarded a flight from Sydney to JFK and signed a lease on a new apartment in New York's Meatpacking District. I was twenty-eight years old and that financial year we had turned over $6.5 million.

—

My move to the United States took place in the middle of the oppressive New York summer, a rude wake-up call compared with the romantic, snow-covered or leafy autumn streets I had previously experienced there. It was 45 degrees Celsius and the trash on the New York pavements emitted an odour that I'm sure would have offended even the city's prevalent rat population. The other problem with trying to do business during summer in New York is that no one's in the city; the well-heeled are escaping the burning concrete and taking refuge in their Hamptons beach houses.

My new home was a loft-style apartment, quintessentially New York with large pillar columns and high ceilings. The building was once a refrigeration storage warehouse, a fact I chose to wipe from my mind given that it was highly possible the apartment was once filled with hanging cow carcasses. I had ordered furniture but it was going to take about four weeks for it to all arrive. The only furnishings I had were a small stepladder the previous tenants had left behind to sit on to eat my takeaway Chinese, and a mattress, which I'd purchased in a nearby bedding store that had agreed—with an inflated cash tip—to deliver it to me straightaway.

While the city streets were scorching and desolate, I spent my days bunkered down next to my apartment's air-conditioning unit, its exhausted sighs echoing through the apartment every ten minutes. Propping my laptop on the stepladder, I sat cross-legged on the floor to Skype with the team in Australia every few days. Sarah did an incredible job of managing the team and business as though it were her own, and before too long the Icon rebrand was up and running successfully. Before leaving Sydney, I had recruited a new creative director for Icon who I worked closely with, gradually handing over my Icon commitments to them. Once in New York, I would be free to focus solely on the Samantha Wills brand. Geoff and I had agreed that in order to do the work needed in NYC but still maintain my public commitments to the brand and team in Australia, I was going to spend six weeks in New York and ten days in Sydney consistently.

A new app called Instagram had launched and, as had happened with Facebook, my personal account quickly turned into the business account. Our consumers delighted in getting a behind-the-scenes glimpse of the brand and the design process. I started to share my travels and recommendations, replying not only to comments on my feed but also following and engaging in the feeds of some of our customers. Traditionally, in the relationship between a fashion brand and consumer, the brand is the more senior in the hierarchy. A creative director would work in secrecy for months, toiling away to craft the next season's 'must-haves' and then revealing them through advertising and media, which told their consumer what they should buy. It was essentially a one-way conversation, from the brand to the consumer. But Facebook and Instagram flipped that on its head and gave brands the opportunity to have a conversation *with* their customers, rather than consistently talking *at* them. Not all brands took this route, but it was one that came very organically to us. It could have been part impostor syndrome, part small-town upbringing, but being in conversation with our customers felt much more authentic to me than talking down *at* them.

Before long, the Samantha Wills account had 10,000 followers. The hashtag #SamanthaWills was being used when customers shared special milestones and events in their lives—times they would wear, give or receive our product. Our customers were gracious enough to speak with me daily and invite me into their worlds. They'd show me how they were wearing their Samantha Wills jewellery, tell me how they received a piece for their birthday from their husband, or as a graduation gift from their parents, or if it was something they saved up for themselves. These stories would be accompanied by a photo of them with their new piece of jewellery, the wooden box also proudly displayed. Our customers were using Instagram to become self-appointed ambassadors for the brand. There was no greater marketing outreach than that and I wanted to make sure I returned their generosity by acknowledging as many of the posts as I could. I dedicated at least an hour every day to go through the hashtagged posts and liking them, celebrating their occasions and thanking them for choosing the Samantha Wills brand. That 10,000-person following quickly crept up to 15,000 and while I very much wanted to maintain a personal relationship with our followers, within a few weeks it had hit 20,000. I was aware that I had created a unique connection with our Instagram community. My overarching concern now was that it was becoming impossible for me to physically keep up with the amount of communication that level of ongoing engagement would require and that our valued community might feel that I was ignoring them.

One day, my Instagram notifications started to chime more than usual. I saw a few messages from customers who had recently visited a prominent Australian women's retail chain and noticed a direct replica of the Bohemian Bardot ring. The images they sent were accompanied by messages of anger and outrage that a product they owned was being replicated by a high-street retailer for a fraction of the cost and also at a fraction of the quality. Sarah purchased a ring from the retailer so we could check it out and you could see where the Samantha Wills brand tag had been roughly soldered over. It was the only thing changed on the item, even our signature ring band had been carbon copied. I kept in mind Geoff's advice that if the brand was being copied it meant it was in good health but this was more concerning than flattering.

Our lawyers dealt with the matter with a cease and desist. Our request first and foremost was for the retailer to strip all remaining stock of the ring from their stores, which they reluctantly agreed to do. More importantly, I wanted to recognise and thank our consumers for rallying around the brand.

I couldn't reply to all the messages individually so I took out a piece of blank paper and with a black marker wrote, 'Thank you so much for taking a stand for Australian designers, I really felt like I had my SW Army with me this week—SWx'. I photographed the handwritten note and posted it to Instagram. The responders were bursting with pride at their collective stand against counterfeits. These women were loyal, they treated the brand like their own and they had formed a camaraderie online with each other. They weren't simply customers, this was a community. Without any premeditated objective, writing 'SW Army' on that piece of paper provided the name for the first of many break-out communities that would form within the brand's greater community.

Instagram also provided a platform for our customers to showcase their Samantha Wills pieces and we very quickly saw that they weren't so much customers; rather, they were collectors of the brand! Our Instagram feed was filled with personal collections of Samantha Wills jewellery that often outsized my own. Instagram wasn't just a way for us to talk with our community, it was also a way for them to talk with each other. Samantha Wills 'Buy Swap Sell' groups started to pop up on forums and discontinued styles were sometimes fetching more than four times the original retail amount. Wanting to take these virtual communities over into the real world, these groups of passionate, like-minded strangers would arrange meet-ups across the country.

If I was giving a talk or making an instore appearance at one of our retailers, the community would be there in force. Women dripping with Samantha Wills jewellery would introduce themselves, usually also telling me their Instagram handle and how long they had followed the brand for. In a social landscape that was once vertically tiered, Instagram made things horizontal. These women were a part of our community as much as we were a part of theirs and they were on a first-name basis not only with me, but with every member of our inhouse team. We knew which members of our community liked turquoise and which preferred rose quartz, we knew their birthdays, we even knew some of their children's and pets' names!

At head office, we had to put in a customer experience team member just to look after the most dedicated and passionate communities. The way that social media revolutionised business and branding was most impactfully demonstrated to me one Sunday evening when I was sitting on the couch in my tracksuit watching TV while simultaneously scrolling through Instagram. One of our loyal collectors had taken the initiative to create a competition of sorts for our community via a special post. 'Colour of the next #SamanthaWills #BohemianBardot? We should take a vote—post a photo showing your favourite colour and preferred casing—we can show @SamanthaWills the top five!'

I replied to the post instantly, saying, 'This is a great idea! Also name the colour that you post (we're running out of colour names!) ;)—SWx.'

The comments from community members started to roll in fast. I spent the next few hours chatting online with our community. Right there on my couch, in my comfy old tracksuit pants, I learnt which colours our most engaged and highest-spending customers wanted us to produce our bestselling product in. Hundreds of options started to stream in and by the following morning, we had sent our production houses a brief of the most popular colours so they could source the stones to match. Within a few weeks, we had the stock—imagined into life by our community—in our warehouse. It was one of the most successful, yet simplest, commercial initiatives we ever did.

Saturn Return

sat·urn re·t·urn

definition

in horoscopic astrology, an astrological transit that
occurs when the planet Saturn returns to the same place
in the sky it occupied at the moment of a person's birth;
the influence of the Saturn return is considered to start
in the person's late twenties

While I'd been busying myself focusing on building a community
around the brand, I had neglected to invest in building a personal
community in my new city. For friendships to form, they need
to be nurtured and I totally underestimated the difficulty of this
when you up and leave with a suitcase every six weeks. The people
I was actually spending the most time with were the passengers
and airline crew flying between Sydney and New York on any
given day. Gone were the days of me turning right while Geoff
turned left. We rarely travelled together anymore, but regardless,

we now both sat at the same end of the plane. My passport was working overtime and aeroplanes and airport lounges had, in a weird way, started to feel like home. Needless to say, there is nothing grounding about finding your personal community with strangers who rarely have their feet on the ground.

—

Starting your own brand is a self-indulgent pursuit. As a creative founder and director, my job was to tell comprehensive stories articulated through the brand that engaged and delighted our customers: to have a clear vision of where the brand was going and to lead the team from design through to campaign and marketing initiatives to get us there. As there are no strict rights or wrongs with creativity, a commercially successful creative director needs to act not only on intuition, but also with a clear understanding of who their customer is and where the brand sits in the marketplace. As brand builders, we can want our brand to sit in a certain tier of the market all we please, but at the end of the day it is actually the market that makes that decision.

I had decided I wanted the Samantha Wills brand to sit a tier to a tier-and-a-half higher than where it was. In the Australian market we had found huge success with our bohemian aesthetic, statement-sized pieces and brightly coloured semiprecious stones, with turquoise being our signature. Our styling was layered and our metals were burnished and oxidised. Our core pricepoint sat at around a recommended retail price of $139 and our consumers were highly engaged because our brand narrative was very real and authentic. They knew about my personal journey from small-town

Australia to the Bondi Markets and they celebrated with us as we started adorning celebrities and being stocked by retailers around the globe.

But after months of researching the US market, everything I knew about the success and authenticity of the brand quickly started to get lost beneath the voice of my ego and insecurities. The truth was that in the US market, our brand was best suited to a distribution of department stores like Bloomingdale's and Saks Fifth Avenue and mid-tier retailers like Anthropologie and REVOLVE. But, instead, I decided that I wanted the brand to sit alongside the higher end brands gracing the glass counters at Barneys New York and Bergdorf Goodman and in expensive high-end boutiques and e-tailers. I knocked on all the top-tier doors, and in the American market that's a lot of doors. When I presented the Samantha Wills brand to them, they would say, 'It's too bohemian. It's not really for us. It's beautiful but it's not what our customer is buying. It's too "statement". Try us again next season . . .'

Rather than changing my approach to find the retail market that was authentic to our brand, I responded by making the biggest mistake of my entire career, and went about changing everything about the brand to try to fit into a market. I sat down at my desk to design the new collection. Rather than staying true to who we were, I started to design product for who I thought we should be.

As a brand founder, it was the ultimate act of betrayal—to the brand, to the team, to our loyal community and to myself. The collection I designed that season looked nothing like the style our brand had been built on. The new pieces were minimal and petite, stripped of all colour and life—that meant no turquoise and no statement-sized stones. I got rid of the oxidised and burnished metals we were renowned for and replaced them with shiny polished chains and sterile casings.

And after that, I changed the entire brand language of our offering. Not content to stop at the product, I opened a new file on my laptop and started to rewrite the brand bio. I took out any reference to Port Macquarie and anything that suggested that the brand was started on a Bondi Markets table. The word 'bohemian' was removed entirely, as was any reference to layering and any use of the word 'statement'. I effectively removed everything that had been a key part of our success to this point.

The mood boards I created for our new direction looked cold and intimidating, the opposite of what the brand had been for the past six years. My ego gave me a little pat on the back while my intuition responded with a funny feeling in my gut. I accepted the former and suppressed the latter. I uploaded the new design files to go into sampling, still in complete denial that I had just committed brand suicide.

—

'It was lovely speaking with you!' the passenger next to me said as our flight touched down. 'I hope you enjoy your time back in Australia.'

'Lovely to speak with you also!' The little bars searched for the network as I switched my phone on.

TO: Samantha Wills

FROM: Christine Salter

SUBJECT: Partnership Enquiry, Paspaley Pearls

Hi Samantha,

I would love to speak with you about a possible design opportunity
with Paspaley Pearls. I understand you are back and forth from New
York, please advise when you are in Sydney next and if you would be
available for a meeting.

Sincerely,

Christine

CHRISTINE SALTER

Creative Director—Paspaley Pearls

As a designer, it was the type of email you dream about receiving. Paspaley are the most revered pearl company in the world, with some of their pieces selling for over $1 million. If Christine hadn't used my name, I would have sworn this email was sent to the wrong person. A week later, Geoff and I were in the Sydney CBD walking towards the Paspaley flagship store and head office located in one of Sydney's most spectacular buildings in Martin Place. Built in the early 1900s, the former bank is as grand as you could imagine, the breathtaking heritage stone walls and floor made even more beautiful by the cabinets of precious pearls and diamonds that now reside there.

'Don't fuck this up, Willsy,' Geoff said, opening the heavy glass door.

'Please don't say "fuck" in this meeting,' I replied, through clenched teeth.

A sales assistant let Christine know we were there. Christine was the granddaughter of the company's founder, Nicholas Paspaley. The Paspaley Group not only had the prestigious Paspaley pearl brand and flagship stores, they were also the biggest wholesale suppliers of South Sea pearls in the world. It was incredible to even have a meeting with Christine, let alone the possibility that they might want to work with us.

'So when I asked my friends, they all said the Samantha Wills brand was their go-to for birthday or Christmas gifts,' Christine explained to Geoff and me, as we sat opposite her in the company's boardroom. 'As a brand, we are looking at how we can invite a new, younger type of customer into the world of Paspaley, and it was made loud and clear that you were the designer everyone was talking about,' Christine smiled. 'I wanted to talk to you about a possible collaboration, and about having you create a collection for Paspaley.'

'Well, the thing is, Christine,' Geoff started, as he leaned back in the chair.

Oh god, I thought, my entire body clenching. I had sat in enough management meetings with Geoff to know that when he leaned back in his chair and said 'the thing is', I needed to brace myself.

'Samantha doesn't really care about trends,' Geoff continued. 'She says, "fuck it" and really just designs what she likes, which in turn is what our customers like. That's why it works.'

I wanted the decadent marble floor of the Paspaley boardroom to open right up and swallow me whole. I looked at Christine,

My first day of school, 1987.

A classic early 90s family portrait.

Melanie and me in 1996 in Year 9.

One of my high school jobs: dressing up as Cinderella at Fantasy Glades.

Working at Prouds the Jewellers in Port Macquarie in 2001.

Fashion frenzy and Sam's there

By CLARE HAYES

THE glamour of the fashion world arrives on Sydney's doorstep this Sunday as designers and models from across the globe fly in for the Asia Pacific Fashion Week.

They will bring with them their latest collections as they vie for attention, recognition and sales.

Mingling among some of the most famous names in the industry will be little-known Port Macquarie jewellery designer Samantha Wills.

The 22-year-old former Port Macquarie High School student stumbled upon success while she was working in Sydney and making jewellery for a hobby.

With no formal training, Miss Wills designed extravagant neck-pieces and earrings out of antique gold, crystals and natural stones to sell at the Bondi markets.

Within 12 months her art had been spotted and used in feature pictures by the Sydney Morning Herald, Cleo and Cosmo magazines, Shop Till You Drop and Harpers Bazaar.

Most recently her jewellery was photographed by Women's Weekly on Delta Goodrem and Jodie Packer also owns a couple of Samantha Wills Designs.

"This attention is priceless, because if these big names are photographed wearing your jewellery, you can't buy that sort of publicity," Miss Wills said.

Miss Wills has since quit her day job to keep up with the demand for her jewellery.

Now she has a spot at Circular Quay for Fashion Week to show her jewellery and is hoping for a major contract with Myer or David Jones, who she hears are scouting for designers.

Down the track she hopes to start her own clothing label and set up a store in Sydney.

"My dining room is set up as my work room at the moment, but it's good for starters," she says.

"Throughout school this was my dream job, but I never expected it to turn out like this," Miss Wills said.

"I was quite surprised because what I was doing was a hobby and for someone to want to pay money for my jewellery is great. I am very lucky."

The sole supplier of Samantha Wills Designs is Dallas Boutique in Port Macquarie.

◻ Jewel in the crown: Samantha Wills in Sydney.

One of the first newspaper articles, just before launching at Fashion Week in 2004. (The year is evident because of my boob tube top and pencil thin eyebrows!)

(*PORT MACQUARIE NEWS*)

SAGITTARIUS Nov 23 - Dec 21

If you don't believe in your plan, how can you expect anyone else to? And if you do? How can you sit idly by while it is being doubted and denigrated? It is time to re-assess your relationship with the fence. If you continue to perch so precariously on it, you will surely develop a real pain in the . . . well, let's just say that you now need to give your heart and soul to the pursuit of an essential objective. Add effort to faith and you just can't lose.

My horoscope on the final day of Fashion Week.

My design space in our tiny flat.

One of my first lookbooks.

Delta Goodrem wearing a pair of my earrings in *The Australian Women's Weekly* in 2004.

Some of my very early handmade pieces.

My first professional headshot, 2005.

My 2006 Fashion Week show in Sydney. I'm smiling, but personally I was falling apart.
(TITO MEDIA)

The 'international' lookbook!

A magazine feature shot in 2006 in the sunroom off my bedroom. I had just moved the business back home because I was in debt and couldn't make the rent.

Myself, Geoff and three of our earliest team members, Ashleigh, Tara and Jess, in 2007 about six months after Geoff had officially signed on as a co-director of Samantha Wills Pty Ltd and a few days after he had turned the debt around. (We got him a Moneybag cake to celebrate the milestone!)

Some of the (bestselling!) turquoise that Geoff and I would clash over.

Our beautiful hand-carved wooden boxes, a signature of the brand.

Drew Barrymore wearing our Desert Lagoon ring.

The placement that changed it all: Eva Mendes wearing our Bohemian Bardot ring in Italy in 2008.

The ring went on to have its own cult following: a customer's personal collection. (JULIE WILLIAMS)

P!NK wearing our onyx Aaliyah ring while in Australia on her 2009 Funhouse Tour.

Kate Bosworth wearing our Midnight Nightingale earrings in Los Angeles.

The card we received from Patricia Field and the *Sex and the City* wardrobe team.

Miranda wearing our Isabella earrings in the movie in 2010.

In NYC in 2010, fresh-faced and with no idea what New York would have in store for me.

(CAITLIN MITCHELL)

Taylor Swift wearing our earrings on the cover of *Seventeen* magazine (USA).

I was just about to call it quits and head home, and then I met Freya in early 2011.

With Sarah Moore, who was instrumental in our global expansion, the day our brand launched instore at Bloomingdale's.

Being named as a 'Breakout Star' by *The New York Times* in 2011.

Backstage at New York Fashion Week in 2012 getting a model ready for our couture show.
(GEORGE ELDER)

Our models waiting at the side of the stage, ready to take the runway.
(GEORGE ELDER)

With Australian designer (and divine human) Toni Matičevski backstage.
(GEORGE ELDER)

A review from the launch of Yellowglen Peacock Lane by Samantha Wills in 2013.

A couture piece in front of our mainline collections in our New York showroom.

In Sydney, and newly brunette, at the Prix de Marie Claire Awards in 2013, where we won the Best Australian Accessories Brand Readers' Choice Award.

(RYAN PIERSE/GETTY)

With Annelise Peterson in New York.

(SYLVAIN GABOURY/PMC)

For my role with Yellowglen, in 2015 giant billboards with my face on them popped up all over Australia. I looked like the happiest girl alive.

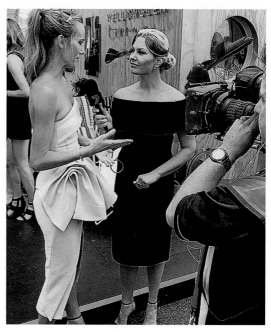

Underweight and barely keeping it together in a live cross with Channel Seven from Melbourne's Flemington racecourse.

Going off the grid in Costa Rica to try to put some of the pieces back together.

In repair . . . in New York City, sweaty after a double spin class with Mantas.

On vacation with Freya and Carolyn in Anguilla in 2016.

Over two decades of friendship: with Melanie in London.

On location in New York City with director Dave Ma, filming the television commercial for Australian telco Optus.

An Optus campaign image that appeared on billboards and bus stops across the country.

In 2016 we were still reinventing our famous Bohemian Bardot! By the time we closed, it had been done in over 300 different colour ways, applications and treatments. The crushed opal style sold out within minutes each time we released it.

Designing at my desk in New York City in 2017. By this stage I had designed well over 10,000 pieces of jewellery. I was designing with my hands, but no longer my heart.

One of our last company Christmas parties, in 2016—a truly incredible group of people to work alongside. By this time, Geoff and I had been in business together for eleven years.

On the red carpet for the Instyle Audi Women of Style awards where I was nominated for Entrepreneur of the Year in 2017.

(DON ARNOLD/WIREIMAGE/GETTY)

Preparing for and shooting our 3 am slot at QVC in early 2018. The live shopping show reached an audience of millions.

Having done the Sydney–JFK route well over 100 times, the Qantas lounges had come to feel more like home than my own home did!

The crossroads at Omega, in June 2018. This is the very spot I stood when I made the decision to close the Samantha Wills business.

My desk in its new position in my New York apartment in 2018. Moving it felt very significant to me.

GRAZIA

SAMANTHA WILLS IS CLOSING HER MULTIMILLION-DOLLAR JEWELLERY COMPANY

'Yes, we are profitable and yes, we are considered successful, but walking away is what I need to do to be creative again with integrity'

Samantha Wills wearing jewellery from her soon-to-close label (Instagram: @samanthawills)

She's the golden girl of Australian jewellery design. The model-like #girlboss who's the perfect front for her hugely successful eponymous accessory brand, which has been a go-to for celebrities, stylists and fashion editor for close to a decade.

But Samantha Wills has shocked industry and fans alike with the shock announcement she's shutting the doors of her jewellery company forever at the end of January 2019. The reveal came, of course, via the millennial creative's news source of choice: **Instagram**.

According to her wordy, four-swipe letter to fans, the brand is both profitable and successful in a commercial sense, but her decision to walk away rather than sell her namesake company was to make room for a new life chapter and "be creative again with integrity, passion and energy". (And GRAZIA, supposes, to preserve control over her own moniker, a challenge experienced by many top designers who have had little control over the way their name is used after cashing out.)

One of the many media articles that came out after we went public in August 2018 with the announcement.

On a national speaking tour for Business Chicks just after we had closed in early 2019. I did this entire tour with searing abdominal pain. (SCOTT EHLER)

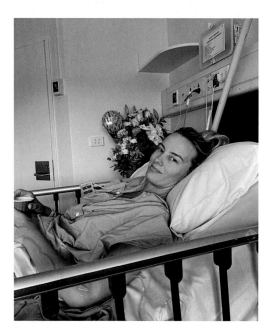

In early 2020, the morning after my endo surgery at Prince of Wales Private Hospital in Sydney. The ketamine still hadn't worn off, but I was told the operation was a success.

At home in Bondi five days after the operation. After sharing my story on Instagram, my inbox was flooded with responses from women all over the world who saw their own story in mine.

In March 2020, we went into lockdown as Covid-19 swept the globe. Minya Rose took this photo as part of a photo-journalling series on how worldviews changed after Covid hit.

At my home in Bondi in mid-2020, working on a new writing project, and doing what I can to make jewellery for the insides of people's minds.

Allowing myself to reflect on the past two decades, and making it a priority to make time to stop and smell the roses.

waiting for either security or the Lord Jesus Christ to come in and escort us out of the building. Christine stared at Geoff in shock, unblinking, then she started laughing.

'Well then!' she said, 'I guess that's a testament to your success, Samantha!' Christine looked at me and noted the horrified look on my face. I returned her kind words with a tight smile that said, *I'm so sorry and thank you.*

'If you are just doing, well, you know, what Geoff said, and designing what you like, it shows that you know what your customers want. I admire that greatly.'

While I could have murdered Geoff in that moment, Christine's reply was one of the most empowering compliments I had ever received. Even with the commercial success we had achieved over the years, impostor syndrome was never too far away. Being self-taught, I doubted myself hugely as a designer because I didn't have a graduate diploma or an official qualification. The importance I gave to that elusive piece of paper was such a ridiculous illusion—it was as though the permission I thought I so needed were written on it. Sometimes, the permission we can't give ourselves is delivered to us in other ways, and on that day to receive that validation from someone like Christine was very significant for me.

Before the meeting came to an end, Geoff dropped a few more profanities and we spoke about the design possibilities within the price bracket they had in mind for the collection. Then Christine invited me to spend a few days up on their pearling ships in Darwin as they were doing the season's harvest. I was floored.

'I still can't believe they want to work with us!' I said to Geoff as we were walking back up Martin Place, 'and I definitely cannot believe you said "fuck" in the Paspaley office! I mean, seriously?'

'Relax, it went great!' Geoff said.

'I also can't believe you told her that I don't design to trends!' I said, as my mind ran through every offensive thing Geoff had said in the meeting. 'Why would you say that?'

'Because,' he said, 'it's the very thing that makes you different to everyone else. You stay true to what you believe in and you know our consumer. That is why the brand is so successful, because it's truly authentic. It's the very thing that makes you Samantha Wills.'

—

At the end of 2011, I came home for Christmas. I had been looking forward to the week between Christmas and New Year, which in Sydney is a social nirvana. Everyone seems to have shifted into relaxation mode: the stress of Christmas is over, the weather is postcard-perfect and the return to work seems a lifetime away. I ran into an old friend, Lisa, down at Bondi Beach late one afternoon. It had been years since we had worked together at Surf Dive 'n Ski, and as the sun went down we decided to head to a local bar for a drink. One drink turned into another and by the time our third cocktail arrived, Lisa and I had caught up on the key events in each other's lives in the seven years since we had seen each other.

'Wait! I can't believe I haven't told you this yet!' Lisa exclaimed. She put her drink down on the bar and sat up like she was about to deliver a parliamentary speech. 'There is this clairvoyant. She's amazing. She does readings from her caravan. You have to go and see her, she is truly incredible!' Lisa's face was intense and mischievous at once, like she was letting me in on a magical secret. 'I've got her number,' she added, scrolling through her phone. 'Text her now!'

One drunken text to the clairvoyant later, I was booked in to see her the following Saturday. Her name was Sandra and she lived an hour's drive away, in Sydney's Western Suburbs. Her house sat at the end of a cul-de-sac, and the caravan Lisa had told me about was there in the front yard, looking as though it had not been moved in twenty years. Grass grew up around its tyres and rust had formed along its vintage window frames. The caravan door was open and I ducked my head as I stepped into the van.

'Come in! Sit, sit,' Sandra said warmly. Sandra was in her early sixties, had short reddish-brown hair and was wearing a maroon top and freshly applied lipstick. I had half-expected her to be sporting purple velvet and a wizard's hat, but she looked like she could be one of my mum's friends, and I felt instantly comfortable with her. 'It's bloody hot out there, isn't it?' Sandra said, as she shuffled a deck of tarot cards. 'You could fry a bloody egg on the driveway.'

I'd been careful not to give Sandra my surname so she couldn't google any information on my story but I was still sceptical as I took a seat across from her at a small round table.

'Let's see what's going on with you then, shall we? Shuffle these and split them into three piles, face down,' she said, handing me a deck of cards. I did as I was told and took a deep breath as she started to turn them over. 'You're feeling a bit ungrounded, a bit up in the air,' she said, perusing the cards. 'They're showing me the Statue of Liberty and the Sydney Harbour Bridge,' Sandra said.

They, I thought, quickly scanning the caravan not sure what exactly I was checking for.

'Have you ever been to New York?'

'Yes,' I said, surprised that she could see the landmarks of my two homes. 'I spend a lot of time there.'

'You live there?' she asked. 'In New York, I mean?'

'Yes. Well, I split my time between there and here,' I explained.

'You're going to be very happy there. You'll be there for many years,' Sandra said, 'but it's tough right now. Hard to put your roots down.'

My desire to move back to Australia had been growing stronger every day I'd been home on this trip. The thought of going back to New York, to the hustle, the continually closed doors and the isolation I was feeling in my personal life, was unappealing. I kept returning to the thought that the company had found its success in Australia and that focusing on that and our local market would be so much easier than going through the entire startup process again to try to expand to an international brand. It had less and less appeal each time I swam in the Australian salt water and caught up with my friends.

'You have to stick it out, it will be worth it,' Sandra said, as if able to see the debate that was playing out in my head. 'Who's Geoff?' she asked.

'What?' I replied, shocked at her calling him by name.

'Geoff. Well, he's a bloody firecracker, isn't he?' she added before I even confirmed I knew a Geoff.

'He's been called a lot worse than firecracker!' I said. 'Geoff is my business partner.'

'Ah,' Sandra said, and paused for a few moments. 'He's good for you, keeps you in line. It may feel like he is being a bit of an arsehole at times, but he means well and admires you greatly,' Sandra said, turning over more cards.

'Yeah, I know he does,' I said. 'Can I ask you a question?'

'Of course, darling!' Sandra said, looking at me. 'Ooh, before you do, your grandfather is right next to you, he guides you, you know? He's saying he is incredibly proud of you, baby doll.' My eyes filled with tears. My grandfather, or Ga as I had called him, was my Dad's father and for as long as I could remember had always called me baby doll.

'Can I ask you, um,' I said, stammering my words. 'Well, how do you receive this information?'

'They tell me, they either whisper in my ear, or they show me a vision, maybe a letter or a name, it can be different, depending what they are feeling at the time, I guess,' Sandra said flippantly, handing the deck of cards to me again. 'Shuffle. Cut into three. Face down.'

'They?' I replied.

'Spirits.' Sandra said. 'Angels, gods, nature, source, the universe, higher self—whatever you want to call it. Whatever it means to you, whatever your higher power is.' I nodded as I recut the cards. I was mesmerised.

'Urgh. How old are you, darling?' Sandra said, her face wincing as she looked at the new spread of cards.

'I just turned twenty-nine, last month,' I replied.

'Hmm, I thought so,' Sandra said, her concerned gaze fixed on the cards.

'Why?' I said, 'is something bad going to happen?'

'Well, yes and no,' Sandra said, her eyes meeting mine. 'The good news is, it's all going to work out fine, exactly as it's meant to. But before it does, there's a bit of, how would you describe it . . . a bit of universe fuckery ahead.'

'Okay,' I replied cautiously. 'How bad is this . . . fuckery?'

'Are you familiar with Saturn return?' Sandra asked.

'*Satan* returns?!' I yelped, instantly thinking back to my Sunday school days.

'No!' Sandra said, laughing. '*Saturn* return.'

I shook my head.

'In astrology, Saturn return is a period in our lives when the planet Saturn completes its orbit around the Sun,' Sandra explained. 'It coincides with the time of our birth, it's like a . . . scheduled crisis, I guess you could say. Saturn return brings us face to face with our deepest fears. Everything we thought we wanted comes into question, and it's like the universe tests us to see how much we really want it.'

Sandra's eyes met mine, now wide as dinner plates, as she continued. 'In addition to testing us with a form of crisis, Saturn return also strips things out of our lives that may be obstacles on our path, things that are distracting us from our mission in life, so to speak. Does that make sense?'

'Hmm. Should I be concerned?' I asked.

'No. Never concerned, just aware,' Sandra said, her voice calm. 'Saturn return happens to everyone, in different ways, but it's inevitable. It comes and it goes, and that's the thing to remember: everything passes. Saturn return can be a bit of a dick, but it's necessary, it brings with it important lessons and growth. It happens every twenty-nine years, give or take.'

'Okay,' I said, not sure what else to ask. The little clock on the table showed that our thirty minutes was almost up. I had so much to take in, and while it all felt very overwhelming, receiving the information also felt oddly calming.

'Well, darling, that's about all for today,' Sandra said, piling the cards back into one deck. 'Oh, wait! They have one more question.'

'Yes,' I said, hoping it was Ga again.

'Who's Freya?' Sandra asked.

'Freya?' I asked. 'I don't know anyone called Freya. I've never even met anyone with that name before.'

'You're going to meet a Freya in New York City,' Sandra continued, pausing as though she was waiting for 'them' to finish what they were telling her. 'She works in events or marketing of some sort.'

'Okay,' I said dismissively. I was less taken with this information than with my Saturn return.

'Freya. Yes, definitely a Freya,' Sandra said, like she was fact-checking with a colleague. 'She's going to have a huge impact on your life.'

—

'I thought it was a really . . . *interesting* presentation, SW,' Sarah said to me after I presented the creative on the brand's new minimal, non-bohemian, non-statement direction, the expression on her face as hesitant as her tone, 'I think changing the direction so drastically is a . . . brave move.'

'I think this is what we need to do to find success in the American market,' I said, trying to convince both of us that the new direction was a good idea.

'Oh! I totally forgot!' Sarah said, clapping her hands. 'I have to introduce you to my friend in New York. I went to school with her here, and she moved over about a year ago.'

'Oh, that would be great!' I replied, 'thank you.'

'No worries at all. I don't know why I didn't think of it sooner! You guys are *so* similar,' Sarah said cheerfully. 'Her name is Freya, I just know you will get on so well!'

'Sorry,' I said, 'what did you say her name was?'

'Freya,' Sarah repeated, 'I'll introduce you guys on email. You're going to love her.'

—

Back in New York, the late-January freeze meant that heavy snow had created a bright white coating on every building and pavement. A few nights after I landed, I was fifteen minutes early to meet Freya. Sarah had put us in touch and we agreed to have a drink in Chelsea. Freya's beaming smile appeared through the door and I instantly saw why Sarah described her as an Australian Reese Witherspoon. It was all I could do to hold the clairvoyant story in, and by our third glass of wine I thought, *Why the hell not?* She would either think me batshit crazy and promptly call for the bill, or she would share my interest in the mystical nature of the meeting.

'So,' I began, taking a large sip of my wine. 'I have to tell you something.' Freya sat, wide-eyed, as I told her about what the clairvoyant had said about us meeting.

'That is *crazy*,' Freya exclaimed, her eyes sparkling. 'It's like the universe arranged for us to meet!'

Freya and I sat and chatted that night until the bar closed and we locked in plans to see a film the following weekend. We both had the strong sense that our meeting that night was the start of a lifelong friendship. Freya's energy reminded me a lot of Mel's and I discovered they were born only four days apart, both Pisces and both incredible, genuine, kind, funny and smart women. Sandra had warned of good and bad news, but right at that moment I wanted only to focus on the good, and that was Freya. Finding Freya made New York all of a sudden feel much more like home.

—

The stock for the new-look, turquoise-free collection started to arrive from our production houses into the warehouse. Australian retailers trusted us as a brand and given that we'd been commercially successful for them for the past few years, they'd increased their order numbers on this collection.

The sell-in numbers—how much stock each retailer ordered—for this new collection looked strong, some of the best we had ever seen, but no matter how great the sell-in is, it's the sell-*through* that really counts.

In New York, I had meetings lined up for the following week and once I had finished those showings, I was to spend the next three weeks designing the Samantha Wills for Paspaley collection. I was encouraged and slightly relieved by the orders and hoped this would be replicated by the tier-one American buyers who had agreed to revisit the brand with its new direction.

I took a highlighter and ran it across each buyer's name and appointment time in my diary. As I did, a piece of folded paper fell from its pages. I reached down to pick it up. It was the notes I had taken during my reading with Sandra. Listed by dot points and slashes, I could only just make out some words within my shorthand.

Scheduled crisis . . . Saturn return puts . . . face to face with our deepest fears . . . universe tests to see how much you really want what you said you wanted . . . things get stripped from your life . . . obstacles on path . . . things that are distracting us from achieving our purpose.

Getting Freya's name must have been a one-off fluke, I thought, folding the note back up and tucking it back between the pages of my diary. It had been a few months since my reading with Sandra and everything seemed to be going just fine.

—

Samantha,

Thank you so much for your time in presenting your latest collection to us last week. It is not what we are looking for at this time, we wish you every success . . .

Ms Wills,

I am writing to thank you for thinking of us as a retail partner for your brand. Unfortunately, we already have similar products in store and won't be proceeding with a purchase order at this time . . .

Hello Samantha,

While we love your brand, we feel that the current collection is not really suited to our consumer. We won't be placing an order this season, but please keep us in mind for upcoming collections . . .

The emails from the tier-one American buyers continued to arrive—a succession of polite declines. Not a single order was placed. And to make matters worse, by the time the New York retailers had emailed me, the same collection they'd all declined had been in stores in Australia for just over two weeks, and it wasn't selling. Given that retailers had backed the collection strongly, they were now all holding increased stock quantities, which made the lousy sell-through number even worse. The reports from our own online store were slightly more optimistic, but not by much.

It should not have come as a surprise that when your customers are highly engaged in the bohemian aesthetic and the relatable story and authenticity of your brand and you go and strip all of that out of it, a sure-fire outcome is a very unengaged customer with the spending patterns to match. Our community was still buying the collection, but not nearly as enthusiastically as they previously had. Cart sizes in our ebusiness were significantly smaller and returns were significantly higher.

When you have lost the trust of your retailers and disengaged your community, the unpleasant flow-on effect is that you will lose the confidence of your team. I was meant to be the creative captain of this ship, steering it forward with integrity and authenticity. Instead, I had shipwrecked us. In one season, I had managed to demolish seven years of brand-building. The severity of what I had done enveloped me. The ego that had patted me on the back only a few months prior had now changed to self-loathing and had then joined forces with good old impostor syndrome, leaving me with an incessant commentary playing like an echo chamber in my mind. *What a fucking failure you are! You know you just designed a collection that is SO far off brand all because you were trying to be someone you are not. This charade of a career that you have somehow gotten away with, it's not just you at the kitchen table anymore. This level of fuck-up affects people's lives, you know? Think about all the people who rely on you, and then you go and do this? Think about that.* I very quickly learnt that the ego is no ally.

I was mired in self-loathing and if you pile enough of it around you, it becomes heavier than concrete. I didn't leave my apartment for the next six days. My computer remained closed. It was time to admit defeat, head home and see if I could somehow salvage the brand for the Australian market.

'I've been trying to call you for days,' Geoff said after I finally picked up my phone.

'I know, I'm sorry.' *What type of company founder disappears for almost a week?* 'I've been . . . sick,' I said.

Geoff had seen the numbers coming through on the sales reports and had heard the consistent retailer feedback that the collection didn't *feel* like the Samantha Wills brand they and their customers had come to know and love over the past seven years. As my business partner, Geoff had every right to demand to know why I altered the brand language so significantly, putting not only the brand at risk, but the business too, given the impact it had on us from a cashflow and commercial perspective. I had known that Geoff's call was coming, and as I sat there in my darkened apartment, I braced myself to face the music.

'You know, global brands aren't built overnight,' Geoff said. The kindness and calmness in his voice shocked me. 'They are not even built over five years. Global brands are built over a decade. They experience growth, they experience failure, they experience change, and if they experience all those things and are still standing, what they actually experience is evolution.'

His words felt like they reached through the phone and opened the blinds in my apartment a little bit, allowing a glimmer of light to peek through. I sat there in silence with the phone pressed to my ear, hot tears gushing down my cheeks. 'Now, I know this is not the best time to deliver this news,' Geoff said gently.

'There is no news you could tell me that could eclipse this situation,' I replied, wiping my face with my sleeve.

'I just got off the phone to Christine from Paspaley,' Geoff said. 'They have just brought a new CEO in and have put a hold on all marketing and collaborations. Including ours.'

'So it won't be proceeding at all?' I asked.

'No. It won't,' Geoff replied. Any other time I would have been filled with disappointment, but in that moment I simply had no available bandwidth.

'Okay,' was all I could say.

'I know that it is not the best news,' Geoff said, 'but, given the current circumstances, I think it might be a blessing in disguise. Our focus right now needs to be on getting the brand back on track and the fact of the matter is, the only person who can do that is you.'

———

The next day, I sat on the floor of my apartment among a spread of art and craft supplies. Surrounded by magazines, photographs, paint, beads, stones, art books, markers and pens, I went back to the beginning. I went back and sat with the girl who started making jewellery on her kitchen table. *Why did you start this?* I asked her. I translated her reply with images and words in my art folio. She and I talked a lot over the next few days. We spoke about our customers and what was important to them as a community. We looked back at the origins of the brand and everything that had brought us to the point we found ourselves at. We then looked forward and collated notes, drawings and quotes of where we wanted to go as a brand. I told Geoff I was working on a rebrand document and that I hoped to have it to him within the week. When I finally hit send on the document, it felt like I breathed out for the first time in months. I knew there was a long road ahead to rebuild what I had broken, to regain the trust of our retailers, our customers and my team, but finally, through the darkness, I could see a ray of light.

—

I was due to fly back to Australia to present the new brand strategy to the team. On that trip I had also planned to have a conversation with Geoff where I would offer a white flag of surrender on the US market expansion strategy. It hadn't worked, and I was prepared to take responsibility and accept that. My flight back to Australia was booked for the Sunday and Freya and I had arranged to have brunch on the Saturday morning before.

'Hi!' I said, smiling as I joined her at the table at one of our favourite little West Village restaurants. The crisp November temperature hinted at an arctic winter ahead. 'Sorry I have been a bit quiet the last few weeks, there's been a bit going on,' I said.

'Um . . . how could you not tell me about this?' Freya said, barely looking up at me. Her face was buried deep in the Saturday edition of *The New York Times*. 'Holy! Shit!'

'Tell you about what?' I asked, sitting down.

'THIS!' she squealed, slapping the newspaper down on the table. 'Australian jewellery designer, Samantha Wills, break-out star!' Freya exclaimed, beaming. '*The New York Fucking Times!*'

It was a giant half-page profile feature in which *The New York Times* hailed me as one of their selected break-out stars of the year. There on the page in full colour were four of our most bohemian, earthy, statement cocktail rings—all of which were from our archive of past collections and represented our authentic brand identity.

'What?' I said, staring at the newspaper in disbelief as Freya called the waiter over to order a bottle of champagne.

My phone buzzed with a text message from Sarah. It was late at night in Australia and unlike her to message me on a weekend.

SW—the website has just crashed. It looks to be a huge surge of traffic from the USA and the Facebook page is getting inundated with comments from people asking for the ring that appeared in the New York Times. Do you know anything about this? Call me when you can!

For the next few days, the phone in our head office rang consistently with calls from both customers and retailers. As the pieces featured in the *NYT* feature were true to our authentic design language, unsurprisingly the retailers that called were in alignment with our brand. The majority of them were based in California or the Midwest and most of them were premium tier-two retailers. I had removed all the authenticity from our brand to try to fit a market, when the entire time I should have been seeking out the market that appreciated our authenticity. Now wasn't the time to quit. It was the time to rebuild.

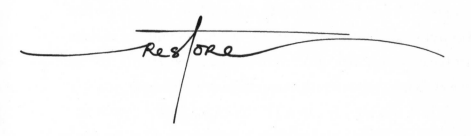

re·st·ore

verb

return someone or something to a former condition,
place, or position

I knew it was going to take time to get the brand back on track.
Product was actually the easiest thing to realign. But I also
had to articulate how we were going to evolve as a brand while
still honouring our origins. I decided to base it around the core
aesthetic of 'luxe bohemian'. 'Bohemian' honoured where we had
come from and 'luxe' was a nod to the refinement we wanted to
give to the brand, part of our commitment to be always evolving
our offering.

At around this time, an Australian events company called
Fashion Palette sent me an email—they were inviting five
Australian designers to do a joint showcase for the 2012 New
York Fashion Week and wanted me to take part. When I saw

that Toni Matičevski and Akira Isogawa had already signed on, I was thrilled to be in such prestigious company. I knew there was an important reason the email arrived when it did—the timing was just right and New York Fashion Week was the perfect platform to announce who we were as a brand with a showcase that honoured our bohemian roots while demonstrating that we were evolving and entering a new stage of refinement.

My desk was already covered with designs for the new collection, so I sat down on the polished wooden floor of my New York apartment to make eight couture outfits for the show and set about cutting wires, threading beads and affixing crystals, pliers in hand. As the elaborate pieces started to take shape, my apartment slowly turned into a medieval armoury. Once again, I found myself working twenty-hour days to ensure the collection was ready, right up to the night before the show. I affixed the final elements and stepped back to look at the eight dressmakers' mannequins in my living room draped in decadent armaments. Car headlights passed on the New York streets below, causing the metal, crystal and beaded luxe bohemian costumes to sparkle as though they were telling me, 'We're ready'.

The day of the show came with the usual pre-show pandemonium. The backstage area was abuzz with models and make-up artists and designers making last-minute changes to their collections. As the models sashayed out onto the catwalk in their Samantha Wills couture armour, I knew instinctively that I was back on track with the brand—it just felt right. I didn't feel that I was trying to be someone else or trying to make the brand fit somewhere it wasn't meant to go. Backstage after the show, the confidence I felt in the new refined brand direction was reflected back to me in the flurry of camera flashes from the journalists and fashion media clamouring to photograph our couture pieces.

The following night, I held a small showcase at The Bowery Hotel so the media could get a close-up look at the couture pieces and also see our full new luxe bohemian retail collection on display. A nod to where we were going as a brand while remaining true to our origins. The evening was attended by international fashion media and the night affirmed to me that we were on track and heading in the right direction. The next morning, as I was waking up and reflecting on the night before, a *Vogue Australia* review popped up on my phone.

NOTHING COULD BE MORE RED-CARPET FRIENDLY THAN THE CHUNKY RINGS AND WHIMSICALLY ORNATE ADORNMENT CREATED BY HOT JEWELLERY LABEL, SAMANTHA WILLS.

In the weeks that followed, Drew Barrymore, J.Lo and Taylor Swift were photographed wearing pieces from our new collection. The evolution of the brand was being received beautifully. Retailers were relieved to see our core aesthetic was back and were supportive of the evolution as well. Gaining back our customers' confidence, however, was going to take more than just product. I spent the next six months investing every spare second I had into talking with our customers, both online and through scheduled instore events. The team was heavily invested in defining this new chapter of the brand together and everyone seemed genuinely excited about the new direction. It was the true loyalty of the team and our retailers and customers that made the evolution possible. The lesson I learnt about brand inauthenticity was one of the most significant of my career. I was enormously grateful to the team and the momentum that we were able to quickly regain as we moved into the next phase.

Professionally, the brand was back on track and would soon be operating more strongly than ever before. And I felt like I was exactly where I was meant to be in my career.

But as life goes, when one area is running beautifully, it is likely that another area is not. I had turned thirty the previous December and my Facebook feed was starting to flood with engagement announcements and wedding videos. As a child and a teenager, you look at adults celebrating milestone birthdays and think them *so* old, but when you actually reach the milestone number yourself, you realise it's not that old at all.

'When are you going to bring home someone nice?' my dad would ask, when I visited my parents on my weeks back in Australia. 'You've been single for a while now. You're not getting any younger you know!'

'So, tell me, are you seeing anyone?' my friends would politely nudge each time I was home.

'You'll be next!' my friends' mums would say at each wedding, as they pushed me onto the dance floor to catch the bride's bouquet.

In the solitude of a long-haul aeroplane journey or in the stillness of a night, the self-doubt started to trickle in. *Was thirty really that old? Had I sacrificed everything by dedicating all my time and energy to building a business?* Fear will always knock on the door of our minds and, left untreated, fearful thoughts can become viral fiction.

Thousands of years ago, when we had to protect ourselves from predators in the wild, a feeling of fear would alert us that something wasn't right, telling us we had to act or we would die. Our fight or flight mode would kick in and we would either fight or run and find somewhere to hide. Now that we no longer have to fend off carnivorous predators, I think the modern-day equivalent is the negative voice in our own minds. Once those fear-based thoughts have spread, they can run rampant, and our decision-making is centred around how to feel safe in that moment rather than looking at why we feel unsafe in the first place.

At thirty years of age, my dominant fear-based thought was triggered by comparing myself with others—so many people around me were getting married and that made me think I should be doing that too. I didn't ask myself if I actually, in my heart, wanted it—I simply let my fear mentality lead that conversation, which very quickly morphed into a self-worth issue.

Friends would set me up on blind dates that would go nowhere and rather than taking a perspective that maybe now was not the right time for me to be in a relationship, I instead took the view that there must be something wrong with me if the same dead-end outcome kept occurring. This kind of thinking then changes how you assess if a person is a good match for you or not. Because when you start looking for a partner to validate your self-worth, what you often get instead is a painful lesson that the only person who can actually do that is you.

I met Jasper when he walked into the bar in New York my friends and I were at one Sunday afternoon. Jasper looked like Heath Ledger—tall, scruffy and handsome. His generous smile was equal parts cheeky and charming. My friends and I already had our fourth round of cocktails on the way and when he joined his group of mates behind us, I turned slightly on my bar stool to face him.

'Hi,' I said, reaching out my hand. 'I'm Samantha.'

'Hi!' he replied, reaching out to shake it. 'Are you . . . with this group?' he said, gesturing to his eight friends.

'No,' I replied, smiling.

'Well, okay then!' he said, still shaking my hand. 'I'm Jasper.'

Jasper was only in New York for the weekend, but he had just accepted a new job and was moving to the city in four weeks.

'Well, I would love to take you out when I'm back here in a few weeks,' Jasper said, his eyes light and his smile dangerous.

'I'd like that,' I replied.

That night, in a bar on the corner of West 4th and West 10th Street, I all but decided that Jasper was to be my knight in shining armour. The one who would slay all my inner self-doubts and dragons and whose affection would no doubt validate my worth. It's a hell of a thing, choosing to hand that type of power over to someone, when all he asked for was my phone number.

illusion

il·lu·sion

noun

a deceptive appearance or impression

Treasury Wine Estate is one of the world's biggest wine companies and the maker of Yellowglen, Australia's bestselling sparkling wine. With a very commercial pricepoint, the brand reached cult status in the mid-nineties, when they ran a modelling competition each year to cast the Yellowglen 'Bubbly Girl'. The winner would appear on billboards and magazines across the country. They decided to move away from the Bubbly Girl campaign in the early 2000s and had gone through a few brand overhauls since.

In 2013, they contacted me to talk about a possible collaboration, so Geoff and I headed to their Melbourne offices for a meeting. The Treasury portfolio was significant, with almost fifty wine brands. The halls in their head office were lined with wine barrels and thousands of trophies, awards and prized vintage bottles. As we sat in the boardroom, the marketing team explained that while the product was accessible, over the past few years the brand had lost its identity a little. It maintained its commercial success as the country's bestselling sparkling because their core consumer base was incredibly loyal, but they were failing to attract a new, younger customer.

'So, we really like what your brand aesthetic is about,' the Yellowglen brand manager told me. 'I feel there may be a large crossover in our core consumer base.'

'I agree,' I replied, studying the consumer slide from their presentation that was projected onto the boardroom wall. 'How do you see us working together?'

'Our idea is to have you design a limited-edition bottle— Samantha Wills for Yellowglen,' the brand manager said. 'You could design it in your signature style and it would run for a period of twelve weeks. It would be sold in over 900 liquor stores across Australia.'

I scribbled the key points in my notebook. 'And if we were to proceed with this, what would the next steps be?' I asked.

'From here, our suggestion would be for you to come back to us with a mood board, say six pages or so, for the bottle design and we can go from there,' the brand manager said.

'Sounds easy enough!' I said. 'Let me come back to you.'

'I think this could be a really good opportunity from a commercial perspective,' I said to Geoff as we walked out through the building's large glass doors. 'The size of their market share could grow our brand awareness significantly.'

'I agree,' Geoff said, 'but do you really want your name on hundreds of thousands of bottles of cheap wine across the country for three months?'

'Not particularly,' I said.

'Well then, I'm late for my next meeting, I've gotta run but I look forward to seeing what you come up with and how you plan on turning pig shit into strawberry jam!' Geoff said, as he jumped in a taxi.

As I sat down to start compiling the six-page mood board, something didn't sit right with me. I hadn't worked on building a brand name for the previous nine years just to have it put on a bottle that would sit on shelves for twelve weeks. I knew the Yellowglen brand well and I knew their consumer, which meant I also knew from a branding and marketing perspective what would excite them. To re-energise the brand and achieve what they wanted to as a company, I thought it would be more impactful to create a new product within the Yellowglen portfolio rather than try to rebrand an existing one. My thought process behind this was that it would garner more attention, which would then filter through to brand interest in their wider portfolio. I came up with the idea for a new offer that I called 'Yellowglen Peacock Lane by Samantha Wills'.

A few weeks later, I hit save on a 72-page brand strategy document I had put together to present to the Yellowglen team. It included everything from six initial mood board creative concepts to logo development and packaging concepts, including shipping and giftboxes. I looked at their current portfolio, which ranged in pricepoint from $9.99 to $49.99, and decided to place Peacock

Lane in the middle tier, with a suggested retail price of $34.99. I looked at what competitors were doing for point of sale and incorporated market analysis, and in the final section I presented the plan for activation launch strategy across digital platforms and events.

The creative idea for Peacock Lane was based on the idea that every time you opened a bottle, you were escaping to a secret midnight soiree. In the presentation, I made this magical make-believe party take place in an overgrown forest which I situated at the back of a vineyard. The vision was decadent and bohemian and best described as if *The Wind and the Willows*, the Moulin Rouge and the Mad Hatter's Tea Party all converged at midnight to drink champagne.

'So, that's the idea I had,' I said to Geoff as I clicked on the final slide of the presentation. We were set to meet with Yellowglen again the following day, a meeting in which they expected me to present six mood boards.

'That's a 72-page presentation,' Geoff said, staring at me.

'I know,' I replied.

'It's fucking brilliant,' Geoff said, turning back to gape at the presentation.

'I know,' I said again. It really was fucking brilliant.

The following day, I suddenly felt very nervous. It felt like I was back in high school and had once again pushed far beyond the boundaries of the required criteria and I was genuinely worried that I had seriously overstepped the line by putting together such a bold brief for someone else's business.

'What's wrong?' Geoff said, as we walked through the Yellowglen foyer.

'I'm just nervous they might think what I have done is a bit . . . obnoxious?' I replied.

'It is obnoxious,' Geoff replied. 'You're essentially telling them that their current brand is shit, so you've gone and created a whole new one for them.'

'That's not what I am suggesting and you're not helping,' I said, feeling my stomach churn.

'Listen, let me rephrase that. It would be obnoxious if it was a terrible concept, but it's not. It truly is an incredible concept and a stunning presentation,' Geoff said.

'Okay,' I said, taking a deep breath. 'I just hope they don't see this presentation as being disrespectful. I've built the concept as if it's my own brand.'

'The brand manager is coming down now to get you,' the receptionist told us. 'He won't be long.'

'Well, Willsy,' Geoff said as we sat down on the foyer's plush couches. 'I thought the concept and presentation was so strong, I actually went and registered Peacock Lane by Samantha Wills under the company name this morning. So if Yellowglen likes your idea, they are going to have to license it from us. Congratulations, Samantha Wills Pty Ltd now has an alcohol brand in its portfolio.'

'What?' I replied. There were a million questions racing through my head but there was no time to ask any of them. The Yellowglen brand manager was walking towards us.

'So you can stop worrying about overstepping the line, it is your brand.'

The Yellowglen team loved the presentation and the new brand strategy and while I'm sure the brand manager didn't love that Geoff had already registered the concept, a few days later we received an email saying that Treasury Wine Estate would love to license the Peacock Lane by Samantha Wills brand from us and, for the duration of the licence, to add Yellowglen to the top of the logo hierarchy. Not only did they want to license the brand, they wanted to put a large marketing budget behind it. They actually assumed the program would run at a loss given how much the bottle design and associated packaging would cost to produce, however they had factored this in and thought the cost of the collaboration was worthwhile to elevate their brand and category. It was on.

Peacock Lane had been in store for two weeks when I received a call from the Yellowglen brand manager to tell me that Peacock Lane had overperformed by 400 per cent on the predicted sell-through.

'When is your next trip to Australia?' they asked. 'We want to talk to you about some other ideas you might have for the rest of the portfolio.'

In the months that followed, Yellowglen appointed me creative director and ambassador across the entire portfolio and it became the start of a very successful five-year partnership.

—

The new—but still authentic—evolution of the Samantha Wills brand was gaining momentum in America. The US sales and distribution was being managed by an American sales agency and while they were servicing the territory and retailers well, we knew that the brand had found its success in part through storytelling, and that it needed someone from within the brand to do that outside of Australia.

Sarah had now been with us for five years and was the perfect person to drive the brand internationally. She was very keen to live abroad, so she relocated to New York and opened our first international office, taking on the role of global sales director where she was responsible for all international markets. Sarah appointed sales distribution partners around the world, giving us representation in France, Tokyo and Seoul as well as our New York and Sydney headquarters, and she very quickly had Samantha Wills stocked in major US retailers such as Bloomingdale's, shopbop, REVOLVE, Nordstrom and Anthropologie. The further we expanded internationally, the more interest we received from new markets. The trajectory was on the up and the more territories we opened up, the more countries I needed to visit to support the brand in each new market. That year I took forty-two international flights.

Jasper and I had been dating for almost a year and he was generously supportive of my constant travel. I would have thought that being with someone who was heading to the airport every other week would have caused strain on the relationship, but Jasper didn't seem fazed by it at all. Every time I returned from one of my trips to Australia, he would be waiting in my apartment with a vase of fresh white roses and a handwritten card sitting on the bench in the kitchen. Never any other flower, always white roses.

Jasper had a love for life like no one I had ever met. His work demanded long hours from him but he didn't let that stop him enjoying every minute outside of the office. Often, he would race through the door saying, 'Babe! Quick! Let's jump up to the roof, the sun is about to set!' And we would rush up to my building's rooftop to see day turn to night on the Hudson River. We could be tucked up in bed for the night and he would get a notification that a band was doing a secret performance, so off we would go to some hidden underground bar to watch the impromptu set, no matter the hour.

His spontaneity and genuine lust for squeezing all he could out of life was a welcome change from the nine years I had spent working practically nonstop. Jasper made life a little more carefree and a lot more fun. But his addiction to chasing the next experience also made me feel as though he was never truly present in the current one. It was like his body was there, but his mind was already thinking about what was next. This created an addiction of my own. Jasper's light was bright, his energy radiated wherever he was, and I became hooked on the rare moments in which I could actually capture all of his attention. I could feel myself cling to these moments, even more so as I could feel them happening less and less often.

'Have you always been blonde?' Jasper said one morning as he was getting ready for work. He leaned in and kissed me as he held strands of my hair between his fingers.

'I have,' I said, smoothing one side of my hair behind my ear.

'It's pretty,' he said.

'Thanks,' I replied, as I smiled a little.

'It's funny,' Jasper continued, letting the strands of my hair fall through his fingers like sand, 'I've always preferred brunettes.'

Before I could manage a reply, he kissed me again, grabbed his bag and the apartment door closed behind him.

A few weeks later, I was back in Sydney. The brand had been nominated in the Prix de Marie Claire Awards for Best Australian Accessories Brand. One of the industry's most prestigious awards, it was the first time we had been nominated and the competition in our category was the best in the business. The gala was being held at The Star casino in Sydney's Darling Harbour. A coveted night on the fashion calendar, it saw celebrities, socialites and designers making their way down the red carpet as camera bulbs flashed and media posed questions from behind a velvet rope. The who's who of Australian fashion were in attendance—ZIMMERMANN, Dion Lee, Toni Matičevski, sass & bide, Kit Willow . . . the list went on and on.

'Samantha! Can you turn around so we can get a shot of the back of your dress?' I pivoted slightly for the photographer. The Australian brand Ae'lkemi had loaned me a dress for the evening from their couture collection. The floor-length gown was white and embellished with tiny glittering sequins. The back of it featured a deep V and, as I turned so the photographers could get a picture of it, my newly brunette hair fell across my bare back. The dinner was a divine, multi-course feast for the senses; no expense had been spared. I looked around at everyone in the room. It was as though all the glossy profiles I had ripped out of magazines a decade before had come to life, stepping off my inspiration pinboard and into that ballroom.

Dessert had just been served when it was time to announce the winner for best Australian accessories brand. Each category comprised an Editor's Choice and a Readers' Choice Award. I knew we did not stand a chance of winning—I was shocked we were even nominated in such a prestigious pool of brands. When I received the invitation and notification that we had been nominated, my personal assistant had RSVP'd for me and asked if I could bring a plus one to the event, a request that was declined—a fact which further solidified my feeling that we didn't stand a chance. *They would definitely allow category winners to bring a guest,* I concluded. I got comfortable in my seat and as they read the nominees, I felt really proud that our brand was among them. The Editor's Choice winner went to Rachael Ruddick. I knew Rachael well and cheered loudly as she made her way to the stage.

'Congratulations, Rachael!' the emcee said while the room applauded Rachael as she concluded her acceptance speech and made her way off stage.

'Please keep your applause going for our next presenter, Kit Willow, who will be presenting the Readers' Choice Award for Best Australian Accessories brand.'

I had followed Kit's career from her first collection. Her designs were beautiful, as was the brand she had created. Kit spoke a little about her journey before she was handed the envelope to announce the Readers' Choice winner. I spooned the last of the chocolate brownie from my plate into my mouth, careful not to spill any on my white dress.

'And the winner is . . .' Kit said, as the room fell silent, 'Samantha Wills!'

What?! I thought, gulping to swallow the remainder of the gooey chocolate sauce in my mouth. The heavy spotlight was shining on me and my shocked face appeared on the big screens on either side of the stage.

'You have to go up there,' the woman sitting next to me said quietly, her eyes nodding to the stage.

'Do I have chocolate around my mouth?' I asked her, panicking.

'A little bit,' she replied, her tone a delicate mix of pity and disgust. Her dessert plate was untouched.

Fuck, I thought, as I tried as fluidly as I could to wipe my mouth with my napkin and get out of my seat. I don't remember anything I said in my acceptance speech that night, but afterwards, waiting for a car outside, I remember looking down at the award I held in my hands. *Best Australian Accessories Brand, Samantha Wills—Readers' Choice,* was engraved on the heavy glass trophy. It was our community who had voted for this, our gorgeous, loyal community. I couldn't stop smiling.

'We won!' I said to the driver, gesturing to the glass trophy in my hands as he held the door open for me. 'I didn't think we had a chance!'

'Congratulations, Miss,' he said. I slid across the back seat as he gently closed the door.

I took a photo of the award and texted it to Geoff. 'WE WERE VOTED THE BEST AUSTRALIAN ACCESSORIES BRAND BY READERS' CHOICE!!' I typed.

'CONGRATULATIONS, BUDDY! AWESOME NEWS!' Geoff replied instantly.

Back at the hotel, I wanted to celebrate the news of the win with someone other than the taxi driver. I excitedly called Jasper and let it ring until his voicemail picked up. Not wanting to leave a message, I hung up, slipped out of my gown and into the hotel robe and decided to close my eyes for a few minutes. I put the phone down on the pillow next to me so I'd hear it when he called back.

I woke up the next morning as the first light peeked through my window. My brown hair was messy and still filled with hairspray from the night before as I reached for my phone.

There were no missed calls.

—

For my birthday, I had been given a reading with a New York astrologer. He had a reputation for being brilliant at what he did; a lot of Hollywood actresses would fly out to New York from LA just to see him. His waitlist was long, and between that and my unpredictable travel schedule it was a few months before I was able to lock in a time with him.

John, who I guessed to be in his late fifties, had been practising astrology for over thirty years. He lived on the bottom level of a brownstone in Chelsea and did the readings from his front living room. The type of astrology he specialised in was natal charting. I'd never had my natal chart done before, and when John's assistant asked for the time, date and location of my birth, I was careful again not to share my surname, still sceptical that a simple google search would reveal information that he could then just relay back to me.

John had a very calming energy about him and on the piece of paper in front of him was my chart. A clock-like circle, segmented into twelve sections for each zodiac sign and with planets dotted sporadically across the chart, it looked more scientific than spiritual and John's demeanour was more therapist than theologist.

'So, if we look at where the planets are for your house of career,' John said, looking down at the chart, 'it shows that you haven't had a strong career year yet.'

'It does?' I replied. My scepticism felt very validated. 'I would say that out of any area of my life, my career has been the one constant that I would deem a success.'

'Well, that might be,' John replied. He was incredibly thoughtful about the words he used, I could see him working through the information in his mind to be able to deliver it in the clearest way possible. 'I don't know what you do for work, but the chart is showing that your real career doesn't actually start till 2018.'

'2018? That's four years away!' I said. 'What do you mean by real career?'

'By real career, I mean what you were put on the Earth to do,' John said. 'Whatever you are doing now is the precursor to what you are actually being called to do, and the chart shows that it is likely to do with writing.'

'I'm not a writer,' I said.

'Writing will be a part of what you do,' he said, as if it were a fact, not a suggestion. 'I also think you will work on a project that is very focused on women, focused on bringing them together in some way.'

The entire session went for an hour and a half. I thanked John for his time and insight and he said he would send me the audio recording of our session that evening. I walked the ten blocks back to my apartment disappointed. Disappointed because I wanted to believe in astrology, I wanted it to be a guidance in my life, but the reading couldn't have been more wrong. The business was booming and showed no signs of slowing down. *I'm a jewellery designer, that's what I do*, I thought. I had never entertained the idea that one day I would not be doing this. I had always assumed that I would have the company forever, that it would be something I passed on to my children. The more I thought about it, the more it frustrated me that I had just spent ninety minutes listening to someone—someone who was hailed as one of the world's best astrologers—tell me things that couldn't have been further from the mark.

We had just launched a new division, Samantha Wills Bridal. I was tempted to email John to prove to him how wrong his reading had been. The sell-through numbers were through the roof and I knew the numbers well enough to know they suggested anything but 'you haven't had a strong career year yet'. We had identified that our loyal, long-time community was growing with us. I had just turned thirty-two and was the same age as a lot of the women who followed the brand. Just as my Facebook feed was continually flooded with engagement and wedding posts, Samantha Wills customers were at the same life stage. We had started to receive a lot of enquiries from brides-to-be looking for jewellery for themselves and their bridesmaids. We started to include a more neutral palette within the main collections and very quickly saw the gap in the market for a specific bridal range.

In designing the bridal collections, I took our core aesthetic but reduced the scale of the pieces. The mainly gold metals we used in the main collection became silver for bridal, and moonstone, crystal and rose quartz become the core stone palette. We knew our wooden box packaging was a bridal favourite; it featured in every shot that photographers took of the jewellery as the brides got ready on their wedding day.

Our new bridal division allowed us to also expand our retail channels as we opened new accounts with bridal-specific retailers. The Bohemian Bardot ring was an entity entirely of its own by 2014, so we added a selection of them specifically with brides-maids in mind. Brides would go instore or to our website and buy Bohemian Bardot rings in quantities of three or four or five, one for each of their bridesmaids. As well as the bridal jewellery performed, it was the bridesmaid offerings that were the biggest commercial success, due to the quantity per sale.

The first year that we had Samantha Wills Bridal in our offering, it made up 48 per cent of our annual revenue. Seeing the growth that was available with new lines, 2014 also saw the launch of four other new divisions under the Samantha Wills brand: Samantha Wills Fine, Samantha Wills Stationery, Samantha Wills Handbags and Samantha Wills Eyewear. The additional divisions had put a heavy strain on our website and it was not uncommon for it to crash due to the traffic it attracted.

SamanthaWills.com required a major rebuild. It took a team of developers a few months and hundreds of thousands of dollars to build us a fully customised platform. The new site had a much more sophisticated backend and allowed us to have access to data, consumer behaviour and insights that we didn't have before. These insights made us change our thinking and, as a result, our behaviours. We were no longer acting like a brand with an ecommerce store, we were slowly merging our practice to behave like a branded online retailer, and with that came the need to have product delivered more frequently. Our traditional way of doing things and working to a wholesale calendar of four main deliveries per year had to change. Our consumers were wanting fresh stock more frequently, so we started to release smaller product capsules every two weeks. With Bridal and Fine now part of our jewellery portfolio, this saw me designing close to twenty-five collections a year.

unravel

un·rav·el

verb

to disengage or separate the threads of

Having been together for nearly three years, Jasper and I were at the stage of a relationship when it is time to move in together, so we began the hunt for a New York apartment. I would shortlist a few properties that we would go and look at, but there was always something about each of them that Jasper didn't like.

'Okay, we'll keep looking,' I would say with resignation each time he found something minor that was a deal-breaker. As with any relationship, when you look back, you begin to see all the red flags you missed. I had subconsciously tethered my self-worth to being in this relationship, and in doing so I had lost all perspective on what was healthy. I would often find myself compromising on things that were important to me, staying silent rather than speaking up so as not to cause a fuss or rock the boat. But compromising values always leads to a compromised outcome. I wanted him to love me the way I loved him, but what I thought was love, really wasn't love at all. What it wouldn't take me too much longer to realise was that while I was treating Jasper like a priority, he was treating me as a mere option.

The company was overachieving beyond our forecasting and, with the expansion of divisions, we were on track to hit the $10-million mark in 2015. My work with Yellowglen had increased as they made me creative director and spokesperson across their entire portfolio. Entrepreneurialism, and specifically female entrepreneurialism, was a hot topic in the media and I started to receive invitations to speak at events focused on small businesses and startups. My time was spent on a heavy rotation of designing, travelling to our factories in China, and working between Sydney and New York along with the other international markets we had opened, as well as the speaking engagements. Add to that trying to see my family every chance I could when I was back in Australia, investing in my friendships and in my relationship with Jasper, and both personally and professionally, it felt like there were a lot of moving parts that depended on each other. Like a Jenga tower, all it would take was for one of the parts to wobble and the whole thing would come crashing down.

We were set to celebrate Jasper's birthday in April and we had organised a black-tie dinner for all our friends.

'How do I look, babe?' Jasper said, straightening his bow tie as we were about to leave. 'Do I scrub up okay?'

'You look very handsome,' I said.

'I figure I've got to put in extra effort if I'm going to be seen with you!' he said, winking at me. 'You make me want to be better, you know that?' His tone was suddenly serious.

'Oh, shush,' I said as I helped him with his tie.

'No, really. I'm a much better person when you are here.' He kissed me. 'I love you, you know that, right?'

'I love you, too,' I said, smiling. 'Now, before we are late to your own party, I want you to open your gift.' I handed him a box I had carefully gift-wrapped.

'Babe, what is this? You didn't have to do this.'

'You don't even know what it is. You might hate it!' I said, knowing he wouldn't. Jasper had a love of fine watches and I had found a vintage Omega from the year he was born. I had been excited all week to give it to him. 'Just open it already!' I said, tugging at the black ribbon.

As Jasper peeled off the wrapping and opened the leather box, his face was expressionless. 'It's vintage,' I said, thinking he may not realise the sentiment behind it. 'It's from the year you were born.'

Jasper placed the box on the table, the watch still in it and looked at me.

'Babe,' he said quietly, 'this is too much, I can't accept this.'

'What do you mean? Don't be silly!' I said, reaching to remove the watch from its case. 'It's your birthday!'

'It's . . . it's beautiful, babe,' he said. 'It really is.'

'If you don't love it, we can go look for a different one,' I suggested softly. His response was not what I expected.

'No, no. I love it, I truly love it, it's beautiful,' he said quietly. 'I just . . . I just don't deserve it.'

'Stop saying that,' I said. 'Of course you do. It's your birthday!'

'No. I don't,' Jasper replied, raising his eyes to meet mine. 'And I don't deserve you.'

A friend who attended Jasper's party was a photographer and a week after the black-tie dinner a beautiful, framed black and white photo of Jasper and me arrived. I was looking at the camera laughing; Jasper's arms were wrapped tightly around my waist as he pulled me close to him, kissing my cheek. I placed the frame on the shelf alongside the other smiling photographs. It would be the last picture we had taken together.

—

'What's taking you up to Brisbane?' the passenger next to me, a woman in her mid-sixties, asked after we had taken off from Sydney airport.

'I'm heading there to speak at a conference for women in business,' I replied, nodding to the pad I was writing on. 'I'm presenting the keynote, so I am just going over it to make sure I know it by heart.'

'Well, congratulations,' she replied. 'That is an incredible honour. You must have some story to share?'

'Thank you. I don't know, I guess so,' I said. She asked me what I was speaking on and I gave her a quick overview of the past eleven years.

'That is a great story!' she said. 'It's important, you know? To share what you have been through. I've worked in corporate my whole life, the finance sector, which was daring enough in itself—a woman in finance! But what I really wanted to do was start my own business. I guess the truth was I was simply too scared to. I didn't know any other women doing it, so I just . . . didn't. There is a lot of truth in that quote by . . . who was it?' she said, closing her eyes to summon the name. 'Marian Wright Edelman! That's it. She said, "You can't be what you can't see." Have you ever thought about writing a book?' she asked.

'Me? Oh no. No. I'm not a writer,' I replied.

'Well, don't dismiss it too quickly,' she said as the flight attendant stopped in front of us with the drinks cart. I shrugged and gave her a small smile. 'It's funny, isn't it?' she said. 'How we feel we need permission for certain things, you know what I mean?'

'Yes, I do,' I replied. I knew all too well.

'Well, however you decide to tell your story, even though we shouldn't need permission from anyone but ourselves, I think you will find it may give other women the green light to follow their own journey,' she said.

I mustn't have looked convinced because she added: 'It's our vulnerabilities that connect us. It's in the sharing of our stories that we see a little bit of ourselves, and that's important.'

I nodded and gave her a small smile as I let the words sink in. 'I'm Samantha,' I said, reaching my hand out over the partition between our seats, embarrassed I hadn't introduced myself earlier.

'It's a true pleasure to meet you, Samantha,' she replied, smiling warmly. 'My name is Rose.'

That afternoon in Brisbane, I peeked through the curtain from backstage. There were well over a thousand women in the audience—it was by far the biggest event I had ever spoken at. I had my presentation planned out, the notes I had made on the plane were scribbled with talking points. The stage manager signalled a five-minute warning as the sound tech fitted my microphone. I looked down at my notes documenting the rise of the brand and our milestones and achievements along the way—it read like a highlights reel. As the speaker before me was finishing up, all I could hear was Rose's voice. *It's our vulnerabilities that connect us. It's in the sharing of our stories that we see a little bit of ourselves.*

'All good to go, Ms Wills?' the stage manager said.

'Yep,' I said, 'ready.'

As the emcee invited me on stage and the crowd started to applaud, I put my notes down, leaving them on a chair backstage as I walked out to do my presentation. In that moment, I knew I had to present more than just the highlights reel and share more of the hurdles and hardships that had occurred along the way. I hadn't prepared to speak about them but Rose's advice made me realise that some things couldn't be read off a piece of paper. Some things needed to be said straight from the heart.

Rose was right, but I had underestimated exactly how right she was. While I still touched on some of the highlights in my presentation, I also spoke about some of the most challenging times in my journey. I told the audience about the time I had gone to present the brand to buyers ten years earlier and they thought I was the intern. I shared the story about the isolation of sitting in my first little Alexandria studio while going through a break-up that felt like it had wrenched my internal organs from my body. I told them that I knew how to build a brand, but in the early days I did not know how to run a business and got myself into $80,000 of credit card debt, triggering crippling anxiety. I told them how I nearly signed 51 per cent of the company over to a business partner because in my desperation I couldn't see any other way out, and I told them how I almost destroyed the entire brand by letting my ego get the better of me. After the presentation, I stayed three hours longer than I was booked to because a line had formed around the auditorium of women who were waiting so graciously to tell me *their* stories. Every story I was told that day started along the lines of, 'I really related to the bit in your story about . . .'

These women who were starting their own businesses didn't want a presentation of facts and figures and the highlights reel, they wanted to hear about the hardships and hurdles— because they were facing the same and hearing about someone else's struggles made them feel less isolated.

Coming off the stage that afternoon, I saw the true importance of sharing our stories. As I boarded my flight back to New York the following morning, I felt inspired and excited and couldn't wait to tell Jasper all about the conference and the serendipitous encounter of sitting next to Rose on the plane. Most significantly, in sharing my story—the whole of my story, not just the highlights—with other young entrepreneurs, I felt an alignment that I'd never felt before.

—

Twenty-four hours later, I landed at JFK and returned to my apartment, where Jasper greeted me. I was used to Jasper checking his phone a lot for work but over dinner at a nearby restaurant that night he was checking more often than usual.

'Who are you texting?' I asked, getting frustrated as I was trying to tell him about the conference.

'Oh, it's just Derek,' he replied quickly. 'He and Ashley are in the area and want to catch up with us.' Derek was a good friend of ours and he and Ashley had just starting dating, but I had caught a glimpse of Jasper's phone screen when he'd picked it up and Derek's name hadn't been on the screen. I didn't say anything. We finished our dessert and as we walked out of the restaurant, Jasper turned to walk towards my apartment.

'Aren't we going to catch up with Derek?' I asked.

A look of confusion appeared on Jasper's face.

'Oh yeah, um, sorry, I forgot to tell you, he said they've called it a night,' he replied after a beat, turning to face me.

'Can you show me your phone?' I asked quietly.

'Huh?' Jasper replied, shocked. I was shocked I had asked to see it too.

'Your phone. Can I please see it?'

'Why?'

'Because I don't think you were texting Derek,' I said, my voice calm and my gaze direct, but my heart beating furiously.

'You're being ridiculous,' Jasper said, looking me straight in the eyes. We never hid our phones from one another. We knew each other's passcodes, and we would use whoever's phone wasn't streaming Spotify for Google Maps or to browse restaurant reviews or look things up, that kind of thing. But that night, his unwillingness to allow me to see his phone made me feel sick to the stomach.

'If you don't let me see your phone, then it's probably best if you stay at your place tonight,' I threatened, assuming he would hand the phone to me and this would all just be a big misunderstanding.

'But I haven't seen you for two weeks,' Jasper said, now unable to look at me.

'Well, it's up to you,' I said softly as I started walking towards my apartment.

He didn't follow me.

That night, I lay staring at my ceiling for what felt like a hundred hours. The suitcase I had collected from the baggage carousel at JFK only a few hours before sat untouched on the floor. My jetlag mixed with this anxiety was a terrible concoction. The shadows from the headlights of the late-night traffic danced across my bedroom ceiling as unwanted thoughts invaded my mind. Out of nowhere, I had an image of the bottom drawer of my desk and in that moment I remembered that Jasper and I had upgraded our phones at the same time only a few months earlier, and that our old phones were still in my desk.

Wearing just a pair of undies and one of his old T-shirts, I walked over to my desk. The cold surface of the chair pressed against the back of my thighs as I sat down and slowly pulled the bottom drawer open. It was like a mini-electrical cemetery, a mass of orphaned cords tangled around each other having long lost their mates, along with phones, international adaptors and an old external hard drive. I started to pull things out of the drawer and there it sat, face down in the clutter. Even his phone couldn't look at me.

The few minutes it took for the phone to get enough charge to turn on felt like months. It was as though the universe was giving me one last opportunity to abort the mission but, in reality, I think it was the universe that had sent me the mental reminder of where his old phone was resting. The Apple logo finally appeared on the screen and my hands began to shake as I entered Jasper's passcode. I took a sharp inhalation of breath as I started reading the messages. I don't remember breathing out.

For the hours that remained before the sun rose, I lay on my bed in a state of shock and exhaustion. Finding out through text messages that your partner is cheating is not uncommon. I wished I felt angry, because anger is at least a sign of energy and strength. I had neither. The days that followed played out in a silent film of shadows waltzing on my bedroom wall and ceiling; the clock ticked interminably and I was barely capable of putting a sentence together.

Freya would kindly come over before work and leave Tupperware containers of food she had cooked for me, and they would be in the exact same spot, untouched, when she called past in the evening. She would get me out of bed just long enough to change my sheets, then I would crawl straight back into them. Freya held my heart together in those few awful weeks that followed my discovery. Privately, I was falling apart, but publicly I had some very big jobs that I was contracted to fulfil.

Two weeks after I found out Jasper's truth, I had to be back on a plane to Australia. Yellowglen were shooting me for their new campaign and I was also scheduled to do two other big shoots. One was for the cover of the business magazine *The Collective*. The other was for the cover for the launch issue of a new fashion publication, *Façon*. As I boarded the aeroplane at JFK, I prayed that the seat next to me would be empty, fearing I would end up in uncontrollable tears at the slightest attempt of conversation from a stranger. By some grace, my request was granted and for the next twenty-four hours I travelled without a neighbour. In the darkness of that aeroplane cabin, somewhere over the Pacific Ocean, I slept when I could, cried when I needed to and held my hand over my chest the entire way, willing my heart not to abandon my body.

Twenty-four hours later, I stepped off the aerobridge in Sydney as I had done countless times before, only this time I was hollow. It felt as if a ghost were wearing my clothes. The three shoots I was scheduled to do all had big teams on set. Determined to show up and do the best job I could, I set my alarm for ninety minutes before I actually needed to wake up. That way I knew I had ninety minutes to fall apart and pull myself together to get ready.

On that trip, and a few that followed, I would spend those ninety minutes lying on the floor of hotel bathrooms, trying to simply breathe. I thought I was consumed entirely by heartbreak, but the reality was that it was a convergence of everything. Not only was I exhausted, but my body was trying in many different ways to tell me to take better care of my health. But I did not listen to what she was trying to tell me. Between work, the travel and trying to hold a broken relationship together, when it came to my health, my constant refrain was, *I don't have time right now, I'll deal with that later.*

In those ninety minutes each morning, I commanded all the tears to pour out of me, hoping that my body would be in drought by the time I got to set. I would go and smile for the camera and do the interviews and breathe a huge, silent sigh of relief when the photographer or interviewer called it a wrap for the day.

The pain that was washing over me during this time was not just from trying to process Jasper's betrayal but also because I was reckoning with the fact that I had attached every ounce of my self-worth to this relationship. I think that may be the hardest deceit to process—that of self-betrayal. The danger of affixing your self-worth to anything or anyone external is that your sense of worthiness evaporates when that person or thing is gone.

Everything felt like it was crumbling around me, and the only strength I had at this point was a bottle of prescription-grade sleeping tablets. I knew I was going to have to find a way to get myself back together, so through a fresh lot of tears, I called Geoff and told him what had happened. Sharing something while you are still navigating it yourself is never easy. He was incredibly supportive, as always, and suggested I should take a little bit of time off.

'I'm so sorry,' he said. I could hear the empathy in his voice. 'I know right now it's fucked, buddy, but it's going to be okay.

Might take a while, but it will be okay. You are surrounded by people who love you and we are here for whatever you need.'

His reassuring words wrapped around me like a hug. The support Geoff provided me in the eye of the storm is something that I will be forever grateful for. I was the one meant to be leading a team and brand, but there were many days in this period where I not only failed to lead, but struggled to even function. As my business partner, Geoff kept everything moving within the business and, as my friend, he held space for me to figure out how I was going to put the pieces back together.

bathyal

bath·y·al

adjective

describing the zone of the ocean that lies between the
continental shelf and the abyssal zone—the place where
sunlight does not reach; also known as the midnight zone

Back in New York, the darkness continued to pool around me—
I could feel it thickening. No matter how much I tried to numb
or outrun it, it would always catch up with me. Jasper and I had
spoken on the phone a few times, but I knew he and I had to
sit opposite each other and have a very honest conversation. The
thought of it terrified me and I guess that's the best and the
worst thing about seeking the truth: once you have it, you also
have instant results. After finding the messages on his phone,
all I'd wanted was for Jasper to apologise, to beg and plead for
me to forgive him. But he didn't.

We had agreed to meet that Sunday afternoon. His all too familiar knock echoed down my hallway. For the last three years, the sound of that arrival would have had me running towards the door. Today, my feet moved slowly and silently towards it. The large hall mirror reflected back the frame of a woman I didn't even recognise. The anxiety of the last three weeks was evident in my body—my shoulder bones protruded and my once tight jeans hung loosely on my hips. I opened the door.

'Hi,' he said. His eyes were as sad as I had ever seen them.

'Come in,' I replied.

We sat on my couch and like strangers made polite small talk until the small talk turned to silence. Unable to sit in it any longer and gathering every ounce of courage that I could muster, I finally turned towards him.

'I need to ask you,' I said, quietly, 'how long has this affair been going on?'

He was quiet for a while. I didn't try to say anything. He looked up at me, then back down to the floor.

'Which one?' he said.

I took a sharp, short breath. 'How . . . how many have there been?' I asked.

Silence.

'At least eight,' he finally replied.

I couldn't breathe.

'Please,' I said, begging, 'please don't leave me,' my eyes desperately pleading with him. He stood up without looking at me and said he had to go. As the door closed behind him, the darkness flooded into my apartment. Without standing, I found my way from the couch to the floor. I curled up in the tightest ball I could, hugging my knees to my chest and I just sobbed. I had finally reached the bottom.

A few hours later I retreated into my bedroom and lay there as the days kept melting into one another. Waking up became the heaviest of tasks, so I started taking a larger dose of sleeping pills to combat it. The only time it didn't hurt was when I was asleep, but numbing yourself doesn't resolve anything, it just postpones it. The state I was in saw my body simply reject any food I tried to offer. I soon had to be back in Australia again for my commitments with Yellowglen for the upcoming Spring Racing Carnival and I had no idea how I was going to fulfil them. I was barely managing in survival mode.

I landed in Melbourne two weeks later. The morning was spent in hair and make-up, and only four hours after stepping off the plane, I was dressed for a day of hosting the Yellowglen marquee. The eyes of the nation fall on Flemington during the Spring Racing Carnival in Australia, which for many is more about the fashion than the sport of horseracing. As with any ambassador role, contracts stipulate a certain amount of social media posts you have to publish over an agreed period, and posting multiple times a day across multiple platforms provides a large podium for people to weigh in with their thoughts and opinions delivered via comments and direct messages.

@SamanthaWills You're much more fuckable now you've lost the chubby weight. That's a compliment BTW. Hit me up, baby.

@SamanthaWills Eat a fucking burger, you anorexic bitch!!!!!!!!!!!!!
#anna

@SamanthaWills I'm sure u get thousands of messages like this.
U probably won't even c this. But I just wanted 2 let you know how
much of an inspiration u r to me. I want 2 b exactly like u! Not like in
a weird way! LOL!!!! UR life is SOOOOOOOO perfect. I feel like we
are friends, even though we haven't met in real life, you know what I
mean. Is that weird?! LOL! I really hope u c this message. If u could
give me a shout out on one of my Insta pics, I would literally DIE!!!!!!!
I check ur Insta every day!!!! I rely on ur posts! Please post more!!!!
UR such an inspiration. U r so perfect!!!!! xxxoooo #LOVEUSOMUCH
#MYINSPIRATION

@SamanthaWills You're hot, but you look like you'd be really
stuck-up. I'd still fuck you though. And you'd like it.

Spring Racing was the biggest event on Yellowglen's marketing calendar. Everyone on the team had worked so hard on the new packaging and brand direction, and it was at this carnival that we were launching it all. In a weirdly dystopian experience, giant billboard-sized images and decals from the new Yellowglen campaign with my face plastered across them were on every flat surface at the Flemington racecourse. The image was from the photoshoot we'd done just after I had found out about Jasper, but in the image I look like the happiest girl in the world. I stared at the girl on the billboard. I didn't even recognise her.

'Samantha, the Seven Network film crew are on their way here now,' Justine, Yellowglen's PR manager said. 'You good to do a live cross in five minutes?'

'Sure am!' I said, flashing my best forced smile in her direction.

'Great!' she said. 'Stay put. I'll grab you when they are ready.' I nodded. 'You look amazing by the way!' she shouted over her shoulder. The megawatt smile I had somehow managed to turn on had started to wilt, but I forced the corners of my mouth upwards in acknowledgement of her compliment. I picked up my phone while I waited for the news crew to arrive.

> @SamanthaWills Do you think actually think you're a fucking celebrity or something? Your PATHETIC. Get ova yourself. Just because you live in New York now, don't think 2 highly of yourself, everyone knows where you came from. You seem like a real fucking bitch, and what, U R 2 good to reply to me? This is the 4th message I've sent you this week, are you fucking for real? Go fuck yourself. No one gives a fucking shit about you, you cunt. FUCK YOU.

'Samantha, this is Jade,' Justine said, introducing me to the Channel Seven reporter.

'Lovely to meet you, Jade,' I said, smiling and extending my hand to shake hers.

'We are just waiting for the news anchor to cross to us, we have about sixty seconds or so. I just have to send a quick work text, I'm so sorry. Do you mind?' Jade said.

'Not at all,' I said still holding my smile in place. 'Go ahead, I'm ready whenever you are.'

> @SamanthaWills I love you! You are looking SO fit lately! I would kill for your body!!!!! Can you do a post on your diet & work-out regime? You are so inspiring! #BodyGoals

@SamanthaWills Why are you starving yourself, SW?!?! I thought
you were a better role model to women than this. You've just lost
a follower. Hope you're proud of yourself for adding to the body
dysmorphia epidemic. What a fraud you turned out to be. That blood
on your hands sure will be hard to wash off.

The cameraman hoisted the large camera onto his shoulder.

'We're live in about thirty seconds!' the producer announced, pressing his hand to his right ear. I had done enough media over the past fourteen years to know that you paste your best smile on when you hear, 'two'. TV producers never count all the way down to one, it's always '*two*!' then they point at you to tell you the cameras are rolling. I could see my reflection in the large glass lens of the camera. The girl in the lilac dress staring back at me looked like someone I didn't know. Her eyes were glassy and her cheeks were sunken. Her collarbones showed sharply with nothing to disguise them in the strapless designer dress she wore that day, two sizes smaller than anything she had fitted into in her adult life.

@SamanthaWills Eat something. You look disgusting.

'Okay, guys, we're rolling. Stand by for cue in,' the producer said, as Jade and I put our phones on a table close by.

'You ready?' Jade asked, smiling warmly.

'Yep, ready,' I smiled back.

'. . . and we're live, in three, two . . .'

'I am here on this gorgeous September morning with the lovely Samantha Wills!' Jade beamed down the camera. 'Samantha, thanks for speaking with us today. I know you have flown in all the way from New York City to host the beautiful Yellowglen marquee here in Melbourne. Now, let's talk about fashion—who are you wearing today and what are the biggest trends you are seeing trackside this year?'

My reflection looked calm in the camera lens, but there is a very big difference between calm and numb.

chrysalis

chrys·a·lis

noun

a transitional state

With any break-up, as someone leaves your life you're not just dealing with that loss but are also grieving the future that you *thought* you were going to have together. You also have to redefine your day-to-day routine. A self-berating monologue played on a loop in my mind. *What could I have done differently? What was not good enough about me for him to stay? Why didn't he love me enough?* It was a dark place to reside. For many weeks I would wake up, answer any urgent emails and then shuffle to the bathroom cabinet and take whatever I had to numb my feelings and put myself right back to sleep. But no matter how much I wanted the world to stop for a little bit, the sun continued to rise and get on with its job. I knew it was time that I started to do the same.

Indoor stadium cycling was a new take on the traditional gym-based cycling classes, and SoulCycle studios were popping up in every New York neighbourhood. Freya had been doing SoulCycle classes for the past two years and every weekend she had tried to get me to go with her.

'Today. You're coming with me today,' Freya said before I could even say hello when I answered her call one Saturday morning.

'Where?'

'SoulCycle. Get up. I've booked your bike. Class starts in ninety minutes,' she said. 'I'll text you the address.'

The studio at SoulCycle was like a nightclub, pitch black and windowless with strobe lighting and speakers that boomed with music demanding you move. In contrast, however, there were also candles on the floor and a piece of raw amethyst behind the instructor's bike. I truly didn't know what to expect. I was the worst rider in the class that day; everyone else in the room seemed to be able to do it with ease, however I was gasping for each breath, certain I was going to pass out at any moment. Freya had the choreography down pat as she moved with the whole class in perfect unison. It was clear my fitness needed some attention. Working from home had many benefits, but when processing any type of grief, it becomes an easy place to hide away from the world and that is exactly what I had been doing.

I desperately needed something to get me out of the house to start my day and I decided that SoulCycle could be just the thing. That afternoon, I logged on and created my own profile on the SoulCycle website. I looked at the studios closest to my apartment, remembering that a friend had told me that she had an instructor called Mantas. Out of the hundreds of instructors in New York, when I clicked on the link for a nearby studio, there was Mantas's schedule. His classes were early mornings and evenings, so I booked a class each morning for the rest of the week.

I felt as though grief had wrapped its arms tightly around me, almost as if we were clinging to each other. I knew I had to find a way to pry myself from its grip, because if I didn't, it would surely suffocate me. When my alarm woke me the next morning, rather than make my morning pilgrimage to the bathroom to numb the pain, I pushed the doona off and put my feet on the floor. *Get up*, I told my grief, which was trying to pull me back under the covers. *We've got to go to class.*

I had purposely booked a bike at the back of the studio. I had heard of the unspoken hierarchy at SoulCycle. While anyone *can* book the front-row bikes, it is only experienced riders who are *meant* to take those positions. The front row keeps pace with the instructor so that the riders behind them follow their lead. The very top of the hierarchy belongs to the five bikes in the centre of the front row. Grief and I found our bike in the middle of the back row in Mantas's class. Mantas looked like a young Matthew McConaughey, with wild blond hair and a smile to match, and he did not fuck around getting the class started. There was no easing into it, it was all systems go from the minute the studio door closed. I felt as though I might die there on that very bike—the speed and endurance Mantas demanded from his riders was extreme. If I managed to survive, I figured I needed to get home as quickly as possible to cancel the remainder of the classes I had booked with him. I was nowhere near good enough to be in this class.

'You are not a number. Forget the number!' Mantas yelled over the loud beat of the music, commanding the attention of the sixty riders in the studio. 'You are not the number on the scale, you are not the size of your jeans, you are not defined by your age, you are not how many SoulCycle classes you have done. Do not define yourself by numbers. Define yourself by showing up. Showing up is the hard part.'

It was one of the most jolting exercise classes I had ever done, both physically and mentally, but before I knew it, the forty-five minutes was up. I could barely breathe and was drenched in sweat, but I had survived. I didn't cancel the remainder of the classes I had booked. Instead, I chose to show up.

Soon Mantas's classes became the bookends to most of my days. I would get up, do his 9.30 am morning class, then come home and work, and then return to the studio for his 7.30 pm class. I soon started to observe that whenever I was riding, my mind was focused on that very moment—there was no thinking about work or going through a checklist of what I could have done differently with Jasper, no replaying it over in my head, and any reprieve from that thought process was welcome. Grief and I had slowly inched our way forward to a bike in the second row. It felt safe in the second row; I was still participating but could easily hide behind the front-row riders. Then, one day, my hiding spot was exposed when the person who had booked the bike in front of me didn't show up. Mantas had a direct line of sight to my safety net.

'You should move forward,' Mantas said, looking at the empty bike, then at me.

'I can't,' I replied, terrified by how exposed I felt. 'I can't ride in the front row.'

'Yes, you can,' Mantas said, his tone no-nonsense, 'you're choosing not to.'

'But it's a centre bike,' I said, stating the obvious.

'Move forward,' he replied as the music started for the class to begin. Part terrified and part angry to have to leave my safe space, I unclipped my shoes and moved to the bike in the front row. That day, grief and I didn't ride together. Grief stayed where she was. I moved forward.

Mantas's classes were like a stent that created space for my heart to repair. Every class I went to in that darkened studio, I released anything that belonged in the dark, and doing so allowed me to move back into the light.

Mantas and I became friends outside of the SoulCycle studio and he told me about a retreat he was leading down in Costa Rica. He was taking a group to Nosara, a beautiful village where the jungle meets the ocean, for a week of surfing, meditation, yoga and organic food. Mantas convinced me to join the group on the retreat. It was something I never, ever would have done, but that was why it seemed like the perfect time to do it. I told Mantas to count me in. He tried to hide his laughter when I asked what hotel we would be staying in.

'Hotel?!' he spat. 'We're going to a remote part of a tropical jungle. We're literally staying in tree houses!'

'Tree houses?' I replied, picturing Peter Pan and the Lost Boys.

'Oh, and,' Mantas said, his tone serious, 'after we land, a local minibus picks us up for the five-hour trip into the jungle. There will be thirty of us on it but it only seats twenty-five, so it's strictly one backpack per person.'

'Backpack?' I said. 'I don't even own a backpack.'

'Well then,' Mantas said, laughing at me, 'you better go get one!'

Mantas emailed me the flight details and I booked my ticket. We were flying to Costa Rica the following week. I had done so much travelling, but I had never done anything like this. I swapped my make-up for mosquito repellent and my Louis Vuitton luggage for a Lululemon yoga mat as I prepared to go off the grid. This is something I would never have done if I had been in a relationship. I was well out of my comfort zone, and I felt proud of myself for that decision.

After Jasper and I broke up, another decision I made was to go off the pill for a while. I had been on the pill since I was sixteen, having gone on it as a teenager to regulate my cycle, and I wanted to give my body a break from it. For seventeen years, using the hormones in the pill, I'd been able to instruct my body to behave in a particular way—including having a regular cycle and, on many months, skipping it altogether. But once I was off the pill, it was as though my body was finally given the chance to communicate honestly with me.

Very quickly, I started to experience monthly pain like I had never experienced before. I took some painkillers and thought that this just must be what it is like when you come off the pill after so long. I trawled the internet and found a tidal wave of reasons for period pain—everything from age to going off the pill to some women just having heavy cycles (heavy compared to what, I did not know). I took false comfort from the generic headlines, WebMD symptoms and side-effects lists. *Oh, good! It's normal!* I thought, accepting what I was experiencing as my new normal and thanking my lucky stars that my now painful period had ended a few days before I boarded a plane to meet a group of strangers in the jungle in Costa Rica.

The arrivals terminal at Juan Santamaría International Airport was lined with little wooden huts staffed by local operators offering taxis and guided tours. My backpack was heavy and its padded straps absorbed the sweat from my shoulders. I wasn't used to either the backpack or the tropical heat.

'Hi,' I said to a girl standing near me. 'Are you here for the retreat?'

'Hi!' the girl replied. She was tall with shoulder-length blonde hair and the most perfect teeth I had ever seen. 'I am. My name is Carolyn.'

Carolyn, I found out, also rode in Mantas's SoulCycle classes.

'I would never ever book something like this,' she explained. 'But it's my thirtieth birthday in a few days, so I thought I would do something a bit different and, well, here I am.'

She had an infectious, warm energy about her. She would not have looked out of place as Zack Morris's girlfriend on *Saved by the Bell* and would have been very intimidating if not for the fact that she smiled every time she spoke.

'It's a bit out of character for me too,' I said. 'Do you live in New York?'

'I do. I'm downtown, West Village, Meatpacking area,' Carolyn replied.

'Oh, me too!' I said. 'I'm on Horatio Street.'

'No way! I'm on Horatio Street!' Carolyn laughed.

I had always wanted to be drawn to the practice of yoga, but could never turn my mind from work for long enough to focus on anything more than a downward dog. But in this environment, I had no choice. There was no phone reception and Mantas would wake us up before the sun rose to sit in silence on our yoga mats. The mornings were filled with surf lessons, and when I finally found my balance, the weightlessness and flow of it symbolised so much more to me. I felt removed from the heaviness of the past few months, and that was a feeling I welcomed with open arms.

Carolyn and I didn't stop talking the whole trip. In between yoga and surfing lessons, we would walk along the winding dirt roads into the local village together, getting smoothies at a tiny cafe and watching the afternoon downpour of tropical rain. It was a friendship that clicked instantly. Carolyn told me she had studied nutrition and now had a private practice in the city. She spoke about her family and where she grew up and she also told me about the therapy she was doing in a conscious effort to move on from a relationship that ended badly.

She asked me how long I had been in New York and if I was seeing anyone, and I told her about Jasper and what had happened. She sat and listened, beaming when I told her about the better times and downcast when I told her how it ended— her reaction was visceral, almost as though she was feeling the emotions with the same rawness I did.

'I'm so sorry,' she said, 'that must have been so awful to go through. How many years ago was that?'

'It was a little over three months ago,' I said.

Carolyn's face turned to shock, and she put her hand over her heart as if experiencing my pain. 'Three months? Oh my god, Samantha! I'm so sorry!'

'It's okay!' I assured her. 'I'm actually doing really well.'

'Okay, well, that's amazing, I would be a mess!' Carolyn said empathetically. 'Now, listen, I'm not one to push therapy onto anyone, people have to get there of their own accord, but if you do want me to introduce you to a few different people, please just let me know.'

'I'll think about it,' I said, grateful for my new friend. I couldn't wait for Freya to meet her—I knew they would get on brilliantly. 'Carolyn?' I said as we finished our juices.

'Yeah?'

'I'm really grateful we have met,' I said.

'I am too,' she replied.

Of the millions of people that live in Manhattan, and of all the streets to live on, Carolyn and I worked out that we had been living five doors apart for a few years. Yet somehow, it took each of us going on a spontaneous jungle retreat for our paths to cross. The magic of that cosmic choreography was not lost on me.

—

I followed the directions on Google maps to the address of the woman Carolyn had recommended I see. I had never felt more like a New Yorker—I had a therapist!

Dr Huber looked as though she was in her early seventies. Her long grey hair was parted in the middle and she wore a black top and pants and chic camel-coloured ballet flats. She reminded me a bit of an alternative Diane Keaton.

'So, I know this is your first time to see a therapist,' Dr Huber said kindly as we sat down in her office, which looked like the set of a bohemian 1970s fashion shoot. The room was white with raw timber floors, contained a couple of large oak chairs with embroidered olive-coloured cushions and was naturally lit by oversized windows. There were interesting knick-knacks on the coffee table—a large quartz crystal, a beautifully embossed brass tray, and other objects from her travels.

'So, let's just start wherever you would like to,' she said, picking up her pen and notepad.

'Um, well,' I said, 'I'm here because I found out my boyfriend was cheating on me.' My eyes brimmed with tears—I hadn't thought I had any more left to cry but, apparently, I did.

'It's okay,' Dr Huber said calmly. She nodded to the tissues on the table next to me. We weren't two minutes into the session and I had already soaked a handful of them.

'First,' Dr Huber said, 'what a motherfucker. Second, let's forget about him for a second. Why don't you tell me how you came to be in New York instead?'

'Dr Huber, did you just say motherfucker?' I said, laughing as tears rolled down my face.

'Yes, honey, I did,' Dr Huber said. 'I call it like I see it. Now, please, call me Jean.'

I started seeing Jean twice a week. It's amazing what comes out of your mouth when you stop worrying about what the other person might think. Jean made our sessions such a safe space, I knew I could tell her anything and she wouldn't dismiss it as silly or unimportant. She would absorb it with empathy, dissect it with care and then we would talk it through, pulling back layer after layer until we got to the core of it.

'I dyed my hair brown because he said he preferred brunettes,' I told Jean on my fourth visit. 'I'd always been blonde,' I pointed to my hair. 'As soon as I found the text messages on his phone, I dyed it back. I was so sad, then I was so angry. Sad that he had left, angry at myself,' I said, expecting myself to cry. I didn't.

'You know,' Jean said, putting her notepad down and leaning forward in her chair, 'sometimes it's not only the act that hurts us, it's also how others respond to us in times of pain and trauma that impacts us. How did he respond when you confronted him about his infidelities?'

I stopped and thought back to that conversation in my living room, playing it back in my head like a silent movie.

'He breathed out,' I said finally.

'How do you mean?' Jean asked.

'Most people would hold their breath at being caught out like that but Jasper . . . he breathed out,' I said. 'Like a sigh of relief. Like the lie he had been living no longer had to be hidden. I think he was relieved.' I'd never seen it that way before.

'And how did it make you feel?' Jean asked softly. I was still watching the silent film, up to the part where Jasper got up and left, the apartment door closing behind him. The girl in the movie fell to the floor. I turned to Jean.

'It made me feel disposable,' I said.

'Disposable is a pretty awful feeling,' Jean said.

'Yes, it is.'

—

As per my prediction, Freya and Carolyn got on brilliantly and one night in early December I sat with them both in a restaurant in the Flatiron District, and we clinked our festively named cocktails together. The conversation covered our usual topics of work, dates anyone had been on recently and the vulgar things we had witnessed on the subway that week.

'Have you heard from Jasper at all?' Carolyn asked gently.

'No,' I replied, 'I haven't heard from him in nearly five months now.'

Freya shook her head like a disappointed mother.

'I have done four sessions with my new therapist, Jean,' I told them. 'Thank you again for the introduction, Carolyn.'

'To therapy!' Carolyn proclaimed, as we all raised our glasses.

'My therapist told me I drink too much,' Freya said, taking a dramatic sip from her champagne glass, 'so I stopped seeing her.' She winked at me. 'No, but truly, I am proud of you for going,' she said.

'She's great, I really like her, we're getting through a lot and I'm learning *so* much,' I said.

'I'm just going to run to the bathroom,' Carolyn said as she stood up. 'If the waiter walks past, can you order me another cocktail?'

'Of course,' I replied.

A few moments after Carolyn had disappeared to the bathroom, laughter erupted from a large group sitting at the table by the front window. There, on that very night, of the nine million people in one of the 25,000 restaurants in New York City, sat Jasper. He was telling a very animated story to his adoring audience and with the crowd still applauding him, he looked up, his eyes met mine and he excused himself from the table.

'Fuck! Jasper's here,' I said to Freya, through clenched teeth. 'He's walking over here right now.' I didn't know whether Freya was going to throw a glass at him or punch him in the face, so I stood up and met him a few feet from our table.

'Hey! What a surprise seeing you here!' Jasper said, smiling as he leaned towards me and kissed my cheek. 'It's been a while, huh? How have you been?'

How had I been? Is he fucking serious? I thought angrily.

'Great!' I lied, smiling. 'I've been . . . great! . . . You know . . . busy!' As I stood there in front of him, there was still a part of me that wanted him to tell me that he was sorry, that he had made the worst mistake of his life, and that he would do anything and everything to make it up to me. But the only emotion he was showing was impatience to get back to his table. 'What about you? How have you been? How's work?' I asked politely.

'Good! Yeah, work's good. Things are good,' he said.

'That's good,' I replied, not knowing what else to say. So many 'good's.

'Well, we should catch up! Maybe grab dinner soon?' he suggested.

'Okay, yeah! That'd be great,' I said. I heard the flicker of hope in my own voice and cursed myself for it.

'Okay, great . . . well, I'll call you Thursday?' Jasper said.

'Perfect,' I said.

Then he quickly kissed my cheek and gave a half-wave to Freya who glared back at him. I wouldn't have been surprised if she'd stood up and announced to Jasper, 'I curse the day you were born!', but instead she shot him the kind of look of disgust that only a best friend can as he walked away, and then smiled warmly at me as I returned to my seat.

'Are you okay?' Freya asked gently.

'I'm good,' I replied, as she squeezed my hand under the table. She didn't let go of it the entire dinner.

'What'd I miss?' Carolyn said, returning to the table.

That December night in 2015 would be the very last time I saw Jasper. We never had dinner. He didn't call that Thursday. I never heard from him again.

—

The way that I worked meant that I spent a lot of time in my apartment—it was my workplace as well as my personal space—but it was now the scene of a crime I would much rather forget, as memories of Jasper lurked in every corner. Even with the photos of Jasper and me long gone and new sheets on the bed, there was a darkness that lingered and I wanted it gone.

'Maybe we could do a sage cleansing ceremony?' Carolyn suggested.

'I think it's going to need something stronger than a smudge stick,' I replied.

'What's stronger than sage when casting out ghosts of fuckboys past?' Carolyn replied.

'Paint,' I said. 'And tequila.'

The next weekend, I had the Salvation Army come and collect all my furniture for donation as I made way for the new pieces I had selected. Freya and Carolyn came over and together, with 20 litres of Dulux—and almost as much tequila—we painted over the memories of the last three years, turning the entire apartment bright white. By the time we were finished it not only looked like a brand-new apartment, it felt like one too. Confident that the paint fumes had evicted any remaining ghosts, I looked over to see Carolyn light some sage, waving it around doorways and window frames as she did a cleansing ritual.

'What?' she said, looking at me as I tried not to laugh. 'There's no harm in covering all bases!'

With our faces, hair and hands covered in specks of paint, my girlfriends and I ate pizza and drank wine sitting cross-legged on the floor. It was the very same spot that I had curled into the fetal position almost six months ago, crying tears that felt like they would never end.

That night, the same thing happened. By the time the pizza was finished and the third bottle of wine was opened, I had tears streaming down my face and found myself gasping for air. We all did, from laughter. The type where you are laughing so hard it's silent, except for the occasional loud snort—which only makes you all laugh harder. The type of laughter that makes your tummy hurt. It might have been the wine, it might have been the paint fumes, it might have been the sage, but whatever it was, Freya, Carolyn and I laughed till 3 am that morning. And laughter, I think, is the most powerful ritual of all.

alchemy

al·chemy

noun

transmutation of matter, in particular with attempts
to convert base metals into gold

Even though we'd been in business for twelve years, there was
still an assumption among the media that the Samantha Wills
brand had popped up out of nowhere. When a reporter would
ask me what the secret to my overnight success was, what I really
wanted to respond with was, 'Are you fucking kidding me!?'
Instead, I would take a deep breath and say, 'It took me twelve
years to become an "overnight" success.'

I was increasingly frustrated by this misrepresentation; first,
because it simply wasn't true, and second, because I knew that
touting such a narrative was harmful for young entrepreneurs.
I thought back to my startup days and the glossy, styled designer
profiles that I pinned above my workbench. Yes, they were

aspirational, but they also made me feel isolated and intimidated. None of the profiles reflected where I was at the time and none of them were relatable. I wish there had been somewhere I could have read real stories about what other women in business were experiencing. Maybe then it wouldn't have felt so out of reach and the 4 am stresses and second-guesses wouldn't have been as lonely.

As I started to do more speaking engagements, the number of people who would line up afterwards to speak with me and ask me often very similar questions about their own business just kept growing. I really wanted to engage with these women, but I was also conscious that I had to get through the line of people who were so graciously waiting to speak with me.

'I just feel like I am not giving each person the level of response that I would like to,' I said to Freya over dinner one evening at a West Village restaurant we loved. 'I wish I could answer all the questions in more detail because I don't feel like I am doing them justice trying to reply in such a short amount of time.'

Sometimes, we say the answers out loud but we still don't really hear them. I decided that I, at least, could share my truth. So I started to write about the ups and downs of my twelve years in business. I wrote about my vulnerabilities and the hardest challenges along the way, and I wrote with more authenticity than ever before. I was publishing these stories on Instagram and found that the character limit was restricting what I wanted to say, so I started writing these articles and saving them in Word documents on my computer.

When I would sit down to write them, I pretended that I was writing them for the young girl making jewellery on her kitchen table. I wanted *her* to have a portal that she could go to when her hands were bleeding or anxiety was choking her at 4 am. Somewhere she could read stories that would let her know she was not alone in her experience. I decided to publish them, and in a very simple Squarespace template I created a website that I named the Samantha Wills Foundation, calling it that because I was sharing stories about the foundation on which my brand and business was built.

The response to the website was significant and I knew within the first week of launching it that it was an important venture. The more real and raw the article, the better feedback it got. I started to reach out to women I admired in business, profiling them and their stories too. But there was a prerequisite to being interviewed. I didn't want the highlights reel—to be profiled you had to speak about your hurdles and hardships. What were the biggest anxieties you experienced in building your business? Not the fluff and the glamour. What was it that had you crying in the shower or lying on the bathroom floor? I wanted to share the true realities of startup, not just the high points. So I wrote it like it was, profanities and all. Writing the articles felt very cathartic. It was as though the stories I had collected over the years had a purpose—and now they had a place to go. I could feel my professional role expanding from just jewellery design and it felt very true to my soul.

You never know who is watching, but people are, and if what you are doing is authentic, you will attract who and what you are meant to attract. As my work with Yellowglen continued, I was also approached by Mount Franklin and Nespresso to front campaigns for them. I felt very humbled that such renowned brands were interested in working with me, but the brand that reached out next would provide one of the most surreal experiences of all. One evening, my phone buzzed and Karen's name appeared on the screen. I hadn't heard from her since we'd met up in a tea house in Los Angeles almost nine years before, when she'd introduced me to Annelise. I swiped to open the message.

> SW! Hi! Sorry to text at this hour, I know it's late there! Just a quick one: my friend is a brokering agent and—confidentially—she is working on the casting for a new Optus campaign. I don't have a lot of details, all I know is that it is centred around small business. They are keen to talk with you more about it. I told her I would reach out and see if it is something you would be interested in?

To be considered for what I assumed would be a corporate speaking job for a company like Optus, one of Australia's telco giants, was very flattering and certainly something I was interested in hearing more about. But before I could even start to type a reply, the three little dots started to bounce on the screen. 'P.S. Mark Wahlberg has already signed on.' Had she not typed 'SW' at the start of the first message, I would truly have thought she had sent it to the wrong contact in her phone. I replied that of course I was interested and would love to know more. Karen promised to make the introduction between myself and the agency managing the campaign when she had more details.

'It was your work on the Samantha Wills Foundation that really solidified it,' the account manager said on one of the early briefing calls I had with them. 'Many of the small business owners in the testing group spoke about how reading your articles made them feel not only more empowered on their own journey, but also as though you were in the small business trenches with them.'

It wasn't a corporate speaking gig at all; it was a full-blown marketing campaign that included a national television commercial, print billboards and digital advertising. They had signed Mark Wahlberg on as the international talent and wanted to sign me on as the national one. Mark was in the middle of a movie in Boston, so they were going to film his section there and I was to film mine in New York. They explained that they would shoot me over two days: the first day, we would shoot a representation of my current role as a business founder and owner. It would be shot in a beautiful industrial-style warehouse in New York, where they would build out a set and sound stage and create a replica of my design table. The filming on day two would be a series of flashbacks to 2004 and 2005, where set designers would recreate the little flat Melanie and I lived in and the kitchen table where it all started. It felt like preparing to enter a time machine. The account manager said they would be sending over the contract that evening and outlining my payment for the job. I felt like it was such an honour and rare opportunity to have my journey documented in this way, I would have done it for free!

Tears fell down my cheeks as I read the contract that evening. The fee they were offering me to front the campaign was almost twice the amount of the five credit cards I had maxed out starting my business twelve years earlier. On the two days that we filmed in New York, as I sat at a replica of my old table and opened replica credit card bills, the irony of being paid to do this wasn't lost on me. The director called action and I started to open the fake bills at the fake table, but it all felt very real. It was a unique opportunity to relive that moment in my journey, but this time with twelve years of added experience, growth and resilience. Sitting at that table with a whole lot of my old handmade jewellery pieces laid out in front of me, I instinctively ran my thumb over the rough skin on my fingers which used to be covered with bandages. What had been open wounds for so long were now just calluses and scars. It had taken some time, but as with most things, they too had healed.

What wasn't showing any signs of healing, however, was the increasing pain I was experiencing every month. I went on and off the pill a few times, in an attempt to suppress whatever was happening with my cycle. It had worked for me for seventeen years, but the pain just continued to get worse and worse. As I was travelling so frequently back and forth between Australia and New York, I would schedule all doctor's visits for when I was back in Sydney. My body was crying out for me to help her, but rather than see this as a cry for help, I viewed it as an annoyance, a hindrance to my already busy work schedule. Each month when the pain started, I would curse my body and take a handful of Nurofen to try to silence it.

If I was back in Sydney but didn't get my period on the days I was there, instead of proactively going to the doctor to discuss it, I would simply add it to the 'It's not a problem *right now,* so I'll do it later' list. But later always came, and when it did, I was always 'too busy'. Instead of scheduling a doctor's appointment as a priority, I would schedule work meetings and just do whatever I had to do to get through the eight or nine days of pain each month. Rather than helping and nurturing my body, I was angry at it.

Samantha Wills was now stocked in retailers in France, Japan, Korea, Australia, Canada and the United States, with our online store shipping globally. Samanthawills.com was running seamlessly, with the intelligence of our platform seeing our ecommerce numbers and therefore our gross profit spike. As romantic as the idea of having a flagship retail store was, and Geoff and I had spoken about it at length, the spend involved in rent, staffing and associated costs was huge in comparison to operating the ecommerce store. Running the wholesale side of the business—that is, selling our stock in large quantities to retailers—was also becoming more costly in a quickly moving digital market. Our P&L blatantly showed us the expense, energy and minimal profit involved in running wholesale, in contrast to the condensed output and high profit of the ecommerce platform.

'I've been thinking,' Geoff said to me as we sat in the Sydney boardroom after a monthly management meeting. 'I think we should shut down the wholesale side of the business.'

'What?' I replied, shocked at his announcement. 'But our entire business was built on wholesale distribution.'

'You're right, it was,' Geoff said. 'You've seen the numbers. The cost that is involved to have reps out on the road, the distributor fees, the freight and logistics—all for wholesale pricing. We're in a rare position in that we actually have the structure and brand presence to operate a very successful online retail business.'

I sat and listened. The part of me that didn't like change held on to the way we used to do things, but I knew from the work I was doing with Jean that holding on to old ways was sabotaging, not serving. I nodded my head as Geoff spoke.

'You don't have to decide right now,' he said, 'but I want you to think about it. The money we are spending for wholesale marketing could all be redirected to promoting samanthawills.com.'

'But what would we tell our retailers?' I asked.

'We'd tell them the truth,' Geoff replied, 'and we do it in a way that is considered and planned and based around integrity.'

'Okay. I'll think about it,' I replied.

I sat with Geoff's idea and the more I thought about it, the more I could see the next stage of our evolution. The Australian and US markets were our two biggest consumer bases. Closing our wholesale operations in Japan, Korea, France and Canada was not going to affect us too greatly. We were shipping direct to customers there through our website already, so I was confident we could maintain the market through our online store.

But I had a harder time letting go of the American wholesale business. It had felt like such a huge mountain to climb to get traction in that territory and Sarah had done such a great job of building our US portfolio to include department store giants and online retailers such as Bloomingdale's, Nordstrom, shopbop, Anthropologie, REVOLVE, and many small multi-doors and independents. And while we had a growing American direct customer database, the majority of our US sales were through retailers, not our website. I didn't know if we had the market power in that region to convert these retail customers to shop at samanthawills.com.

A few days later, Geoff and I sat down with the management team to work out the best way to implement the brand's global wholesale closure. We had agreed that we would continue stocking only two external retail accounts, David Jones and The Iconic, both of which were Australian based. We decided that the best way to implement the wholesale closure strategy was to give a two-season, six-month lead time on the decision and to offer retailers the option to cancel their pending orders should they wish to replace our brand straightaway. Of our 570 retailers worldwide, only three cancelled their existing orders.

Our sales team was tasked with calling all of our retailers to tell them of the decision. These were emotional conversations—many of our sales reps and their accounts became teary as the news was delivered. Some of our retailers had been with us for a long time and were very attached to our product—both because they'd stocked it for so long and because they knew how much it meant to their customers.

Almost all of our retail accounts said how much they appreciated being called and having the situation explained to them, rather than receiving a generic mass email. The response was a true credit to our management team and to the care that was taken through the whole process. It was an exhausting and emotional week and the aftermath was a strange mixture of sadness and celebration. Sadness for the end of an era of being a wholesale-driven business, but excitement for what was to come as we evolved into a true branded online retailer.

—

It had been eighteen months since Jasper and I had broken up and while I dreaded the dating scene, I figured getting out there might help bring a bit more work–life balance into my world. Having never been on a dating app, I was sceptical when a friend mentioned a new one, an invitation-only app called Raya. She explained to me that it was designed for creatives, a way to bring like-minded individuals together. 'You should give it a go,' my friend said to me over coffee one afternoon in Soho. 'Worst-case scenario is that you meet some cool, creative people?'

'I don't know,' I said, hesitantly.

'What if we just apply for you, you know, just for fun?' my friend urged, picking my phone up off the table.

'It doesn't sound like fun to me,' I said.

'Well, not with that attitude,' she replied, looking up from my phone like she was scolding a bratty teenager. 'There,' she said, handing me my phone back. 'You've applied. Now we wait.'

The next day a pop-up notification on my phone welcomed me to Raya.

Over weekend brunches, Carolyn, Freya and I would swipe through the limited number of profiles that Raya would allow you to see per day. Models, celebrities, company directors, designers and creative entrepreneurs populated the platform. You wouldn't believe some of the dating stories I amassed over the following few months.

I went on a date with a very well-known tech entrepreneur who told me within five minutes of meeting him that he was looking for marriage and that he was *such* a good catch and was *so* well off, he just couldn't understand why women didn't want to marry him. I just smiled politely and feigned shock to go along with him. I met a guy who lived in a tree house who was running an eco-startup and spoke for the better part of forty-five minutes about how tomatoes communicate with us. I had a very short and very meaningless message conversation with John Cusack and an only slightly longer one with Bryan Adams. I was disappointed that John Mayer's Raya profile didn't have one of his own songs as his profile soundtrack.

A guy who'd seemed lovely in our text messages asked me out for dinner. I accepted and then between starters and mains I began to tell him about the Samantha Wills Foundation and how I had launched it to empower women in business.

'Oh, you aren't one of those feminist types are you, Samantha?' he responded.

'I am,' I replied. He looked bitterly disappointed and I looked for the quickest exit.

Another time I agreed to be a plus one to a black-tie charity fundraiser. While it seemed a lot to attend such an event with someone I barely knew, I rationalised my decision by thinking, *What's the worst that could go wrong in a crowded auditorium?* Turns out, a lot. My date proceeded to drink no less than nine martinis within the first ninety minutes and when I was making small talk with a group of women who I had just met he stumbled in to the middle of our conversation and yelled at the top of his lungs, 'We should date!'

I responded by suggesting that this was something we should talk about in private, to which he very loudly replied, 'Well, if you don't want to date me, I'll just hang out with you and fuck other chicks then!'

In exhaustion, I finally decided that dying alone in my apartment was preferable to enduring another terrible date. I deleted all of their numbers, as well as the app. I was done with dating. And I was especially done with Raya.

—

The Samantha Wills Foundation was gaining lots of momentum, and I was splitting my work time between designing jewellery and writing business and brand articles for the foundation. When I spoke or wrote about business and brand, I felt more alive than I had in years. Meanwhile, the very same electricity I used to feel when designing jewellery had started to dim. I had designed well over 11,000 pieces of jewellery by 2017, so creative fatigue was not a new feeling to me. Each time it surfaced, I thought it was just part of the process. It would take at least another year to accept that this time it might be more than a temporary creative block.

I knew by this stage that the universe was always eavesdropping, and no conversation or prayer went unheard, even if the timing of its response was not up to us at all. That week our head office received a call from a representative of the American home-shopping giant QVC.

'They want to open with a half-a-million-dollar order!' Lucinda, our general manager based in our Sydney office, said when she called to tell me the news. 'We'll ship direct from here to their warehouse. This is bigger than any retail contract we could ever hope to sign in the States!'

It had been seven years since the night I'd sat in that New York Fashion Week tent watching Rachel Zoe present her QVC collection live on American television—seven years since I had wished for the opportunity to do the same.

'You're going to be presenting Samantha Wills jewellery into hundreds of thousands of homes across the USA! QVC is a juggernaut!' Lucinda exclaimed. 'This is huge, SW! Oh my god, you must be so proud! And for them to open with half a million—*and* they said that is just to test it! This could be beyond huge! How do you feel?'

While it was still a wholesale account, it was one big account, which meant streamlined logistics. My enthusiasm should have mirrored Lucinda's.

'Excited!' I lied. 'It's really exciting!' But the truth was that I didn't feel anything at all.

Lucinda had been liaising with a woman named Sage Ladiner, who was the director of an agency that sourced brands that she felt would be successful for QVC. The filming for QVC was all done in a studio in West Chester, Pennsylvania. It was about a two-and-a-half-hour drive from Manhattan and filming timeslots were allocated twenty-four hours a day, live around the clock. Sage would accompany me every time I had to go into the QVC studio to film our segments. It was a platform like nothing I had ever seen. Stepping into the studios was like stepping into a whole other world. Some of our slots were for one hour at three o'clock in the morning, others were six-minute spots in prime time. The hour-long slots we filmed were no joke, nor was the preparation.

I would sit in the hair and make-up chair in the QVC studios, my reflection staring back at me, as segment producers and set dressers moved around holding clipboards and speaking into headsets. It was everything I had ever dreamed of for the brand, but rather than relishing it, I felt as if everything was simply moving around me, almost like I was just watching it. Everything about presenting on television is over-the-top: the smiles, the enthusiasm, the lights, the hair, the make-up—all of it.

'Tease it to Jesus,' Noelle, the QVC hair and make-up artist, said as she took to my hair with a comb the first time we met. 'That's what they say where I'm from. The higher the hair, the closer to God.'

'That sure is some big hair you've given me!' I replied, smiling at Noelle as she hair-sprayed my roots and then teased them some more. 'Where are you from?'

'Texas, by way of Georgia,' Noelle said in her southern drawl. *Spray. Tease.* 'Folks there love this type of hair, and they just gonna love you and your cute accent!'

'Oh yeah?' I replied, smiling. 'QVC is popular there?'

'It's popular everywhere, sugarplum,' she replied. *Spraaaaay.* 'I don't think we've had many people on from Down Under before though. Sweet baby Jesus, that is a long way away! How long is that flight?'

'It's about twenty-four hours door to door,' I told her.

'Oh Lord above, no!' Noelle shrieked. *Tease. Spray.* 'They'd have to tranquillise me to get me to be on a plane for that long. Have you been back since you left?'

I didn't have the heart to tell Noelle I had done the flight well over a hundred times—she'd either think I was lying to her or would have a small conniption.

'Only a few times,' I replied.

'Well, sweet angel, you are all done,' Noelle said, standing back to admire her work. 'And don't you just look a picture!'

I didn't recognise myself—my make-up felt like it was an inch thick and my hair was so big I thought I might need to duck when walking through doorways, so as not to hit my hair on the doorframe.

'I love your work, Noelle,' I said. 'Thank you!'

'You're more than welcome, honey child! Oh wait, one more thing before you go,' Noelle said. *Spraaaaaaaaay.* 'There! That should hold. Go get 'em! Have a great show!' I was certain I had enough hair spray in my hair for it to hold this style for the next four years.

The studio's green room was filled with screens: two large screens that streamed both the QVC channels live and a bunch of smaller screens, which were filled with numbers and charts showing minute by minute how each segment was tracking.

'She's on in five!' a producer called to Sage.

'Okay!' Sage replied. 'We'll head out now.'

I stepped on to the set, the bright studio lights almost blinding me.

Smile.

'Good evening, America! And what a treat I have for you tonight!' The show's host beamed down the camera lens. 'I am here with Australian jewellery designer, Samantha Wills!'

That night we sold $80,000 worth of jewellery in twenty minutes. We did four more segments over the next two days, selling more jewellery in those three days than we would in a whole month on our own website.

'Samantha, this is the start of something really big,' Sage said, hugging me after I came off air. I smiled back at her, hoping she couldn't see through me.

It was around this time that I started reflecting on what the brand had achieved over the past thirteen years. Everything was running brilliantly, which made the detachment I was feeling even harder to make sense of. *Who was I to feel anxious when everything was going so great?* I berated myself. No matter how much jewellery we sold or how well the business was running, I felt little excitement for it—it was honestly as if I was watching it happen to someone else, to a stranger who I had no emotional connection to. I was operating fine, still designing and doing all the things I was required to do, but having to create twenty-two collections a year was no longer a creative venture, it was a hard slog of logistics and production, timelines, pricing matrixes and delivery schedules. I could do it, but I knew I was designing with my hands, not with my heart. And as a creative person, that is a real problem.

Geoff and I decided that I should do some work with a brand coach. The objective of having a brand coach is similar to that of going to a therapist—they're an external third party who can look at the situation and try to identify what is blocking it. I met with the brand coach every few weeks and she would ask me questions and have me do creative exercises to try to shift my perspective, with the end goal of assisting me to get that creative spark back. But the truth was, the creative flame I once had for creating jewellery had all but died out.

I decided to call my Freya-predicting clairvoyant Sandra to try to get some divine guidance on how I could summon my creative energy back. I had spoken to her many times over the years and appreciated not only her clairvoyance but also the friendship we had developed.

'I was wondering if you could give me any insight into my work,' I said to Sandra hopefully.

'Work . . . hmmm,' Sandra said down the phone, as I could hear her turning the cards over. 'No. there's nothing here about work.'

Great, I thought.

'But there's a very handsome man coming into your life,' Sandra said, sounding excited.

'I've given up on dating,' I said flatly.

'Well, dating hasn't given up on you,' Sandra replied.

'Oh yeah?' I said, the words coming as half-heartedly as I felt them.

'But he's not Australian,' Sandra replied.

Well, that makes sense, I thought. I had been in New York for seven years and assumed purely as a numbers game that any prospective suitors would be American.

'He's not American either,' Sandra added, almost as though she'd read my mind.

'Of course he's not,' I replied, laughing a little. 'Because that would just be too convenient, wouldn't it!'

'I think he's from Europe. They are showing me the letter I,' she said confidently. 'Maybe . . . Italy?' she added a few seconds later, with much less conviction.

As I always did, I scribbled her words in my diary as she spoke, putting question marks next to anything she didn't seem to be 100 per cent clear on herself. 'Europe. Letter I, maybe Italy?' I wrote.

'Okay, but my work?' I prompted. 'Are you sure you don't see anything you could give me guidance on?'

'Shhh. Nope. Nothing on work. But there is a letter N,' Sandra said.

'Okay?' I said with slightly more hope, wondering how a letter N related to my career.

'His name starts with the letter N,' Sandra said.

'Whose name?'

'The European!'

'Oh,' I replied. *We're still on that.* 'But I don't want to date a European. I don't want to date anyone right now,' I told Sandra.

'I don't make the rules, honey. I just tell you what they tell me,' Sandra replied. 'Now listen, they are telling me that his name begins with an N, but that he doesn't go by that name. It's like no one calls him by his Christian name. But I'm certain, he's on his way!'

After the reading was finished, I hung up and looked down at my journal page. It was peppered with random letters, scribbles and lots of question marks. With no guidance on my career and even more confused than I'd been before the reading, I put the journal in my desk drawer and vowed to bury the feeling of unease for a little while. I had two days to finish the latest collection and then had to be on a plane back to Australia to speak at a conference about living your passion.

The irony of the timing and the topic was not lost on me.

—

I was walking down Hudson Street one afternoon to meet Carolyn for coffee, and on my way I saw an ad for Gotham Writers Workshop, a writing college in New York. I got to the cafe a few minutes early so I brought up and scrolled through the college's website on my phone. They offered all types of courses and I noticed they had a memoir class that ran for a semester and was due to start in a fortnight's time.

'I just signed up for writers' college,' I told Carolyn a few minutes later as she sat down at the table.

'What?' she replied. 'When are you ever going to find the time to do that?'

'I don't know, but I have to do something different creatively to try to get through this block. I have to start on the next collection soon and my creative well has runneth dry,' I said, dramatically.

I'm not convinced that either Carolyn or I believed I would follow through, but two weeks later, I walked into the Gotham

Writers Workshop building on 8th Avenue and 38th Street. I hadn't been to school in almost twenty years. I found a seat at a desk that would end up being mine for the semester and exchanged polite small talk with the other students. It was a small class of only about fifteen people and it felt as though everyone there had the same trepidation that I was feeling—not so much wondering whether they had a story in them, but more so whether they'd be able to put the words on the paper to tell it. In our first lesson, the teacher explained to us the difference between writing autobiography and memoir.

'Autobiography is a set start-to-finish timeline, it's like filling in a calendar,' she explained, 'but memoir, memoir is one moment, one place, one time. You could write an entire memoir on just one single night of your life. Memoir is expressing how you feel about that experience, what you learnt and how it affected *you*. Your job—as writers—is to tell that story in a way that makes the reader feel like they are in the memory with you. They are there experiencing the pain, joy, passion, heartache—whatever you are writing about—with you.'

I hung back to speak with the teacher after our first lesson. With my class schedule in hand, I was instantly transported back to high school.

'You're going to miss how many classes?' my teacher asked when I explained to her that I would have to travel back and forth to Australia three times over the semester.

'Four. Hopefully only four,' I repeated, feeling like my teacher was already disappointed in me. 'It's for work. I have to go to

Australia for work. I promise to keep up with the assignments. I won't miss any,' I promised.

'Okay, well your first assignment is due next week,' the teacher replied.

And so I started to write. Our assignments were 1500-word papers, telling stories about our lives that had to be focused on one moment, one place, one time. Every third week, each student had to be in the 'booth'. The booth was a metaphorical soundproof booth and the class had to provide constructive criticism of your work.

I loved it, not so much the booth process, but the writing and learning how to construct stories in a way that was coherent and meaningful for your reader. The feelings I used to have when creating jewellery were now flickering again, but this time it was about words and intertwining them into stories. I became friends with one of the women in my class and she promised she would take notes for me when I had to travel.

On my next trip, rather than putting on headphones and turning on a movie as soon as I boarded the flight, I started to write instead. I had been looking so intensely at how to bring back my creative passion as it related to my career responsibilities, that I hadn't yet looked at what it might mean for me personally. For so long, I had only known myself and the brand as a single entity. Typing on my laptop made me feel like I was in work mode, so I pulled out a pen and paper and wrote that way, which felt different. I started to write down the things that were important to me personally:

- To feel more grounded.
- To be able to sleep unmedicated.
- To reduce the head noise and anxiety.
- To feel at home in my apartment, not in an airport lounge.
- To find the next avenue in my career that I am truly passionate about, that in turn impacts women by empowerment—possibly writing?
- To achieve these things, I need to travel less and invest in building a home, both physically, emotionally and spiritually.
- I need to make a change.

I underlined the last point. I knew I had to make a change, but I couldn't quite understand what it would look like. I couldn't step away entirely from the public commitments required for the brand—you don't get that luxury when you decide to name something after yourself. Did it maybe mean stepping down as creative director of the brand? Did it mean moving a creative team to work with me in New York so I was travelling less? They seemed like pretty drastic measures to me, and my heart wasn't sold on either of them. But any change to the only thing you've known your entire adult life is going to feel drastic in some way. It felt like taking a step into the unknown.

A couple of weeks later, I had checked in at Sydney airport and was sitting in the lounge, early for my flight back to New York. I picked up my passport; its cover was ratty and it looked about as worn out as I felt. I started to flick through the pages covered in stamps. Then I went right back to the first page and started to count the American entry stamps. Forty-nine.

Forty-nine stamps into America meant I had done the flight between Sydney and JFK ninety-nine times. The flight I was waiting for would make it a round one hundred. The journey took twenty-four hours each way, so that meant I had spent 2400 hours in the air on these flights. And this number didn't even include all the time I had spent flying to other places, like China and Europe, in between. No wonder I didn't feel grounded. With my passport still open on the last page, I stared blankly across the all too familiar lounge.

I took out the notes I had written just a few days before. I was thirty-five and I knew I wanted to start a family. I wanted to live somewhere that felt like a permanent home, not a transient place I would crash at in between airport runs. In that moment, sitting in the Sydney airport lounge, I knew I had to make a change and that what I was doing and the way I was feeling was not sustainable. Maybe it was time, after fourteen years, to hand the product design over to someone else. Time to recruit a designer, so I could step out of the day-to-day business and focus on just the overarching creative direction. In that moment, I had an idea of what I could write about for my upcoming class assignment—I was going to write my letter of resignation to step down as head designer of the Samantha Wills brand.

Writing the words on paper felt incredibly liberating, and I submitted it in class a week later. It strangely felt like the safest public place to test the feeling of resignation. My most honest truth, read by strangers, made me feel vulnerable, but not scared. Instead, I felt a fair bit of relief. I sat with the letter for a few days. Geoff was visiting New York the following week. I knew a change had to happen and my hands shook as I handed him the letter. He looked at me, bemused, and asked me what it was.

'It's my letter of resignation,' I replied, my voice quiet. 'I can't do it anymore.' The familiar feeling of tears pricking my eyes began, threatening to spill over as Geoff read the letter.

'Okay,' he said, nodding. 'It's okay.'

I explained to him that I was tired of being on an aeroplane every other week and also talked him through the creative exhaustion I'd been feeling and how I felt I was designing for mass production and no longer to create.

'I understand,' Geoff said, still looking at the letter. 'Leave this with me for a few days and then let's reconvene on it, how does that sound?'

I nodded.

When we talked again, Geoff and I came up with a strategy. The first objective was for me to travel less. The other, harder, step was to recruit a new head designer. We agreed that I was going to continue with my public-facing commitments for the brand, but within the business I was going to take the title of executive creative director, a role that would allow me to still be involved at an advisory level, but not on a day-to-day one. We also agreed not to make the announcement publicly until we had employed the right person, so we briefed the senior management team on my decision and set about searching for my replacement.

Back at my design desk, I began working on yet another new collection. As I sat there sketching and arranging semiprecious stones for the new designs, a notification popped up on my phone:

'This is a courtesy notification to let you know your subscription to Raya is about to renew for another year.'

What? I thought, putting my pliers down and picking up the phone. *I thought I deleted that ages ago?* I didn't have to look too far to see that I had only deleted the app from my phone, not my actual account, and that to delete the account you had to re-download the app. I re-downloaded the app and was met with a new message from a guy called Niall. 'Hello from Dublin, where absolutely no one uses this app . . .'

I had forgotten all about Sandra's prediction and wouldn't remember it until I came across my journal in a drawer a couple of months later. But there he was. The European man whose name started with an N, who was from a country that started with an I—not Italy. Ireland.

'Hi Dublin,' I replied, 'the app's sure to catch on soon, otherwise you're just going to end up with a lot of penpals.' I'd logged in to close my Raya account that day, but I ended up opening up something else entirely.

Niall and I started messaging. He knew nothing of who I was, and I knew nothing of him. Our messages started as short and polite small talk but soon became longer and more personal, each one revealing something new about ourselves to the other. It is an incredibly beautiful way to get to know a person, writing. Our correspondence felt like a traditional method in a modern format. Niall was a musician and writer and we talked about our respective creative processes, our favourite eighties movies and the ever-sacred exchange of Spotify playlists. We had the exact same sense of humour and the daily updates from my Irish penpal very quickly became the highlight of my day.

Melanie was still living in London and she and her husband had welcomed a baby girl, Naya, the year before. Mel had asked me to be Naya's godmother, a role I was so honoured to accept and we had already planned for me to visit in January 2018. I told Niall that I was heading across the pond and was soon on my way to spend a few days in London with Mel and her little family.

And so, three months and thousands of messages after that first exchange, Niall and I finally met for dinner. It was easy and lovely and it felt like we had known each other for twenty years. With broad shoulders and standing six-foot-six, Niall was as tall as he was handsome, but even bigger than his giant frame was his gentle, giant heart. It was truly like none I had encountered before.

We didn't stop talking for the following forty-eight hours until we said goodbye at the airport as I headed back to New York. Dublin and New York didn't get any closer over the following months, but Niall and I did. He would send me new music he was working on and I would send him my writing assignments from college. He would send me photos from the studio when he was recording and I would send him pictures of the new jewellery collections I was designing. Niall introduced me to the work of his favourite singer–songwriter Tom Waits and gave me an insight into the process of songwriting. I had never been with someone who inspired me to create like Niall did. Spending time with him didn't reinvigorate the old creative energy I had lost, it opened up an entirely new channel altogether.

At one therapy session, Jean had suggested that I try the practice of meditation, saying it could be a way to allow new creativity to find me. I set about getting a chic Goop-recommended meditation pillow, scented meditation candles and fancy crystals, which I placed carefully around the designated spot in my apartment. Hoorah! I was ready to meditate! I would light my fancy candles and sit on my overpriced pillow and close my eyes as tightly as I could, willing the meditative peace and clarity that everyone spoke about to come to me. Needless to say, I had all the gear and no idea.

Niall was finishing up his Master of Psychology with a focus on mindfulness, and a big part of his work centred around mental health and exploring ways to calm the mind. He taught me about mindfulness and how it relates to everything: the act of acknowledging and accepting emotions that arise, and using mindfulness to guide yourself towards calmness and the present moment. We would speak about how mindfulness related to energy and how we show up in the world and, above all, the impact that it could have on conscious kindness.

'Mindfulness *is* meditation,' he said.

Something in me changed in that conversation. I made peace with the anxiety I held around my fading creativity. The uncertainty didn't disappear, but I began to understand how to live alongside rather than underneath it, acknowledging it in my periphery rather than letting it cloud my line of sight. Meeting Niall changed a lot of things—in my heart, in my creativity and in my awareness of where my internal world met the external one. The serendipitous way in which I met him felt like a poignant chance encounter, and one I could not have been more grateful for.

I had started to read more on meditation and had been reading a book called *Intuitive Being* by Jill Willard. The book focused on different energy centres in the body, including ways to calm the mind and nervous system through meditation. One night in New York, I finished and closed the book and then decided to take a look at Jill's website. It said that she was holding a week-long meditation and workshop with a focus on intuition at the Omega Institute, which was about a ninety-minute drive north of Manhattan up in Rhinebeck in New York State. The workshop was in mid-June, still six months away, but that night, I booked my spot to attend.

On one trip, Niall took me to one of his favourite places in Ireland and we spent the weekend hidden away from the world. Knowing how much room he took up in my heart was a scary feeling. But no matter how hard I tried, I found myself plagued by past experiences—the narrative I was holding onto was that men leave and they did so because I wasn't good enough for them to stay. Even despite the work Jean and I had done, I still knew this narrative was lurking within me and I wanted to be rid of it.

In the past, I had moulded myself into what I thought the person I was dating wanted me to be, thinking that if I did so, they would stay. The charade was exhausting, and I didn't want to do it anymore. It was time to extend the vulnerability I was sharing in my public career to my personal life. But, my god, being vulnerable and revealing your truest self in a new relationship is a terrifying thing to do. However, I had come to learn that true intimacy comes in the sharing of our vulnerabilities. It is the exchange of information about yourself, your past, your fears, things you're working on, things you're hoping for.

And so on that trip, one evening over dinner, I told Niall everything. I told him how I had let my ego get the better of me and nearly ruined the entire brand in one season. I told him that even though I was still creating jewellery, I wasn't *being* creative and at times it felt like it was killing me on the inside. I told him about Geoff and how a lot of the time I felt I was letting him down by wanting to step away from the business, and also about how finding a new head designer was proving to be much more difficult than I had anticipated. I told him how my true passion was actually the Samantha Wills Foundation and that I felt like because of that, I had failed so many people, particularly those that had worked alongside me building the jewellery brand to what it was.

I told him about my therapy sessions with Jean and I told him about Jasper and how much that experience had wounded me. I told him I had spent more nights simply trying to breathe on hotel bathroom floors than I could remember, and that some nights I took sleeping pills because the thought of lying awake with my thoughts between midnight and dawn was absolutely terrifying to me. He sat and he listened and I just kept talking. I told him things I had never told another soul.

And for the very first time in as long as I could remember, I felt like myself. I didn't tell him only the parts of my story that I thought he would want to hear and I didn't gloss over the messy bits so he wouldn't think I was too broken or maybe too much of a liability. It felt like I was showing him my open wounds, pointing and saying, 'This one, this one here is the deepest, here's how I am trying to mend it, but here, right here—here is the place it hurts the most, so here is the place I need you to take the most care with.' And he did. The kindness of his soul wrapped around mine and it felt like the safest place in the world.

'Why did you enrol in writing school?' Niall asked me.

'To see if I can write,' I replied.

'You can,' he said, 'and you have to.'

'Have to what?' I asked.

'Write,' he replied. 'You have to tell your story.'

'I don't know if I've got it in me, it's a big thing, to share that with the world,' I said.

'I understand,' he replied, and I knew that of all people, he truly did. 'I think sharing your story is important, but you have to be comfortable to do so, and you'll know when the time is right for that,' he said reassuringly. 'But I think you should start to write it and I promise you, you will start to feel lighter with every single word you put on the page.'

I once again said goodbye to him at Dublin airport and on the flight back to New York City, I started to write this book.

—

'Welcome to Sydney. If you would like to adjust your watches, the local time is 6.37 am. As we have crossed the International Date Line, the date is Tuesday, the first of May,' came the cabin supervisor's voice over the plane's PA system. The week ahead was filled with back-to-back interviews as we continued our search for a new head designer. We had been interviewing for months with not a lot of success. Lucinda had already done first-round interviews with all the new candidates, creating a shortlist for me to meet with. I hadn't told any of the team about my growing internal disconnect from the product and the brand. I was still trying to work through it myself, especially the guilt of it.

The truth was that the Samantha Wills brand had become much bigger than me many years ago. So many people had worked on it over the years, each pouring such love and energy into it; it belonged to all of us. It meant something to our community and it meant something to our team. It wasn't just the brand that was my name, though—logistically, the creative workings of the business had been built to rely on me. I should have trained up a head designer to work alongside me years ago. A resource to hand some of the bigger design projects and creative tasks over to. But I didn't. Instead, I'd held the creative direction and design close and driven them personally. It had been a blessing to the brand in many ways, but now at this juncture, it was anything but.

When a brand is a person's name and that person works actively within the business, it can come with a unique set of issues and frustrations for the team. In some ways, the business actually ran better when I wasn't in the office, because when I was in the building, people felt they needed to get my sign-off for most things and at times I know I made that experience even harder—particularly when it came to the creative approval. But even though I had made the decision and put the wheels in motion to step back, making that a reality was challenging. It was hard to relinquish control, even though it was me who had instigated the change.

'You're causing issues,' Geoff said to me one afternoon as we stood outside our Sydney office. 'You can't have it both ways. You either have to step away from the business and empower and trust the team to make and stand by their creative decisions, or you step back into the brand and lead it. Being half in and half out, changing things at the last minute . . . it's frustrating for the team.'

It was hard to hear, but I knew he was right. The last thing I wanted to do was make anyone's job harder or less enjoyable, but I knew I was doing both. It's no good being there in body if your heart is no longer in it. Part of me was still hopeful that my creative passion for jewellery would just one day magically reappear, but it didn't and the longer I waited for it, the more I was disrupting the team.

For example, marketing would create campaigns and activations that had a progressive feel and brand language. They were beautiful, but I didn't feel that they were on brand for us and so I would request changes be made, usually at the last minute. This not only demotivated the team, it also started to affect timelines and workloads. It was not the type of leader I wanted to be.

I had to either get out of the way, decide on a new head designer and give the team my blessing to take the brand forward without my play-by-play input or step back into the business and continue to lead the brand.

I told Geoff that I understood what he was saying and that I was committed to finding the right candidate to take on the head designer position. By this time, I had designed over 12,000 pieces of jewellery and was still designing more in the interim. I couldn't wait to get a new head designer into the role.

I've now come to recognise that universal guidance often comes in the guise of roadblocks such as closed doors, frustrations, misalignments or having a desired outcome that just won't fall into place. But sitting in our office boardroom for the final round presentations with the head designer candidates, I didn't see that once again the universe was giving me very clear guidance on this situation. Rather than seeing the major roadblock we were facing in finding the right candidate for the role as a sign to reassess the situation as a whole, I instead pushed on and asked Lucinda to go back to the recruiters again to continue the search.

———

While there was a major heaviness in one area of my life, there was also an incredible lightness in another. Niall and I spent a long weekend together in London and it was lovely to have him meet Mel and her family.

'I know there is a lot going on with work right now, but I haven't seen you this happy in a long while,' Mel said. 'He is amazing. You two look very at ease in each other's company. I am very excited about this!'

Niall showed me where he used to live when he was based in London and we enjoyed late breakfasts, room service and the anonymity and disregard for time that comes with holidays in foreign cities. Spending time with Niall felt like a safe haven where I could take refuge from the business-related angst I was feeling. But as lovely as being with him felt, we were realistic that it was not without its complications. We both had demanding careers and often conflicting schedules, factors that put pressure on any relationship, but on top of that we also lived on different continents. But if that was the way it had to be for the time being, I was happy to accept the distance and demands. Having him in my world felt, in many ways, that the universe had given me a sacred gift.

—

My body didn't know what time zone it was in as I once again touched down from New York to Sydney to continue conducting the second- and third-round interviews for the head designer role. We had twelve people to interview and I was also booked to speak at a women in business event for Westfield. The presentation went well. The same couldn't be said for the interviews. Every person we interviewed either didn't have the experience required to lead a jewellery program the size of ours, or if they did have the experience, their design language was not a fit. No matter which way we tried to slice it, it seemed like we were searching down an empty trail.

'Am I being too unrealistic?' I asked Lucinda after we had finished the final one for the day. 'Tell me honestly.'

'No, not at all,' Lucinda replied. 'It's going to be a very hard position to fill. The brand has such a longstanding aesthetic and language and all of that has been crafted from your mind and your hands. This recruitment is tough, but we will get there!'

I appreciated her optimism, but I wasn't as confident.

—

There are times in life when the universe pulls the rug out from under us. This can happen at many different moments in our lives, and for reasons we may never fully understand.

That week, neither my heart nor my mind expected the call I received from Niall, and just like that, the gift I had nurtured so sacredly was no longer able to be held. My relationship with Niall ended as a result of a force greater than the both of us, for reasons I couldn't fight and had to accept. My heart broke equally from the sadness in his voice when he told me as it did from the relationship ending. There was no anger, no yelling, no resentment, which left only a deep sorrow. Our hearts were as heavy as each other's. That night, for the very first time since I was six years old, I dropped to my knees beside my bed, and with silent tears pouring down my face, I looked up to a God I had never believed in and said, 'Please. Please . . . if you're listening. *Please* let this be okay.'

I guess it's true what they say. Everyone prays in the end.

cross·roads

noun

an intersection of two or more roads; a point at which a
crucial decision must be made that will have far-reaching
consequences

The meditation workshop I had enrolled in was due to begin
the following week in upstate New York. The only thing I felt
was numbness, but as I pulled into the campus, I noticed that
there was definitely something a little magical about the place.
The Omega Institute campus looked exactly like the pictures I
had seen on the website: lush green lawns, a large still lake and
white wooden cabins dotting the picturesque acres of rolling
hills. It was a world away from Manhattan. There were large
trees lining the main roads around the campus and little wood-
chipped paths that wound through organic vegetable patches,
flower gardens and outdoor meditation areas.

I felt like damaged goods entering sacred grounds. The internal creative disconnect that had been rumbling for the better part of the past two years refused to be ignored anymore and with my relationship no longer a sanctuary to escape to, my life currently only existed in jagged fragments. I dropped my bags at my cabin and followed the map to the main hall for orientation. Walking in, it was like my first day in a new school and I was sure that everyone could see the brokenness I was feeling. I took a seat at the back of the small auditorium.

'Everyone here has a story,' the campus director said, after he welcomed everyone into the hall. 'Everyone here is expected to show considered kindness.'

The Omega regulars nodded and put their hands over their hearts, while I and the rest of the newcomers awkwardly scanned the room, looking every bit as self-conscious as we were. All I wanted was to go home. But when I really thought about it, I actually didn't know where that was. And so there I sat, in a hall full of strangers, not knowing what the week ahead would present.

Being in the quiet surrounds of the Omega campus felt foreign—I had become so used to either New York sirens or the hum of an aircraft at 30,000 feet. I had made the decision to disconnect from social media for the week and to only check my texts and emails in the evening, keeping my phone turned off throughout the day. The grounds were said to be sacred and I had read about a beautiful meditation temple atop one of the hills that overlooked the campus where an early morning meditation was held each day. I decided that seeing I was here, I might as well throw myself into the experience entirely and committed to doing the pre-sunrise trek each morning to the meditation temple.

That first night, I didn't fall asleep until after midnight and I jumped as my alarm started screaming at 4.30 am, cursing the commitment I'd made the night before. I got dressed in the dim light of my cabin and started the short pilgrimage up to the temple. The majestic wooden building was surrounded by Japanese-style ponds filled with koi fish and lily pads. I removed my shoes at the entrance, added them to the pile of my fellow early risers' sandals and well-worn Birkenstocks and found a spare cushion at the back of the room. I closed my eyes and took a few deep breaths.

What if you feel this lost for the rest of your life? my mind heckled me. *What are you even doing here? This temple is for real medita-tors, you're wasting your time . . .* My mind clearly had no regard for the 'This is a place of silent reflection' signs that hung all around the temple. I wanted to stand up and leave but was worried that the other meditators—the *real* meditators—would judge me, so instead I willed myself to stay for at least twenty minutes. After what seemed like an eternity, I heard the person in front of me getting up and jumped on the opportunity to leave when they did. It was still dark as I made my way back down the hill, tired, angry and frustrated.

The Jill Willard workshop that I had signed up for was set to begin at 9 am. To pass the time, my impostor syndrome and I went back to my cabin to discuss all the reasons why everyone else who was visiting Omega was significantly more spiritually qualified than me to be there. We came to this conclusion with steadfast certainty, even though we hadn't spoken to a single other person since we'd arrived. It's truly amazing the narratives that impostor syndrome can come up with. He is the ultimate con artist, dressed up as the most convincing of storytellers.

'Welcome, everyone, to the Intuitive Being Workshop,' Jill said. Her voice was soft and steady. Jill was in her mid-forties, was tall and slim and had blonde hair that fell past her shoulders and skin that had been kissed by the Californian sun. I had already read Jill's book twice. Her voice was as nurturing in person as it was on the page. We all introduced ourselves to the group and everyone had a different story to share. There was an older lady who had lost her life partner suddenly and wanted to harness intuitive insight to make peace with her partner crossing over. There was a mother of two college-aged sons from Buffalo, and a middle-aged, softly spoken man who was a computer software sales manager from Ohio. When it was my turn to introduce myself to the group and tell them a little bit about why I had signed up for the workshop and where I was from—introducing myself being something I had done thousands of times in my career—I couldn't get any further than my name. Tears rose and words retreated.

'My name is Samantha, and I signed up for this week because . . . I'm so sorry,' was all I could say, as I looked down and tears fell into my lap.

'It's okay,' Jill said, kindly and calmly. 'This week, we all show up exactly where we are, you are supported in here.' She gave me a small smile, her eyes kind and then she carried on with the class.

I was so embarrassed but no one in the class batted an eyelid, they just offered warmth and empathy. I couldn't help but feel I was ruining the class for everyone and we were only a few minutes in. I was utterly broken. A complete mess, but for all the beauty that Omega held, I rationalised that it had seen a lot of mess. It's the type of place people go to heal or deeply cleanse, neither of which were pretty processes. The fragmented pieces within me started to dance a little quicker. Being at Omega had given the deep rumblings a space to erupt; a space to finally unravel.

On the third night of the workshop, I turned on my phone after dinner to check my emails as I was walking back to my cabin. I waved my phone above my head as I walked—no doubt looking as crazy as I felt—trying to catch some of the elusive campus mobile phone service. When I saw emails start to filter into my inbox, I immediately stopped walking to take advantage of the pocket of good reception.

Over the years, Geoff and I had developed a practice where we would send each other what we called 'observational emails' every quarter. These emails had nothing to do with numbers or the P&L; rather, they were about company culture and things we observed within the company, hence their name. I had known I would receive this quarter's email from him while I was away at Omega, but I couldn't have predicted that this particular email, among the thousands of emails that Geoff had sent me over the past decade, would set off a course of ultimately life-changing events.

FROM: Geoff Bainbridge
TO: Samantha Wills
SUBJECT: Business at a crossroads

Hi SW,

I understand you are upstate this week and I respect you are taking some much-needed time and space both professionally and personally.

As you know, I was hesitant to send this email to you this week, but as per your request, please find my observational thoughts below.

I'm increasingly concerned about the future of the Samantha Wills jewellery brand and feel that it is very much at a crossroads. Our journey thus far has been special, but our future has never been more uncertain.

From my perspective, it comes down to brand ownership/ leadership. While the Samantha Wills business is functioning well, the Samantha Wills brand has stalled and our leadership team is lost in their decision-making framework due to conflicts between Samantha Wills the brand and Samantha Wills the person.

Our success has largely come through building a team to support your brand vision, but increasingly this vision is not widely understood. My role in this partnership is to fulfil your vision but even I am confused about what this is (and I think you would agree that you are even struggling to see it yourself) and thus I am now just running the business to the P&L in the absence of a higher cause or purpose—something I never anticipated would happen.

This is a brand and a business that is crying out for purpose and passion; a consumer who wants to feel valued and loved; a team that wants to feel connected. Ultimately this is your business, your brand, your team and your story.

The time has come when we need to make some hard decisions:

— Given the lack of success we have had in trying to find a head designer to replace you, are you willing to return to Australia to effectively step back into running the company from HQ with appropriate creative support?

— I recognise that the scope of product we produce is significant: how do you feel about handing parts of this over to a larger design team who would work under your vision? Do you think you would be able to hand this creative control over while actively working in the business?

— I have learnt that pain is an important part of anyone's journey and I respect that right now you are experiencing a very painful time. Given this, are you mentally and emotionally able to commit to this?

— If not, what are you able to commit to?

— If you choose not to step into an active role for the next growth phase of the business, are you prepared to watch a steady decline in the business over the coming years? I ask this given how personal the brand and the journey is to you.

One thing I have learnt and may be able to provide as advice is that pain is always difficult, but it's okay and a natural process we all must go through to grow. The good news is, it doesn't last forever, we will always be different on the other side and, if harnessed correctly, it builds resilience and not fear, courage and not resentment.

Of course, no decision needs to be made in haste but given your week away I felt that you may wish to factor some of the above into your thinking (but as I mentioned, I was equally nervous sending it to you at this time because I am very aware of what you are processing personally).

GB

I felt deeply the support in his words and appreciated his generosity in wanting to build a business around what I was prepared to commit to for the brand. I glanced up after I finished reading his email, and a moment of sheer surrealness washed over me when I noticed where I was physically standing. The path I was taking back to my cabin split in two and I had stopped right at a crossroads. The path to my left was the main road that wove around the entire campus. It was tarred with asphalt and you knew exactly where it would take you. The road that went to the right was not a road at all; it was a thin, winding path leading into a section of trees and ferns, and beyond that a flower garden.

I looked back down at my phone. 'Business at a crossroads' was indeed the subject line of the email. I looked at the crossroads I was standing at, the symbolism so significant in that moment that I couldn't separate the physical from the metaphorical. My skin prickled with goosebumps and, in that instant, I just knew. I put my hand on my heart and heard the quietest, calmest of voices say, *It's time to close.* It was the clearest thing I have ever experienced. It was as though I actually felt the words being spoken.

I glanced around. There was no one standing anywhere near me. With my feet still at the diverging roads, I thought about what we had covered in the meditation workshop just that day— how to differentiate our mind's chatter from our intuitive feeling. Jill had described intuition as an instant knowing, a calm feeling that you often cannot logically describe. The mind chatter of the ego always pipes up slightly afterwards, listing all the reasons why your intuition is off the mark, all the things about it that make no sense, listing any and every reason why staying with what you know is the safest option. And as if on cue, the reasons why closing a successful business would be crazy started to roll in. *But what would you do? You've made jewellery for the past fifteen years, how are you going to support yourself now? It's going to look like you've failed. I think you should just stay in the business. Don't be so ungrateful. Being passionate about something creative isn't everything, you know. Why would you risk stepping into the unknown? What if it doesn't work out?* While I understood the concept of intuition versus ego-driven mind chatter, I didn't yet trust myself or my intuition enough to act alone on such a big decision. I needed some sort of confirmation to reassure myself that I was indeed not going mad.

Please, give me a sign of what I am meant to be doing, I prayed, hoping that the silent request would be heard. I put my phone back in my bag and glanced down again at the crossroads. I turned right. The path wound through a flower garden, and the students from the art workshops had tied painted stars that glistened in the dusk light to the branches of some of the trees. The path I was on met back up with the main campus road, right where the Omega bookstore was located. I decided to go in even though I didn't need any more books—I had a pile of waiting-to-be-read books so high I could barely see over it. But that night, I wasn't looking for a book, I think a book was looking for me. That is the best way I can explain why the only book I picked up that evening was *Big Magic* by Elizabeth Gilbert. Its bright cover faced out, its subheading, 'Creative Living Beyond Fear', illuminated in the shop light. It was the only book I remember even seeing. I purchased it at the counter and was lying on my cabin bed reading it not ten minutes later.

In a beautifully conversational way, Elizabeth Gilbert brings to light all the fears and excuses we make that block our true creativity. Every anecdote in the book felt like a little ember landing in the creative depths of my soul, each an optimistic flicker that maybe my creativity had not evaporated entirely, and maybe it was actually alive and well and just seeking a new channel through which to flow. I finished the chapter I was on and placed the book down next to me.

The only identity I had known my entire adult life was Samantha Wills, jewellery designer. Most people had even stopped calling me Samantha years ago. I was referred to as 'SW', because the brand 'Samantha Wills' was bigger than me as an individual, and therefore it got that name, not me. I don't know if it could be classed as an identity crisis, but it definitely felt like an identity conflict. For so long, my existence in the world had been inextricably entwined with the profile of the business. *If I did choose to close the Samantha Wills jewellery brand, would I once again become Samantha Wills?* I thought, wondering if a name could be returned to a person after such commercial use. *And who—or what—was Samantha Wills if she wasn't designing jewellery?*

I had never once thought about closing the business before, meeting this concept for the first time that evening at the cross-roads. It raised a whole lot of new questions, ones I had never asked before. I had always thought I would be involved in the business for life. That was the by-product of naming a brand after yourself, wasn't it?

I picked up the book again and my heart sank a little as I read Elizabeth's words introducing the chapter containing an interview with musician Tom Waits. The same Tom Waits that I had never heard of before I met Niall. My heart sank because Niall was the one person I wanted to talk this decision through with, but I knew calling him wouldn't be fair to either of us and no matter how much I wanted his advice in that moment, I knew this was a decision I had to make entirely on my own. No doubt, reading about Tom Waits reminded me of Niall and as heavy as it made my heart, I do think the universe knew it would take something significant to get my attention, and that it did. The interview ended with this quote from Tom Waits:

You know, artists—we take it so seriously. And we get so freaked out about it, and we think that what we're doing is so deadly important. But, really, as a songwriter, the only thing I do is make jewellery for the inside of people's minds. That's it.

I closed the book. I was in complete awe at the cosmic choreography that had led me to this point. As I went to sleep that night, I felt a presence envelop me. 'Thank you,' I whispered. I wasn't really sure who was listening, but I knew without a doubt they were. As I drifted off to sleep that night, I also without a doubt knew that no prayer goes unheard.

end·ing

noun

an end or final part of something

In the two weeks following my decision, I didn't tell a soul. Instead, I would wake up and pretend that the closure had already happened and Samantha Wills Jewellery was no more. I would ask myself how it *felt* to no longer have a company rather than asking myself what I *thought* about it. I consciously made a point of separating the two, knowing that I probably wouldn't have an answer for the latter. And every single time, the answer to my own question was unequivocally that closing *felt* like the right thing to do.

FROM: Samantha Wills
TO: Geoff Bainbridge
SUBJECT: Re: Business at a crossroads
DATE: June 2018

Hi GB,

Again, I wanted to thank you for your transparency and your care for my wellbeing in your email (and always!).

It feels like a very tumultuous time in my life, but I guess before any growth comes a lot of hard decisions. The unknown that I am experiencing professionally, personally and spiritually feels full of endings, evolutions and lessons. It is incredibly uncomfortable, but I have faith it is all leading me to where I am meant to be in life and I am trying to be guided by intuition, heart and calmness in the decisions I am being presented with. This often feels so severely isolated and lonely, and to have you in my life and my corner and to have your support across all, but especially the professional, decisions ahead of me means more to me than I can actually find words for. I know you know this, and I hope you know how truly full of gratitude I am for you and for everything you have brought to my world.

Fifteen years ago, there was no question in my mind about pursuing the little jewellery business I had started on my kitchen table. It wasn't a matter of weighing up pros and cons—there actually was no question, I just knew it was what I was meant to do.

But here we are.

The promise I made to myself from the very start was that if my heart was no longer in it, it was time to close that chapter and begin a new one. I never expected it to happen, but my heart hasn't been in it for a while now. And I think that time has come.

I looked at the options you suggested in your email, and I know that moving back to Australia and working in the business is what is needed for the brand. I am confident enough in my abilities that I know I could do that, take it to the next phase and continue its commercial success. But when I sat with that idea, there was nothing about it that excited me—and this feeling brought with it much guilt.

The thing that excites me in life is the mindfulness and kindness of the human spirit, and how we can impact the world with those things. I think I was able to combine my love of creativity with this in building a brand that had an impact on people. Samantha Wills has been a brand that has been able to give back in so many ways, and this is something I am incredibly proud of.

I feel the landscape has changed. We are in a different time, and I believe now more than ever we need more kindness and calmness in the world. I now struggle to personally reconcile that message alongside having to achieve brand longevity. To do that for a brand like ours, we have to try to capture the next generation of customer. As such, to hit a younger market, the pricing has to reduce, and as you know, this would mean quality is also reduced. This of course can be done, however all of it, including the communications, has to be done with a quicker, faster, turnaround. It feels very disposable to me in many ways.

If I had called the brand anything, *ANYTHING*, other than Samantha Wills, here is where I would talk to you about how we might sell the company, but as you so wisely advised me in our very first Ballina bain-marie lunch meeting, I am simply not prepared to hand my name (or my heart and soul) over in this way.

I am incredibly aware that there are many people that this will affect and have not made my final decision yet for this reason. I wanted to send you the above to let you know where my head and heart were at in advance of our conversation. I don't know the logistics around this at all and I have a million questions about it and what the repercussions of it will be.

I also want to preface that I will probably burst into tears many times when we chat, but while I may sound like I am in a heightened state of emotion, I have sat with this in more calm moments than emotional ones over the past ten days and have found a daunting yet calm peace with it. As it turns out, it is a much more tormenting decision to close a multi-million-dollar company than to persist with a small debt-ridden one. The spectrum of emotions I have felt in the process of getting to this decision have included both bravery and insanity, as well as pure fear, anxiety, freedom, captivity, selfishness, guilt, excitement, nervousness, steadfast clarity and crippling unsurety; just to list a few—but I am never one for doing things by halves.

If I look back on when my heart departed the jewellery brand, it was probably around two and a half years ago, and for that I apologise to you, and to our team. It has been hard for me to even admit that to myself, but it also might explain why I have felt ungrounded and frozen for the past few years, waiting for another door to magically open. I am very aware of the sacrifice it takes for a business partner and a team to work towards achieving the founder's dream in a creative business and I know I have been absent from that for some time. For that, I am truly sorry.

I look forward to speaking with you and your thoughts on the above.

With a very heavy heart, but with much gratitude,

SW

FROM: Geoff Bainbridge
TO: Samantha Wills
SUBJECT: Re: Re: Business at a crossroads
DATE: June 2018

Hi SW

Great email / great honesty / great vulnerability / great courage.

This brand requires energy, passion and commitment, and without that from the top then it has no future, it just becomes a fallen giant. I am not going to try to get you to stay when clearly you don't want to stay, I am not going to try to get you to commit out of some framework of guilt, but what I am going to do is say listen to your heart and stay true to my mantra of respecting and fulfilling a founder's vision even if this is ultimately the closure of the Samantha Wills jewellery brand.

The process of closing a business is not something I am overly familiar with but shouldn't be too difficult given our common moral and ethical position on how we should treat people. The main discussion is around timing and to understand how this is going to impact specifically on individuals.

First and foremost, I need a final decision from you about the what (and not the when, where, how, etc.) and, in this situation, I can't be your sounding board given my obvious and significant conflicts. Your email—while clear about your feelings—is not final in your decision. Seek appropriate guidance and counsel as required and let me know if there is any information that you might need to help make this decision.

My commitment to you is more than just the brand, and while one chapter may ultimately come to a close, another will as quickly and easily open up, perhaps for both of us, who knows. But how exciting is the unknown!

My best,

GB

Just as saying things aloud makes them feel more steadfast, telling the people in my personal life about my decision started to make everything feel very real. My nearest and dearest people were scattered all over the world, so I reached out to each of them to let them know of my decision. I was overwhelmed with the support and love I received back from all corners of the globe—New York, Sydney, London and Dublin. I also had to call our brand director, Nadia, to let her know we were closing. The inhouse Samantha Wills team all reported to Nadia, and she would be a large part of the closing proceedings.

'So, I just wanted to call you today to let you know something,' I said to Nadia. 'I've made the decision to—'

Saying it out loud to the people it would directly impact was probably hardest of all. Tears intercepted my words, as Nadia waited patiently on the other end of the phone.

'—I've decided to close the business.' I stopped as a few tears escaped. 'I'm so sorry.' Nadia didn't gasp or reply in shock at the news.

'You know,' she said, her tone thoughtful and considered, 'if Samantha Wills the person is not well, then Samantha Wills the brand is not either.'

Nadia had taken over as acting general manager when Lucinda had gone on maternity leave, and in that role she'd inherited a lot of exposure to me, and at that time it included some big windows into my struggles. It was also during this time that I had been the least engaged with the business and the brand and had been unclear in my vision for Samantha Wills in the long term. At that time, I didn't even know who I really was, let alone my brand. I had been operating on autopilot, getting the job done with my hands but not with my heart. Nadia's reply was as kind as it was insightful.

Geoff worked on the logistics with our senior management for our internal team communications. Paramount was that the team felt supported both emotionally and financially in this decision while I worked on how best to make this announcement publicly. Geoff wanted to ensure that renumeration packages were put together that went above the legal requirements, given the circumstances in which the company was closing. Geoff and Nadia were going to meet with each team member to tell them of the decision and the logistics. We had another round of QVC shows that were already scheduled, so I filmed those and then flew back from New York to Sydney where I would meet with the company as a whole to explain my decision openly and honestly to them, answering any questions they might have before we made the announcement publicly, via a media announcement.

The team made their way into our boardroom, having already met with Geoff and Nadia, who had told them that we would be closing the doors permanently in six months' time. As I sat with the team in the boardroom that day, I apologised to them, thanked them and dug as deep as I could to communicate to them the very real journey it had taken to come to this decision. Rather than questioning how I could be so selfish as to take their jobs, they thanked me for having them be a part of the journey. I was floored beyond belief. Their generosity and graciousness that day—and for the six months that followed—is something that was above and beyond anything I could have imagined.

We wanted to honour the legacy the brand had created over the past fifteen years. This involved upholding our commitment to our community and to honour them and the journey we had been on together. We wanted to make sure the final six months was a celebration of all that we stood for. I had spoken with a trusted journalist at Mamamia.com and they were going to break the story just before midday, at the same time as an announcement from me was going to be run across all our social channels. By noon, the news was out there for the world to see. Samantha Wills Jewellery would be closing in six months.

The instant outpouring from our community and what followed over the coming months was something I had significantly underestimated. Our company email and letterbox became inundated with women sharing their stories with us, not just about what the brand had meant to them, but what the jewellery itself signified for them. I would read each email and letter with a hand on my heart. Stories about how by sharing our business journey, we had inspired other women to start their own. A letter about how a piece of Samantha Wills jewellery was the last ever gift a mother gave to her daughter, who wore it every day as a reminder of her mum who now looked down on her from heaven. Another email explained how as a survivor of domestic abuse, on the day she found the courage to leave and file an AVO, she also purchased a Samantha Wills Bohemian Bardot ring as a gift for herself to mark the day she moved her life forward—to her it signified the strength she had to find to start again. 'That ring became my shield and my sword,' she wrote. Jewellery had become the vehicle for what our business did, but stories like these went far beyond jewellery. It was these stories that showed us the strength of our brand and community connection, and it was that legacy we wanted to honour in our closing.

American Express had asked me to sit on a business panel that November—it would be my first public speaking engagement since our closure announcement. After the panel, a Q&A was opened up to the audience and an older gentleman in the crowd raised his hand and was handed a microphone.

'Can you help me understand your decision?' he said, looking directly at me. Even through the brightness of the stage lights in my eyes, I could see the confusion on his face. 'If the business is profitable, in growth, has significant brand market share and a streamlined back of house and supply chain operation in place, I don't understand the logic behind your decision,' he said. 'Why wouldn't you continue the company's legacy by offering it to longstanding members of your team?'

His question was followed by the sound of the 500 people in the audience turning in their seats towards me. I nodded slowly, acknowledging that I had heard him. I would usually have felt anxiety from the 1000 eyes that were looking at me but, in that moment, I knew exactly how to answer his question.

'There's two main words in your question that resonate greatly with me, and I think they are really important to talk to,' I said. 'Logic and legacy. I can't tell you the logic behind my decision, simply because there is none. In the moment I made the decision to close, I did not run it through a filter in my mind, I simply put my hand on my heart and something in me knew it was the correct decision, and I knew because it *felt* right. There is a difference between thinking something and feeling something. Thoughts can get clouded and frantic but you can't fake a true feeling. And legacy, well, we are both talking about legacy, but in different ways,' I continued, still looking at the gentleman who asked the question. 'I think this question is important because the legacy of a business *is* honoured by selling and having it continue on, but the legacy of a *brand*, I believe—and I can only speak for my case—is honoured by recognising when it is time to walk away by choice rather than running it into the ground by obligation. Closing it while it is still alive with great energy, reflecting on it, celebrating it and moving forward—all with purpose. I felt the brand had said all it had to say. Continuing would have seen it as just a business with a product, not a brand with a voice.'

He looked at me for a few moments, his expression unchanged as he still held the microphone in his hand. I didn't know whether this was going to result in a debate or a stand-off. Slowly, he moved the microphone towards his mouth.

'I understand now,' he said, his expression softening. 'Thank you for explaining that to me, I had never thought of it that way before.'

The words that came to me on that stage sounded rehearsed, but they weren't. The answer had only come to me in that very moment. It was as though I was explaining to the gentleman in the audience and myself at the same time. I finally understood my own reasoning.

The marketing team and I had met to plan out our final weeks of marketing and communications. I had the idea to add a watermark to the marketing that we published in the final two months of trade, adding the years '2004–2019' under our corporate Samantha Wills logo. In my mind, it was a way to bookend the journey of the brand and as the 2019 was postdated, I thought it would also be an effective communication to show that there were only a few weeks left of trade and, as such, the final opportunity to purchase the little remaining stock we had left.

It didn't take long for me to realise that it was not my best marketing idea. After we'd implemented it, the next weekly Google analytic reports that documented where and how the brand was mentioned showed that two of the most popular Google search terms were *Samantha Wills Death* and *Samantha Wills Obituary*. I had not realised that, at a glance, it looked like birth and death dates, as used in a death notice or on a headstone. The timing of it made me laugh—also I had to laugh at how truly morbid it was to read that your own death was a highly searched topic.

We celebrated and farewelled the team with our annual, and final, Christmas party in Sydney. It was emotional as we celebrated together for the last time as an organisation. As Geoff gave a speech, I looked around the room at our incredible team—there were a few tears, but everyone was laughing as Geoff recapped some of our best moments over the years.

'It's been a journey for all of us and both Samantha and I are truly so grateful for each and every one of you and all that you have contributed over the years,' he said. The team started to clap and cheer as Geoff went to hand me the microphone. 'But let us all never forget . . .' he continued, retracting the microphone as everyone fell silent, 'let us never forget that around this time eleven years ago, Samantha was getting ready to give away 51 per cent of her company . . . And I'd just like to say, I'm fucking glad she didn't!'

The team cheered even louder and—in true Geoff style—that was how he introduced me to say my final official thankyous to the team.

I thanked the team for their support and dedication over the years, and I also thanked them for the level of graciousness it takes to work for a creative founder. Their decision to come to work each day to help build someone else's dream and the sheer generosity of that decision has never been lost on me. And for the final time, we all raised our glasses and toasted the end of an era.

'Well, this is it,' I said, sitting down next to Geoff as the dance floor began to fill up behind us.

'This is it,' he said as he lifted his glass.

'Just out of curiosity,' I asked, picking up my glass, 'if we *had* sold . . . how much do you think we could have sold it for?' It was a question I had purposely not asked until now.

'After all was said and done and the staff payouts were processed, you probably would have walked away with a bit more than $8 million,' he said. I just nodded.

Geoff was the ultimate in graciousness. Even though we'd had our fair share of differences over the years, his support and dedication to the business was the greatest of blessings. In the end, the amount we each received from the closure was astronomically less than it would have been had I decided to sell. As a business partner, Geoff had every right to be angry with my decision, but it was what he said to me next that proved that, while our eleven-year business partnership had come to a close, our friendship would remain forever.

'For what it's worth . . . I think the decision you made was the right one,' he said. 'Cheers to you, SW.'

'Cheers to you, GB.' We clinked our glasses together. 'Oh, and Geoff . . . for what it's worth, turquoise is a really good seller.' Eleven years later, and I was not about to let him forget it.

'Fuck off, Willsy,' he replied as we both laughed.

—

Our last day of trading was 11 January 2019. I think people were waiting for a big reaction from me, maybe the type you would expect at the end of a fifteen-year relationship, but I felt nothing but calmness. In a way, I think I had done my mourning for the end of this particular part of the journey, not on the day we closed and not even on the day at those crossroads that I made the decision, but I think I subconsciously processed the emotion of the closure in the two or so years in the lead-up to making the decision. The turmoil and inner unease I felt definitely came with a subconscious processing that this journey was coming to an end—it had just taken me a while to catch up to it.

We turned the website off that day at 5 pm and it went to a holding page which read: 'Samantha Wills Jewellery is now closed'.

emergence

emerg·ence

noun

the process of coming into view or becoming exposed
after being concealed; the process of coming into being

It can be so easy to become stuck on something ending, but the truth is that something new cannot begin until something else ends. In the weeks that followed the brand's closure, there were no huge, sweeping changes. In New York, I took a few days to pack up my design desk, carefully storing and archiving all the jewellery components, crystals, clasps and trinkets. It was the same process I'd go through after designing each collection— tidying my work area to be a blank canvas to then immediately begin on the next. But this time there was no next. My tools were the last things I put into the large cardboard boxes that now housed the last fifteen years of my career. I packed them carefully in a cupboard and closed the door.

I had called that New York apartment home for almost ten years and after I'd packed away the contents of my desk, I pulled it out from the wall a little—the marks indented on the floor showed an almost decade of it sitting in the same spot. I kept pulling the desk out from the alcove that had been my jewellery design studio and dragged it all the way across the living room, finally pushing it underneath the window that looked out over The New Whitney Museum and the High Line. My desk was not even a few metres from where it had been, but the perspective was entirely new and the shift felt significant. I knew it was time to revisit the book—this book—that I had started writing the year before on my way back from Dublin, and so I made a cup of coffee, opened my laptop and sat down to write. Moving my desk that afternoon was both significant and sacred to me: it was the physical shift from making jewellery for people to wear to making jewellery for the insides of people's minds.

I had told my manager who handled all my public speaking and ambassador work about the book I was writing. He made some calls to Australian publishing houses and a few had expressed interest in offering me a contract for a business memoir. I was booked on a speaking tour in Australia the following month to talk about the decision to close the business and we agreed I would have an early manuscript to show prospective publishers then.

The speaking tour covered cities as well as areas in regional Australia. The audiences were brilliant and it felt good to be talking about the brand's journey from this perspective after closure. But as good as it felt emotionally, physically I was not in a good way. I had still not gone to see anyone about the pain

I was experiencing monthly, but it was to a point now where even swallowing five painkillers at a time wouldn't help.

When I got to Brisbane on the speaking tour, the pain in my abdomen was searing and all I could do was coil up on the bed and will it to go away. My hair and make-up artist was due to arrive in thirty minutes, but I could barely stand up. By this time, I had completely reasoned with myself that periods were just painful, no one enjoyed having them and cramps were a known side-effect, so it just was what it was. But even with that reasoning, I knew that this pain was new and worse than it had ever been. Two more cities and twenty more painkillers and the tour was over, but the pain I was experiencing was anything but.

On this trip, I had already booked an appointment with my GP as I wanted to discuss fertility testing and the possibility of freezing my eggs. The morning of my appointment saw me yet again in the fetal position, my entire body in full convulsions, and I was haemorrhaging. It felt as though full body organs were passing through me. I reached again for the bottle of painkillers and, an hour later, was in the doctor's office but hunched over and unable to sit up straight. I winced throughout our appointment as she walked me through the process of egg-freezing and then at the end of the session, I told her that my cycle had been a 'little heavier' than usual these past few months.

My body was crying out, louder and louder each month, for me to help her. I can't imagine the relief my body felt when she finally heard me bring it up with the doctor. My doctor referred me to an obstetrician-gynaecologist who I could speak to about the egg-freezing, but suggested I make an appointment with her sooner rather than later to discuss what she described as abnormalities in my cycle. I called the ob-gyn's office that afternoon and her receptionist informed me she had an opening the following week, but beyond that, there was a wait time of a few months.

I had a meeting with a management company that I had been trying to secure for months scheduled in New York the following week. I knew this monthly pain process well enough by now to know that I had about another forty-eight hours of excruciating pain, but that then it would subside and I would have a few weeks of freedom before it would start all over again. *I just have to get through the next forty-eight hours*, I thought. *It's taken me this long to finally get this meeting secured, what's another couple of months?*

I didn't know how to not be busy, to not have a diary full of scheduled meetings and the thought of turning down a possible opportunity was a foreign concept to me, and so I carried on with what I knew. Rather than extend my stay in Sydney a few extra days and take an appointment to invest in my health, I instead chose the meeting—what I thought to be an investment in my career. After my GP appointment that day, I took another couple of Nurofens, signed my book deal that afternoon and boarded my flight back to New York the next morning.

A career is a hell of thing to hide behind. I still had the ingrained belief that soldiering on through pain or illness was a sign of commitment and professional robustness. But there comes a point where your body becomes so exhausted from being ignored for so long that it couldn't care less about your business meetings or career opportunities. That was the point of frustration my body was at: exhausted and tired of the terrible treatment I was giving her. It would be the last time my body was going to allow me to make everything else a priority above my health.

I had another speaking job booked in Australia that November and I *finally* made an appointment with the ob-gyn for that trip. The three months between going back to New York and returning to Sydney were excruciating. My symptoms rapidly worsened each month and no matter how much googling I did, the overarching internet diagnosis was simply that periods change over time, often getting heavier and more painful as we age. So, I just kept going.

I had been referred to a specialist doctor, Dr Ha Ryun Won, and once I was back in Sydney in November, I finally fronted up to an appointment. Her office didn't feel like a doctor's office at all—the decor was very chic and it felt like someone's very stylish living room. There was one corkboard near the reception desk that was overflowing with photographs of babies and handwritten thankyou cards from parents thanking the doctor for their successful fertility journey. While the appointment I had was to talk about the process of freezing my eggs, I knew that's not what we were going to be talking about that day.

Dr Won could not have been nicer in our initial appointment—she was thoughtful, informative and calm. I told her about the symptoms I had just come to accept as normal over the past four years since going off the pill, and also the pain and immobility they were now causing me. As I listed what I was experiencing, the empathy in her eyes reflected a care and concern that I had not once shown my own body. She gave instructions for pathology tests and some scans. We were to meet again in a few days once she had the results.

'There's a few things we have to go through today,' Dr Won said at the start of my follow-up appointment as she brought my scans up on her screen. 'First, you are losing so much blood that your body is not able to keep up. Your iron levels are meant to be around 200 and yours are sitting at seven. How your body has any energy at all is a miracle. We'll get you in for an infusion and see how your body responds.'

Iron infusion. Easy, I thought, *no problem. Tick.* I mentally added it like a meeting agenda item.

'There is also a lot of endometriosis in your uterus as well . . . Now, endo is common, but I'm going to hazard a guess from these scans that yours is around Stage 4, so it's at a very advanced stage. The pill masks most signs of endo, like a bandaid to what's going on underneath, so it's likely that you have had it for a long while, but only started to see the symptoms recently. But let's come back to that in a second.'

I shifted slightly in my chair.

'We've also found two large fibroids—each is the size of an orange,' she said to me, her tone careful and calm. There's something about receiving that type of information in a doctor's office that feels as though you are watching it on a long-running Australian soap opera. She paused for my reaction.

'Okay,' was all I said back. Not 'Oh, fuck!' or 'Holy shit' or 'What does that mean!?' Just, 'Okay'. The leadership role of response I would usually embody in that instant evaded me and I sat there wide-eyed like a new recruit on my first day, too paralysed to ask questions and just waiting for an adult to give me instructions.

'The pressure of the fibroids on your uterus is causing it to be in a state of trauma, and the endometriosis has spread to many of your organs. We need to get you in for surgery.'

I just nodded. *Trauma is an aggressive word to use*, I thought. Or maybe it was a case of it being precisely the right word to use and if I had aggressively sought help when my body first asked me for it, perhaps we wouldn't be sitting here at all. The egg-freezing conversation would be happening another time, but she did let me know that if one day I did decide to try to fall pregnant the significance of the fibroids and the damage they had caused, even after removal, would mean that I would be unable to give birth naturally.

'Okay,' I said again.

Dr Won explained that while she could make assumptions from the scan she wouldn't know the full extent of my situation until she was able to look at it in theatre. The rest of the appointment was spent discussing all the precautions for the surgery. The biggest one was that while keyhole surgery was the preferred option, due to the fibroids being so large they would not be able to be removed whole. Because of this, the fibroids would have to be cut up in the body, then removed piece by piece. She went on to explain that there was a chance that the fibroids could contain cancerous cells and, if that were the case, this method meant the cancerous cells could be released into the surrounding areas.

The other decision was that if, in the surgery, the endometriosis proved to be causing danger to the bowel, whether I consented to have a colorectal surgeon scrub in to remove the part of the bowel affected, a surgery that comes with significant risks, from a colostomy to ongoing reparative bowel surgeries.

It was a lot to take in, and while a big part of me was overwhelmed at the unknowns, I think on some level a part of me was also relieved. I felt my body breathe out a little, an exhausted sigh, saying thank you. Thank you for *finally* helping me. The conversation that afternoon in the doctor's office was an all too confronting example of how I so many times had ignored what my body was trying to show me. Writing this hurts every part of my heart. The vile and horrible way I had spoken to and treated my body, ignoring her when she was trying to get my attention. When she was screaming out in pain, instead of caring for her, I just ignored her and did whatever I could to continually numb her. I thought back to the countless number of times I had just reverted to 'I don't have time', 'I've got too much to do' or 'I'll do it once I finish the such and such project/deal/contract/collection/proposal' or, the most common, 'I'm too busy right now, I'll deal with it later'. I thought I would have known better than this, but even at its worst, I still prioritised everything else ahead of my own health.

My operation was scheduled for a few weeks later. The entire process of it and the shame I felt about why it took me so long to acknowledge and take responsibility for it were sobering and I knew it was time to focus on my health—and time to return home to Australia for a while. To spend less time on planes and more time getting grounded, something I hadn't done in well over a decade.

I spoke to Dr Won on the phone the day before the surgery, and she said that it was good that I was able to schedule the surgery now. A new virus had been identified in China, and she wasn't sure if these types of surgeries would be possible soon. I didn't think too much about it at the time, and definitely did not know the suffering Covid-19 was about to inflict. All I knew at that moment was that it had taken me far too long to get to this point.

On a hot summer Tuesday afternoon in January 2020, tears streamed down my face as I was wheeled into the operating theatre at Sydney's Prince of Wales Private Hospital. Of course, I got my period the day before the surgery and as they transferred me onto the operating table, blood soaked through my surgical gown.

'I'm so sorry,' I said to the nurses through floods of tears. I was in so much pain and embarrassed by all the blood that was everywhere. I was scared at what they were going to find when they opened me up and whether I would wake up with part of my bowel missing . . . and I was ashamed. Ashamed and angry at myself that I had prioritised everything else over this for so many years. The tears just kept coming.

Dr Won was the lead surgeon of an all-female team. As I lay there on the cold operating table in a hospital gown, hairnet, compression socks and with tears running down my face, Dr Won took my hand and with her face near mine said in the most beautiful, calm and reassuring tone, 'Samantha, we're going to make this better,' and squeezed my hand tight. Unable to speak, I just cried harder, as I squeezed her hand in return. Then it was time to go to sleep.

'We're going to take great care of you, Samantha,' Dr Won said.

The surgical lights burned bright above me as the anaesthetist carefully put an apparatus over my mouth. And then, the most beautiful thing happened.

Every woman in that operating theatre came and stood around me and all leaned down and whispered the same thing.

'We're going to take great care of you, Samantha.'

'We're going to take great care of you, Samantha.'

'We're going to take great care of you, Samantha . . .'

Calmness washed over me as the women surrounded me, and I felt held by all their calm and generous energy, care and intention. I closed my eyes, knowing I was exactly where I was meant to be.

The surgery was meant to take three hours, but five hours later I was wheeled out into the recovery ward. I don't remember much of what happened that evening, but I was assured it all went well. The following morning—and once the Ketamine trip had worn off—Dr Won came to see me and explained that the surgery had indeed gone well and that the additional two hours we were in theatre came about because the endometriosis was chronic Stage 4, having attached itself throughout my uterus and bowel. 'Riddled with it' was the term she used. It was like ten years of barnacle build up that needed removing, cleaning, scraping and extracting, but she assured me it was worth it.

The fibroids were successfully removed and the endo had been separated from the bowel without the need for bowel surgery.

While I felt that all my internal organs had had a kebab skewer put through them, I also pictured them down there looking around at each other and being able to breathe for the first time in more than ten years, shocked and grateful at their newfound life, and relieved they were no longer covered in layers and layers of barnacles and soot. I silently apologised to them for not doing it sooner, pleading with them to forgive me for my negligence. If I had treated another body in my care with such neglect, it would be classed as a criminal act. This comparison really hit home.

The day after I was discharged, Dr Won called me to tell me that she had received the results and the fibroids were benign. Relief and gratitude washed over me. She also said I could begin the egg-freezing process in six months, the time needed for my body to recover from the operation.

As my wounds began to heal physically, I vowed to treat my body better. I felt ashamed that I had let it get to breaking point before this realisation reached me.

So often over the years I would be asked in interviews, 'What advice would you offer to women in business to best avoid burnout?' Any answer I gave before being rolled into that operating theatre now seems naive. The answer I can now offer is that to truly understand the importance of boundaries, personal wellbeing and self-care, I first had to burn out. I was only able to have that realisation from the coals. I had no fuel left. No fuel, no fire.

Burnout is the result of an excessive and ongoing imbalance. When we operate so far from our centre that our body has to stop us in our tracks so that we can realign and start to shift the pendulum back towards the middle. But, balance. What is it, anyway? All I know for certain is that whoever it was that came up with the notion of 'work–life balance' most definitely was not a creative entrepreneur.

The concept of balance goes against the very molecules that are in the DNA makeup of entrepreneurialism. It's as if our balance barometer organically skews to the right, a forceful magnetism to our creative pursuit. People will tell us we work too much, but when we are creating, we don't see it as work at all. It's a much-needed process of the soul; it's not something we choose to do, it's simply something we must do. If balance was what we were seeking, we would have stayed with a nine to five job, the security of the safety net. So while I think it an unrealistic goalpost to try to match up balance and being an entrepreneur, I also know that it is going to take something truly significant to realign a chemistry that, in truth, was probably never balanced from the start.

Our soul only ever wants the best for us, and she communicates with us through our body. We can rest in that trust; the body never lies. Be it physically, through haemorrhaging and burning out, or more subtly—an unsettling, an internal rumbling that whispers at first, but if we ignore it, will certainly begin to yell.

You don't have to run a business to be a creative entrepreneur. Creativity is not just a paint palette or pottery class. We create careers and friendships and families and foundations. We create connections and communities; we create homes and safe havens for those that we love. We are all creating every single day; it is our contribution to this world, and we are always being called to give in whatever our creative currency is. Photography or philanthropy. Marketing manager or mother (or both). Goldsmith or good listener. An inner rumbling could be disguised by a cloak of discontent, the belief that there is something else out there for you. It is all those soul whispers and synchronicities that are vying for our attention. It is the cosmic choreography that is asking us to waltz, even offering to lead us to quick step a little closer to where we are meant to be heading, but which we all too often write off as mere coincidence, take a seat in the shadows against the wall and return to what we think we know. It is the ideas that come to us in the shower and dance on our eyelids as we dream at night . . . Once those creative murmurs start to rumble, they never leave. If we don't explore them they linger around us, emerging every so often in a haunted whispering of *what if* or *what could have been* . . .

When I signed the contract to write this book, it was on the premise that it would be a business memoir, the ins and outs of how the Samantha Wills brand went from a kitchen table to a global stage. But the more I wrote about that, the more I realised that there was so much more to the story. Not just the highlight reel and the business hurdles, but the business journey *and* the personal journey—as a creative founder, the public brand and the private life—and I came to realise that none of those existed in isolation. They were intrinsically linked. All this time I thought I had a creative career and a personal life, but the truth was there is no such thing, there is only a creative life. This beautiful, decadent, bohemian tapestry that when we look at it with hindsight and distance paints a big picture, but all we are afforded each day is seeing the intertwining of each of the knots. Golden threads that are weaving through and around each other, that on their own might not seem that significant, but they are. And that's the faith we must keep. We cannot spend our time fearing every knot, because without each one, there would be no tapestry.

I only realised while writing the final chapters of this book the significance of the crossroads I found myself at when I made the decision to close my business. The impact of finding myself at a physical crossroads is obvious, but less obvious are the crossroads we find ourselves faced with in life every day. We stand at a crossroads countless times in our journey, and each time we do, the decision will be between faith and fear.

The soul will always guide us to make the decision that scares us, asking us to have faith in our path and take a step forward, even if we are unable to yet see where that step leads. Doing so is a step towards where our soul is being called to go. The ego mind, however, will always encourage us to stay in the familiar, to make the decision out of fear, seeking instant comfort in the environment or circumstance that we know. No matter how stagnant or uninspiring, the ego doesn't care; it thrives on familiarity. Faith versus fear; that's the decision every crossroad presents us with. I'm constantly trying to return to that realisation, and rather than hold on tight to the familiar, loosen my grip a little on what I thought something was meant to look like and surrender to what is unfolding. Each time I find myself here, I now listen for what my body is trying to tell me. It's not thought, it's felt.

Before I sign off, I would like to leave you with some things that I have come to find great calmness and value in. These are my wishes for both you and me.

If you find a time that you are feeling overwhelmed or in need of some guidance on which direction to head next, send a prayer up to whatever power you believe in and bring your attention to what starts to present on your path. Take a moment and find some silence; quiet your mind so you can hear what your heart is trying to say. Observe what begins to unfold around you, create space so that ideas and intuition can reach you. Maybe it's a knowing to pursue a business startup idea from your kitchen table, maybe it's summoning up the courage to walk away from an established one to allow a new chapter to begin. Notice the people who come into your life and show you something new. That cosmic choreography is not by chance, it is fulfilling a sacred contract that, when we as the student are ready, the teacher will appear. We, too, will play this role for others. And I hope it goes without saying, pay attention to the coincidences—coincidences that I believe are not really coincidences at all.

When you turn the volume down in the mind, I hope that you find an unwavering trust in yourself. A steadfastness to stand confidently in your own truth, not what someone else thinks your truth should be, but yours, your sacred knowing. A calmness and confidence in the life you choose to create.

When the universe asks you to dance, I hope you take her hand. I hope you choose faith over fear.

And maybe in your moments of silence, you will be able to hear your body whispering to you—if so, listen to it before it begins screaming. Our bodies truly want what is best for us; they do not lie.

When personal darkness descends towards us, I understand the heaviness of that, how scary it can be—it feels scary because it is. Scarier still is the fight we put up trying to resist it. Not only the energetic haemorrhaging it causes, a bleeding out of our life force, but also the reeds that entangle us, keeping us stuck and stagnant, unable to move forward. That is when we are being called to travel to the depths of the darkness, to touch the very bottom. We carry our painful experiences with us like heavy rocks, held in our arms and pressed tightly against our chests. We sink with them to the bottom, this process allowing us to be stripped of what we no longer need to hold. And as we lie there in the bathyal zone of our ocean floor, we look around. We shed what no longer serves us. The things we brought down with us start to crumble. In their dissilience, they are not heavy anymore. Now only a weightless fine dust, glimmering like phosphenes. In those particles all that remains is resilience. That's what we keep from our descent into the depths—a newfound knowing and strength that now dance through our bodies like stars.

In that darkness, stay down there as long as you need to, but not a moment longer. Know that what is meant for you will always find a way, and, with that, shed the barnacle-covered anchors that keep us tethered to the shadows as you begin your ascent. Notice the lightness. The gold in you radiates brighter now.

That is our alchemy. A combination of elements and trust.
The very beauty and rawness that runs through our veins,
for it is made up of gold and dust.

heartfelt xx

Writing this book has been, without a doubt, the most in-depth project I have worked on in my career to date. Immersing yourself in bygone chapters of your life and then finding a way to bring them to life literally as book chapters has been a discipline I absolutely would not have been able to undertake on my own. My sincere gratitude and heartfelt thanks to the team, both professional and personal, who surrounded me in bringing this book into existence. Thanks to my publisher, Kelly Fagan, and everybody at Allen & Unwin for the opportunity to share this story and also for the creative integrity you afforded me throughout the entire process. Thanks to my incredible copyeditor, Emma Rafferty, and to my truly magnificent managing editor, Angela Handley, for your talent (and saint-like patience!). Thanks to Sean, Jo and my entire 22mgmt team. To my chosen siblings—Melanie, Freya, Carolyn, David, Sarah and Kirsty—thank you all for wrapping me in love and support throughout the writing of this book, but even more so throughout this life. How lucky I am to call each of you family. Darling Lewis, thank you for providing a safe and warm place for me while I dug to the depths of where I had to go to get this story onto paper. I am forever indebted to you for the love, support and graciousness you have given me.

To every person whose name is in this book, thank you for being a part of my journey and for what you have afforded my life and journey. There was one photo in this book I could not find the original message to credit it, so I wanted to offer my special thanks to the lovely girl (now woman) in the Fantasy Glades picture who a few years ago sent me that photo via Instagram DM saying 'when I was a kid I had my photo taken with Cinderella at Fantasy Glades in Port Macquarie. I just found it in an old family album and thought, Cinderella looks exactly like the jewellery designer Samantha Wills . . . so I know this is a weird question, but was it you?'

Eternal thanks to my incredible mum and dad, Ron and Patsy Wills; thank you both for not only allowing me to chase my dreams but always actively encouraging me to do so. Thank you, Mum, for putting me into that beading class in our local craft store! To my Nan, for your strength and love, and for sharing your story with me in letters so that I could keep it forever in your handwriting.

To my long-time friend and creative collaborator, Scott Ehler: what a privilege it is to create alongside you. I appreciate our partnership so dearly.

My business partner and dear friend, Geoff Bainbridge: thank you for seeing something in me that I didn't see in myself all those years ago. Thank you for celebrating with me in the sunshine and holding space for me in the darker times. You have afforded me so much throughout this journey and I remain forever grateful.

When you ever-so-modestly (!) name a brand after yourself, by default you are then given the public adulation for the brand's successes; but the Samantha Wills brand eclipsed me many, many years ago. Its success is due to every single person who worked on it over the years. To the women who led the company with grace and strength—Tara O'Sullivan, Sarah Moore, Lucinda Grice, Nadia Lotter—and every soul I was fortunate enough to work alongside, while there are far too many names to list here, with my hand on my heart I thank every single one of you. Thank you for taking that journey with me.

And finally to you, dear reader, and now dear friend. Thank you for choosing this book and for allowing me to share my story with you. I hope our paths cross soon so you can share stories from your journey with me. It's been an absolute privilege to spend this time with you. On all your days ahead, I wish you more gold than dust, but above all, I wish you a steadfast trust. Trust in yourself, in your journey and in your knowing. With all my love.

CONNECT WITH THE AUTHOR AT:
SAMANTHAWILLS.COM
INSTAGRAM.COM/SAMANTHAWILLS

tell me, what is
it you plan to
do with your one,
wild & precious life ?
—mary oliver